Jordan Lee Harding

Living in
BERLIN

BARBARA SICHTERMANN   INGO ROSE

Photographs by
DEIDI VON SCHAEWEN

Translated by Deke Dusinberre

Flammarion

CONTENTS

6

INTRODUCTION

12

BERLIN,
NEW AND OLD

54

BERLIN'S PARKS
AND WATERWAYS

88

INTERIORS

136

POTSDAM
AND BABELSBERG

172

RENDEZVOUS

201

VISITOR'S GUIDE

The bear is the mascot of Berlin, symbolizing the pride of native Berliners.

People say that Berlin is perpetually changing, but the same could be said of every city, for they are all organisms that are continuously evolving. In the case of Berlin, however, it could be argued, to extend the metaphor, that the city has not merely experienced growth and development but also ruptures, fractures, displacements. Several times in its history, the city has had to start over. Even today, it is beginning again from scratch. This time, however, it is hoping to forge an image it can enjoy for a good, long while. Because Berlin finally has the time, the money, and the detachment needed to carry out methodical, lasting reconstruction and development.

Ten years or more ago, people drawn to the city viewed Berlin as a kind of picture book of the twentieth century. Due to its provisional, divided status, Berlin could never completely erase the wounds of war and traces of megalomania from its landscape. Ambitiousness, realism, defiance, and destruction all appeared openly, with no make-up or modesty. East and West, of course, tried to demonstrate their respective economic and cultural power through architectural projects, but beneath the new veneer an old, ruined Berlin still spoke of its tragic past in visible, palpable terms. Everyone knew it, and went to see the city and its Wall for that very reason.

In 1989, the Wall fell and Berlin erupted with joy. People immediately picked up sledgehammer and spade. When, in 1991, the German government announced that it would return to Berlin, the capital was seized by a veritable building fever. With astonishing speed, the city shrugged off its nightmare and shed the weight of its past. Plans and blueprints blossomed: some buildings were restored, others converted, new ones erected. The wildest dreams came true. People rediscovered and revived the hidden, dilapidated, overlooked beauty of old Berlin. The numerous vacant lots dotting the now borderless city swiftly vanished.

Cranes temporarily became—once again—the emblem of Berlin. This time, however, it was hoped that the outcome would be final and lasting: a city of bold and

The spectacular dome on the Reichstag is the work of British architect Sir Norman Foster (page 1). Jonathan Borofsky's towering sculpture, Molecule Man, seems to be walking on the Spree (pages 2–3). This vivid depiction a hunt is one of a number of sculptures in the Tiergarten. In the background can be seen the Victory Column (pages 4–5). The Rococo exuberance of the Ephraim-Palais contrasts with the powerfully modern broadcasting tower dubbed "the TV asparagus" (facing page).

Berlin today, with colorful façades by Italian architect Aldo Rossi in the Schützenstraße neighborhood (facing page). Also modern is the Borsigwerke Gate in Spandau (far right, bottom) by French architect Claude Vasconi, which alludes casually and imaginatively to Neoclassical precursors in Kreuzberg (right) and Potsdam (far right, top).

remarkable buildings. The edifices that emerged from behind the scaffolding did not please everyone, of course; that would have been impossible. On the other hand, visitors are certainly charmed by the energy—so typical of Berlin—with which the reunification and rebirth of the city is being engineered. Everyone seems to be helping it turn toward the future.

Many internationally known architects came to work for Berlin. Potsdamer Platz, the Reichstag, Unter den Linden, and Friedrichstraße are now part of a grandiose urban landscape that would never have seen the light of day without the world's finest architects. Yet these designers always took into account the city's old appearance, which they carefully preserved or redesigned—the new Berlin has risen on the foundations of the old. But prestigious buildings are not the only novelty: comfortable hotels with built-in art galleries have opened, and tastefully decorated restaurants now offer regional and international cuisine of outstanding quality. All kinds of markets, shops, exhibition venues, museums, and cultural centers make Berlin an exciting place with many surprises for visitors. And neighborhoods where various nationalities blend their exuberant lifestyles have also been affected by this new spirit—more and more artists, actors,

In front of the Märkisches Museum stands a statue of Zille, an artist and illustrator who remained close to the people. His scenes of working life were accompanied by caustic texts (above). A promenade near Schloß Charlottenhof at Sanssouci, Potsdam (above right).

artisans, and musicians belonging to the alternative scene are moving to Berlin. This is where things are happening, where things are changing, this is where the chiefs of our global villages now meet. People from all corners of the world are coming to see Berlin.

The city seems to be evolving into a beautiful, buoyant, and elegant metropolis. Apart from brief periods in the late nineteenth century and the 1920s, it has rarely had the chance to pursue such a course. But now it looks as though Berlin—former capital of Prussia and current capital of Germany—will devote all its renascent energy to addressing today's pressing issues of art and lifestyle.

Who would want to miss experiencing this wonderful change?

*In fine weather,
entire families establish
their summer quarters
in the Tiergarten and
the lakes around Berlin—
they may sleep at home,
but they eat and play
outdoors. Beer gardens
and cafés offer a range
of drinks and snacks.*

BERLIN, NEW AND OLD

Clocks have always run faster here than elsewhere. Berlin was always in a hurry to prove its importance and creativity to the world. It granted neither pause nor rest, and its charm was largely derived from its non-stop bustle and modernity. Berlin grew at great speed, moving forward with much impatience and little reflection—noisily, boldly, energetically. It epitomized total, straightforward urbanism. Never in the vagaries of its existence did it sink into timid provincialism. If Paris can be compared to a delightfully beautiful woman, Rome to an immortal ancient goddess, and London to a gentleman of the old school (friendly and generous beneath a snobbish exterior), then Berlin inevitably evokes a young man bursting with energy, ambition, spirit, and arrogance, all the while remaining curious and willing to learn. This boisterous, unpredictable city is fond of experimentation.

It has known dark days, however. Destroyed by bombs, it was caught between the two camps after World War II. East and West—the Soviet empire and the free world—each controlled part of the city. There was no longer just one Berlin, but an East Berlin and a West Berlin, the latter a Western isle surrounded by East Germany on one side and its capital, East Berlin, on the other. This island of four million inhabitants was ringed by a wall topped with barbed wire and flanked by mines. There was no longer any question of movement. Berlin was a young man deprived of half his limbs; his feet and wrists were bound, he was floored, and he could barely breathe. The city seemed to be giving its last gasps. People concerned about their future left the Western sector of the walled town; only dreamers, conscientious objectors, and spies moved in. And yet Berlin never lost its appetite for life. Even during the decades of division—"in the days of the Wall"—people built, renovated, and developed. There was even a certain competition between East and West, and so the world continued to keep an eye on a city that had become one of the stakes of the Cold War.

To the left of the Reichstag, where Germany's parliament sits, extends a row of new buildings known as the Band des Bundes (Federal Strip), built to house government offices (previous double page).

On Gendarmenmarkt, the statue of Friedrich von Schiller (1871) seems to be contemplating the cupola of the Deutscher Dom. The monument was the work of young artist Reinhold Begas, whose statue enhanced the fame of the German writer (left). The undulating façade of the Ku'damm-Eck on the corner of Kurfürstendamm and Joachimstaler Straße.

*These façades,
dating from the turn
of the century (1871 to
1913), are found
in the neighborhoods
of Kreuzberg,
Charlottenburg,
Schöneberg, Tiergarten,
and Mitte.*

Then came 1989: Russia released its grip on East Germany and Berlin; the Wall fell; the postwar period came to a close. No one had foreseen the unification of Berlin, and the population's surprised shouts of glee were echoed the world over. The city on the banks of the Spree found itself whole again—it shook itself off, rubbed its aching joints, massaged its muscles, and prepared to make a new start. This time, Berlin was not driven by a vague determination to conquer. It had finally become an adult and, for the first time in its history, envisaged the real possibility of forging its true identity.

In order to do so, the capital had to pull itself together again, flaunting its attractions by stressing and enhancing them. It finally had the time, means, and desire to accomplish just that. Berliners of old had never known a refined lifestyle, whereas Berliners today seek peace and beauty. They also realize that vestiges of the past are precious and have to be retained. They have therefore been building their new city in a way that would show off the beauty of the old one. That does not mean, however, that radical changes have been rejected when designing the new Berlin. Berlin wants to live up to its reputation as an avant-garde city, a laboratory of the future. The results have disappointed neither residents nor visitors. With its usually alacrity, Berlin has transformed itself once again by risking architectural innovation.

*The various styles
exemplify the decorative
diversity of the period,
appropriately called
Historismus.*

The Kaisersaal (Imperial Hall) of the old Hotel Esplanade has been incorporated into the Forum (above). All eyes are drawn to the impressive roof overhead. The continual animation draws both tourists and Berliners by day and by night (right).

POTSDAMER PLATZ

Everyone, whether they be first-time visitors or those who have already been to the city and know it well, heads straight for Potsdamer Platz. Just a few years ago, Potsdamer Platz was deserted. But now a city within the city has sprung up there, forming a new center of attraction on the western edge of downtown Berlin. It is a futuristic amalgam of palaces devoted to leisure and consumption, of skyscrapers packed with offices, housing, and luxury penthouse apartments, of insolent, bold, unusual architecture. The plaza has everything to draw city-dwellers from their homes—cafés, restaurants, tree-lined squares with fountains and benches, and a major shopping mall. In addition, Potsdamer Platz is endowed with a huge movie theater, a live theater, a casino, a grand hotel, and a station. And everything is brand new. Berliners see Potsdamer Platz as a magnificent gift, although they have not yet fully come to terms with its splendor and sheer size. This zone, with its vast, shiny new buildings and new streets, is the most convincing sign of Berlin's revival. Amazed visitors apparently meet there to waste what Berlin used to be so stingy about: time. In Potsdamer Platz, a stroll becomes an urban pleasure, a recent twist to a brand new lifestyle. Up until now, Berliners could only find quiet by leaving town. Today they can go to Potsdamer Platz, with its Sony Plaza and Marlene-Dietrich-Platz. Formerly, Potsdamer Platz was the hub of a hard-working metropolis; now it is a place for promenades. Berliners are experimenting with new ways of walking: strolling, ambling, wandering. And for the first time in their history, they seemed delighted. The area is also a real magnet for tourists.

The New Town. The new Potsdamer Platz is much larger than the old one, which was not a square but a circle (and a lively one, at that). In contrast, Leipziger Platz, nearby to the east, is a large octagonal plaza around which impressive new

buildings now rise, such as the Canadian Embassy and the Mosse Palais, named after Jewish publisher Rudolf Mosse. Potsdamer Platz has now given its name to the entire zone stretching as far as the Landwehrkanal to the southwest and the Tiergarten to the northwest; when people refer to Potsdamer Platz, they mean much more than the streets radiating out from the Potsdamer Platz suburban train and subway stations. They are referring to an entire neighborhood that includes Leipziger Platz and extends as far south as the Kulturforum. It is impossible to take in this new neighborhood, with its conglomerate of heterogeneous buildings, in a single glance. At night, the zone is easily recognized by its signs and logos, the bright green cube set atop the Debis building, and the lighted roof of the Sony Center, which resembles a huge circus tent and gives the neighborhood a playful, artistic feel.

The Sony Center on Potsdamer Platz was designed by German-American architect Helmut Jahn. The tower, right, with its shimmering glass and steel façade, is Berlin's tallest building.

In the foreground is a "wall for art." Next to it is the old building of Huth wine merchants (above).
Italian architect Renzo Piano designed the main building of the Daimler-Chrysler scheme, clad in honey-colored tiling (right). In the background rises the green Debis-Signet building.

The overall scheme called for a mixed use of space, 50% being devoted to offices and 20% to housing, with the rest allocated to community use (shops, restaurants, theaters). Architecturally, the plans called for buildings of various sizes. Skyscrapers over 300 feet were allowed, but this high-rise silhouette had to be balanced by a labyrinth of streets that would persuade conservative residents of the capital to accept this leap into modernity. And the concept has worked, resulting in a creation as reassuring as it is bold. When walking through the area, strollers sometimes feel they are in a kind of lively old town, and at other moments in a typically American towering street with its geometric skyscrapers of steel and shimmering ceramic façades.

Delbrück-Haus, a large, soberly elegant building that houses a bank, is clad in fine, natural stone, pale gray in tone, decorated with bronze doorways and window frames. Designed by Berlin architects Kollhoff and Timmermann, the structure marks the northern entrance to Potsdamer Platz. Its southern counterpart was the work of the same two architects, and is part of the Daimler-Chrysler zone. This huge "slice of the pie," which runs as far as the canal, was bought by the automobile corporation shortly after the fall of the Wall. It has become one of the area's key draws, thanks to the Marlene-Dietrich-Platz, the Imax-Kino movie complex, and the Musical Theater (for Broadway-type musicals). It is best explored by strolling down the old Potsdamerstraße, Eichhornstraße, and Linkstraße. Here is where Paris-based architect Renzo Piano made his mark on the new neighborhood. His most remarkable accomplishment is undoubtedly the headquarters of the service company Debis. Some 300 feet high, the building can be seen from afar thanks to its logo. Open to the public, its imposing atrium has the scale and appearance of a basilica, and is decorated with interesting sculptures such as Jean Tinguely's *Meta-Maxi*. Piano's tall building, which occupies a triangular site, adds a note of refinement to the area and

serves as a gateway to the highly built-up southern perimeter. The cool transparency of the glazing is counterbalanced by the rosewood-colored tiling, which creates a warm feel.

Piano's contribution, however, has not been restricted to the corporate world. He also designed some of the leisure facilities: the Imax-Kino, the theater, and the casino. The latter two overlook Marlene-Dietrich-Platz and form the western edge of the Daimler-Chrysler zone. Their façades, with their silvery reflections, are a nod to the golden façade of the national library next door.

Opposite the Kulturforum, near the Tiergarten, the sharp edge of the Sony-Europazentrale building advances like the prow of a ship on Lennestraße (top). Renzo Piano also designed the strong, rounded forms of the Imax-Kino on Marlene-Dietrich-Platz (left).

Members of parliament sitting in the Reichstag have a view of Potsdamer Platz across the Tiergarten (above). The Filmhaus houses the world's largest collection of items devoted to the most famous of Berliners— Marlene Dietrich (right).

New Berlin's Most Famous Plaza Before work began, plans for the area were the subject of stormy debate. The difficulty lay in balancing considerations motivated by nostalgia with a desire for striking modern architecture. The final result is a compromise, which is probably one of the reasons for the square's popularity. Those who find the Arkaden shopping arcades too "mercantile" like the soberly rebuilt station, whose vast, three-level dimensions only become apparent once underground. The delicacy of the glass and steel street entrance is delightful. Meanwhile, people discouraged by the uniformity of so many office buildings are consoled by the Sony Forum, located on the northern edge of the city near the Tiergarten. The Forum is part of the Sony Center, the European headquarters of the giant Japanese electronics firm. It was designed in 1991 by German-American architect Helmut Jahn and officially opened in 2000. The forum itself is one of the most popular spots in new Berlin. It consists of an oval covered plaza 40,000 square feet in area, flanked by fine modern buildings housing offices, shops, restaurants and cafés. The Forum is also home to the (formerly West) German Academy of Cinema and Television.

Also located in the Forum is the *Kaisersaal* (Imperial Room) of the old Hotel Esplanade, a typical example of the refined decoration of Germany's imperial days; the architects were instructed to incorporate elements of the 1911 hotel into their design. Although the Esplanade had to be moved—via a complex hydraulic system—it now seems at home its new setting. The architects also had to preserve the old edifice called the Weinhaus Huth, formerly a wine merchants, the only other surviving building on Potsdamer Platz. The edifice was converted into a restaurant that now welcomes a clientele as demanding as the original customers.

One key attraction of the Forum is its extraordinary roof, which seems to float above the plaza and can be opened, re-shaped, or closed. It gives the vast space below a more intimate, convivial feeling. This tent-like covering consists of strips of glass and translucent fabric held in place by metal cables. It has a delicate, airy quality, providing the Forum with an artificial firmament.

Potsdamer Platz was conceived as a business district. Its enormous popularity with the public is due to two factors. On the one hand, enough housing and leisure space was added to the office premises to prevent the area from emptying at night. And on the other, the scheme has brought back to life what had previously been a huge, empty site (perhaps the most profound and lasting reason for its popularity).

Below the arcades of Potsdamer Platz, strollers wander among the trees as though in a huge indoor garden (above).
As this landscape of cranes and construction sites at Potsdamer Platz shows, Berlin is an evolving city (following double page).

The Kulturforum. No other site in the heart of a major city has undergone such a dramatic transformation in so little time. At the end of the 1980s, Potsdamer Platz was still an open wound in a capital damaged by war, a vacant lot in a Walled town, a remote spot in a city divided by the Cold War. Previously, it had symbolized the hectic, innovative business district of a booming capital city, where Europe's first traffic lights were installed (nostalgically restored today). In the 1920s, it was considered the busiest square in the Western world, the throbbing heart of an international metropolis, a crossroads where the life and business of an uncertain young republic was at its most intense. But then came collapse. Potsdamer Platz was abandoned like a factory whose products no longer interested anyone. The Wall was right next door. Street urchins, the homeless, and itinerant salesmen used the vacant lot on the eastern edge of town to gamble, to swap or steal merchandise.

Despite the stagnation caused by the Wall, new buildings were erected not far away. In the late 1950s and early 1960s, Hans Scharoun reshaped the landscape by designing the Philharmonie and the Staatsbibliothek (National Library), whose extraordinary, powerful volumes won people over. Another major Berlin building, the Neue Nationalgalerie (New National Gallery) was Mies van der Rohe's last design (1968). Yet even this wonderful structure did not manage to revive Berlin's lifeless heart. Residents of the divided city dubbed the vacant lot with its immense arts complex the *Elefantenwiese* (Elephant Meadow), enjoying the concerts given there. Nowadays, the Kulturforum is taking on new life within the expanded Potsdamer Platz, giving the business district a cultural dimension and a deeper meaning.

The Architects of New Berlin. The new city's architects designed buildings that were often bold, sometimes beautiful, and always costly. By common agreement, it was decided that only the finest materials suited the capital: a good deal of glass to let in light, much natural stone for its sober nobility, expensive woods for their fine feel, ceramic tiling for visual impact, and hard metals to flatter the residents' pride.

And all the representatives of countries who installed their embassies here have done likewise—the Mexicans, the Finns, the Maltese, and the Swedes. Somewhat to the west of Potsdamer Platz, in Tiergartendreieck where, a few years ago, the annual Frühlingsfest (spring festival) was held with its big Ferris wheel and roller coaster, impressive new buildings have appeared. Although they are diplomatic establishments, they are partly open to the public and visitors will discover that there was no stinting on resources and that their sober, elegant forms are resolutely modern. The Mexican Embassy, for instance, is a total novelty for Berlin—its façade is composed of large white shafts of concrete into which have been set blocks of marble that glimmer in the sun. The architects, Gonzales de Léon and Serrano, proudly claim that they deliberately ignored city guidelines because they had no

Various outdoor sculptures have been placed around the Neue Nationalgalerie, such as Herkules *(1971–72) by Maschinksy-Denninghoff (facing page). Hans Scharoun's distinctive Kulturforum houses the Museum of Musical Instruments, the Philharmonic, a concert hall for chamber music, and the National Library (above).*

Bronze statues of Frederick I and Sophie Charlotte with a model of Charlottenburg (top). The copper façade of the Nordic embassy compex (above).

From the top of the Victory Column at Großer Stern in the Tiergarten you get a wonderful view of the city (right). In the background rises the needle-like television broadcasting tower.

desire to erect yet another set of "façades of holes," by which they meant endless walls with windows.

Nordic embassies acquired a certain notoriety when five countries—Denmark, Sweden, Norway, Finland, and Iceland—joined forces to develop their lots on Lützowplatz collectively. It was a world first: never before had diplomatic bodies sacrificed territorial sovereignty and autonomous embassies for a collective project. The resulting building shows that it was a wise decision. A band of copper strips surrounds the five buildings, highlighting that they are each part of an ensemble; their link is further embodied by a communal building, the Felleshus. Architecturally, the various buildings in the Nordic embassy complex are devoid of pomp. They have an appealing lightness and grace, and display a typically Scandinavian predilection for natural materials such as wood.

Also in Tiergartendreieck, the conservative Christian-Democratic Party (CDU) has established its national headquarters in a strikingly unusual building that resembles a ship cutting through the waves of the capital—the imposing prow appears almost menacing. The Social-Democratic Party, meanwhile, also designed a new building for its headquarters: Willy Brandt Haus (1995), located a little further east, near Halleschen Tor on Stresemannstraße, is another open construction, traversed by light. Its triangular shape and sharp angles are surprising and it, too, suggests a ship in the way its bow juts into the corner of an intersection. Apparently, Germany's major national parties see themselves as captains navigating the maelstrom of History.

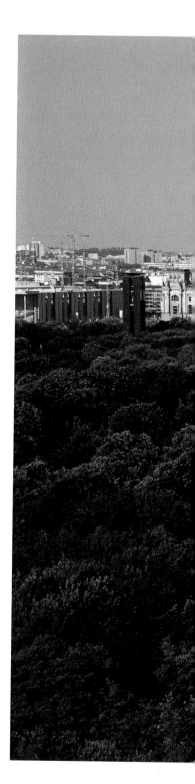

Designed by artist Hans
Haacke for a courtyard
of the Reichstag, this
earth pit contains soil
brought by every member
of parliament from his or
her native region (above).
The Reichstag dome
aroused controversy when
it was first proposed.
The glass cupola,
designed by Sir Norman
Foster, serves as a viewing
platform and has proved
immensely popular (right).

Reichstag and Chancellery. East Berlin's largest contractor is none other than the Federal Republic itself. The new Berlin would never have seen the light of day without the aura provided by a government of national scope and international contacts. One of the best-known official buildings is the Reichstag, erected during the imperial period on a design by Dresden architect Paul Wallot. It was completed in 1894, and can be reached on foot from Potsdamer Platz by heading down Tiergarten toward the Spree; its dome can be seen from a distance and guides the stroller like a lighthouse. This monumental rectangle with four corner towers used to be right next to the Wall, just inside the Western sector. It had lost its original dome and was very dilapidated. Around 1961, it was sufficiently refurbished to host meetings and exhibitions. But it served no authentic purpose. Children flew kites on its overgrown green, officially dubbed "Republic Plaza." When the Wall was torn down, the Reichstag was still there, waiting for its day of glory, along with German democracy. Some people expressed reservations, of course, about making Berlin the capital of Germany and re-establishing the Reichstag as the seat of the nation's parliament—the weight of the past was too heavy, they claimed. "What!" retorted those in favor, "It's just a chamber! Modernize it, move in, and have your debates and arguments, but this time according to the rules, and with the rest of Europe in mind—and you'll see: everything will be fine." Subsequent events have proved them right.

Exactly one hundred years after the original edifice was completed, the distinguished British architect Sir Norman Foster was commissioned to renovate Wallot's unlucky child, preparing it to enjoy better days as the seat of parliament. The architect returned to Wallot's original plans, removing all additions made after initial construction. At the German parliament's request, he even agreed to rebuild a modern version of the dome. The glass cupola admits a good deal of light and seems trapped in scaffolding. From a distance, it

almost looks unfinished. Since this original achievement is a reflection of Berlin itself, it has become one of the main symbols of the new city. Berliners have dubbed it the *Eierwärmer* (egg warmer). It is open to the public, which has been pouring in. The artist Christo contributed to the Reichstag's popularity in 1995, a few years before the elected officials returned, when he made a dream come true by wrapping the entire building in a splendid white garment. Thus appareled, the parliament building awoke from its long and controversial dormancy.

Germany's chancellor also required a suitable mansion. When the Wall fell and the Democratic Republic of [East] Germany collapsed, an entire series of official premises became available to house the new Berlin government. No one, however, really wanted to move into a former East German ministry. So new buildings went up. The new Chancellery, for instance, was built from scratch. It is the most prominent component of what is known as the Band

The main part of the new Chancellery (dubbed "the washing machine" by Berliners because of its boxy shape and round hole), is the centerpiece of the Band des Bundes, the strip of federal government buildings erected along the Tiergarten. Inner courtyards and gardens make the offices a pleasant place to work (above).

Spectacular views of the city can be had from the observation platform on the Reichstag (left). The mirrored cone inside the cupola reflects daylight down into the parliamentary chamber thirty feet below. A computer-controlled shield tracks the sun to prevent glare (right).

des Bundes (Federal Strip), a string of buildings located in the Mitte neighborhood. It coils twice around the Spree, and extends from the Chancellery gardens to the parliamentary offices. The new Chancellery is a colossus of concrete and sandstone some 1,100 feet long, one of Europe's most imposing government edifices. Berlin architects Axel Schultes and Charlotte Frank designed a linear series of sober, elegant, uniform office buildings. Schultes declared: "With this construction, we wanted to incite politicians to show imagination." The "government villa," as this building is popularly known, is nevertheless 12 feet shorter than the Reichstag, thereby deferring to parliament's supreme constitutional authority.

Island in the Spree. The Chancellery is a short distance from the historic center of town—you can either follow the Spree on foot or take the S-Bahn east. Spree Island, in the very heart of Berlin, underwent the same fate as the rest of the city; many things were destroyed, far too many. Yet there remained sufficient vestiges to attempt a reconstruction that offers a glimpse of what Berlin looked like in the past while making room for novelty.

The northern tip of the island is occupied by Berlin's five great museums, which alone justify a trip to the capital. Collectively known as "Museum Island," the area is currently being renovated under the supervision of British architect David Chipperfield. The central part of the island was formerly the site of Berlin castle, now demolished. Currently, it is occupied by the Palast der Republik (East Germany's "Republic Center"), whose future remains undecided. Formerly, the old town of Berlin and its various businesses were located on the southern tip of the island. On the opposite bank, to the northwest, is the old Saint Nicholas neighborhood, Nikolaiviertel, which has been partly renovated; it is delightful to wander through this pretty medieval setting with all the restored inn signs flanking the thirteenth-century Nikolaikirche. The old fishing quarter, in contrast, has completely vanished. Only one row of eighteenth-century houses—a rare sight in Berlin—on the southernmost tip of the island gives some idea of the former beauty of this vanished neighborhood. The finest of the houses is Ermelerhaus, which projects all the splendor of a Rococo palace; it is now a hotel in which you can admire works by the artist Georg Baselitz.

On the north end of the island is Prussian architect Friedrich Schinkel's most handsome and sublime effort: the Altes Museum (Old Museum). The building is the oldest on Museum Island (Museumsinsel), and Schinkel himself considered it to be his most successful work. With its colonnade and large dome, it has an impressive simplicity. The island also boasts another structure by Schinkel, namely the fine Schloßbrücke (Castle Bridge), lined by eight magnificent marble sculptures.

The pointed steeples belong to one of Berlin's oldest buildings, the thirteenth-century Nikolaikirche, which gave its name to the surrounding neighborhood (left).

In this charming part of the neighborhood, narrow streets with old-style shop signs give strollers the impression of being transported back to the eighteenth century (above).

Karl Friedrich Schinkel considered the Altes Museum to be his finest accomplishment. Along with the Pinacotek in Munich, it was the first German museum to be opened to the public (above). The Schloßbrücke spans the River Spree and is dotted with statues by Schinkel. Behind it is the Deutscher Dom (facing page).

Schinkel's Berlin. The Schloßbrücke leads to the foot of the old avenue known as Unter den Linden. That is where many major Prussian buildings are to be found: Humboldt University and the Staatsoper (National Opera House) face one another, followed by the Kronprinzenpalais (Crown Prince Palace) and Zeughaus (the Arsenal), buildings steeped in history and restored with care. Here, too, on the right-hand side (between the National Library and the Arsenal) is another work by Schinkel—the Neue Wache (New Guard House). Inspired by Roman barracks, this was the architect's first construction project in Berlin. It was inaugurated as the royal guard house in 1818, and owes its fame to its lively history as well as to its architectural merit. Today it serves as a memorial and houses a *Pietà* by Käthe Kollwitz.

A great classical architect, Karl Friedrich Schinkel (1781–1841) left his mark everywhere in the capital. He became architect to the court of Prussia during the difficult days of the Napoleonic wars. In addition to being an architect, Schinkel also drew, painted, created theater sets, and invented new styles. He was a designer in the broadest sense of the term.

Schinkel's genius stemmed from his conviction that every artist had to push his abilities to the limit. He wanted to be surprised by his own work. He rejected the Rococo style expected by his patrons because he felt that it lacked dignity and inventiveness. Schinkel refused all compromise with the spirit of his times. He sought a syncretic style that would transcend periods, establishing links with the major phases of the history of architecture. Marked by his long stay in Italy, he was also influenced by Gothic architecture. A later trip to England, just then entering the industrial era, allowed him to discover the austere charm of utilitarian buildings in which function determines form. Schinkel thereby revived antiquity even as he became a prophet of modernity. His Altes Museum, his Neue Wache, and his theater on Gendarmenmarkt are a few of Berlin's buildings that now boast a real patina of age. They incarnated Schinkel's vision of a return to the harmony of ancient Greece. In a way, he could even be considered a forerunner of the Bauhaus, as demonstrated by his academy of architecture (the reconstruction of which is currently being considered), his unbuilt plans for a Kaufhaus (department store) on Unter den Linden, and his Gewerbeinstitut (Institute of Decorative Arts) on Klosterstraße. His legacy has thus been a lasting one, even though his work was dismissed by some as lacking sufficient pomp.

Old Berlin would not be what it is today without Schinkel—nor would new Berlin. Contemporary architects honor him, restore him, quote him. Thus two buildings flanking the gate of Platz vor dem Neuen Tor, the work of Berlin architect Josef Paul Kleihues, manage to restore to the site some of the aura it had when Schinkel built two customs houses there. The new edifices are distinct from the old ones, but they respect the proportions established by Schinkel. Furthermore, a Schinkel museum now exists in a church he designed, the Friedrichwerdersche Kirche.

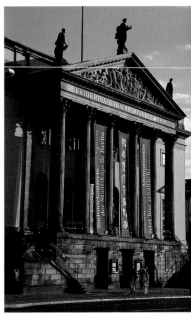

Germany's first
independent Opera House
was built on Unter den
Linden in 1741–43 (top).
A detail from Schinkel's
Neue Wache (above).

Unter den Linden. Right next to the Neue Wache, the Zeughaus (Arsenal) is one of the oldest buildings in the castle sector. It was begun in 1695 and completed in 1706. Architect Andreas Schlüter worked simultaneously on the castle and the arsenal. An extension is now being planned for this Baroque building, whose roof is decorated with sculptures that can be seen from afar. New York architect I. M. Pei has been asked to pursue the concept he began with his pyramid at the Louvre in Paris, namely to add a futuristic construction to a historic monument. For the moment, the Zeughaus is home to the Deutsches Historisches Museum (German History Museum) and to a very pretty coffee house.

But Unter den Linden is not only the avenue of kings and prince electors, it also bears the mark of the burghers who frequented the boulevard (and lived there, if they could afford it). Bettina von Arnim, widow of the great Romantic writer, lived at number 21, on the third floor of the Raczynski mansion. There she held a kind of salon, where she invited all the leading minds of the day. Poet Friedrich von Schiller also moved to Unter den Linden in 1804: "My wife and I are much happier in Berlin than we would have thought. Here there reigns great individual liberty and freedom from the rigidity of bourgeois life." These days, the same liberty can be seen on the avenue where classic and contemporary architecture coexist, as do students and opera singers, bankers and diplomats, the old and the new. Berlin's old freewheeling spirit is beginning to blossom again "under the linden trees."

Pariser Platz. To the west of the avenue, visitors can admire the Brandenburg Gate, which remains the international symbol of Berlin. Designed by Carl Gotthard

The Adlon Hotel, the DG-Bank designed by Frank O. Gehry (left), the Brandenburg Gate (below), and a reminder of the Nazi book-burning campaign in May 1933: a glazed recess in the ground on Opera Platz containing empty shelves (bottom).

The Zeughaus (Arsenal) is the oldest historic building on Unter den Linden, an avenue with a proliferation of lively cafés as it nears the Brandenburg Gate (facing page).

Langhans on the model of the Propylaea in Athens, the entrance to the Acropolis, it was inaugurated in 1791. The monument projects a solemnity worthy of ancient Greece, along with an aristocratic grandeur. It consists of twelve columns in two rows supporting a pediment and roof topped by a four-horse chariot.

The gate and its chariot formerly overlooked the glamorous Pariser Platz (Paris Plaza), but the war left few traces of this elegant meeting place, and the Wall delivered a final blow by running through it and completely depopulating it. Not surprisingly, the square became a vast construction site after the fall of the Wall in 1989. People wanted to restore it to its former glory. The architects of the new Hotel Adlon based their design on the old one; Haus Liebermann (to the west of the Brandenburg Gate) and its twin Haus Sommer (both designed by Kleihues) are similar to the original buildings without, however, disguising their modernity. Meanwhile, on the north side of the square the French Embassy is currently under construction, designed by Frenchman Christian de Portzamparc, an architect known for his bold designs. Opposite this stands another remarkable new building, the headquarters of the DG-Bank. Conservative Berliners shuddered on learning that American architect Frank O. Gehry would design the building, for he was hardly an advocate of classicism. And yet Gehry respected zoning guidelines, erecting a rectilinear classical façade and saving his audacious creativity for the bank's interior atrium, which is dominated by the curved shapes and organic lines typical of his style.

Pariser Platz is finding its unity once again, and now symbolizes Berlin's true luxury: space. The city can expand because it boasts a great deal of space. Visitors who gaze down Unter den Linden from the Brandenburg Gate or who look westward to the Tiergarten do not suddenly feel small. Instead, they are amazed by the vast perspective to be had from Pariser Platz, and the enormous portion of the city that can be viewed in a single gaze.

Gendarmenmarkt

To the east, behind Friedrichstraße, halfway between Wilhelmstraße and Spree Island, is Gendarmenmarkt, considered by some to be the most beautiful square in Berlin and one of the finest in Europe. With three harmonious monumental buildings—Französischer Dom (French Protestant Church), Schauspielhaus (Playhouse), and Deutscher Dom (German Protestant Church)—it has enthralled visitors for three centuries. It was heavily damaged during the war, and the authorities in East Berlin long hesitated over its reconstruction. The work was only completed after reunification. Gendarmenmarkt has once again become one of the city's most attractive spots.

A theater on Gendarmenmarkt designed by Langhans burned down in a fire in 1817 (it was already the second one on the site). So Schinkel was commissioned to build a new playhouse. He saved a few portico columns from the former building and incorporated them into the vestibule of the new theater, at the top of a monumental staircase. Even today, the symmetry and nobility of this temple of performing art are impressive, although Schinkel, as usual, added a touch of joyous if elegant sobriety. The interior is worth a visit. Decoration so colorful and delicate is rarely seen in a performing arts venue. Today the theater is used as a concert hall and has been renamed Konzerthaus Berlin.

The houses on Charlottenstraße, Mohrenstraße, and Französische Straße were highly sought after and a neighborhoud of artists, philosophers, traveling salesmen and eccentrics formed. In the Weinlokal Lutter und Wegner, established in 1811 in Charlottenstraße and immortalized by E.T.A. Hoffmann and Jacques Offenbach, writers, musicians, and actors met to drink and chat. Bismarck dined here, as did Marlene Dietrich. At the turn of the twentieth century, the neighborhood became more affluent and banks opened branches here. But these changes did not alter the square, which has retained its cosmpopolitan atmosphere, as well as its beauty and grandeur.

Gendarmenmarkt is considered to be one of Europe's finest squares (left). Schinkel's Konzerthaus, with its monumental staircase, is sometimes used for official ceremonies (above).

The highly varied architecture on the new Friedrichstraße: in the middle is the glass façade of the Galeries Lafayette and beyond it Quartier 207 (above).
The Quartier 206 building is particularly striking at night when the façade lights up (above right).

Friedrichstraße

From Gendarmenmarkt, take two successive left turns and head west until you run into Friedrichstraße, a famous street that before the war was lined with cafés, bars, and restaurants and was a favorite haunt of prostitutes. Back in the Roaring Twenties, Heinrich Mann wrote: "Men and women stagger and reel from the fury of jazz. Dance has become an obsession, a fixation, a cult. The stockmarket hops, ministers sway, and Parliament leaps about. Poets twist, seized with visionary convulsions, and girls from the new cabaret theaters wiggle their posteriors, carried away by the rhythm." Allied bombing caused widespread destruction, however, and few buildings remain from the prewar period.

These days, there are more jet setters than bohemians, but the street still bustles. The new buildings give this treeless street a certain unity and the intersection of Friedrichstraße and Unter den Linden is one of the city's busiest places. It has witnessed many architectural transformations. Lindencorso, the sober but robust building on the corner, was the first new project, and sparked debate among architects in the 1990s: did the height limit of Berlin buildings (70 feet) have to be strictly respected, or should architects go higher? Should traditional models be followed, or bold innovations attempted? The conservatives won out, and Lindencorso, designed by Frankfurt architect Christoph Mäckler, seems to many people somewhat monotonous. That is not the case with every building on Friedrichstraße, however. Between Jägerstraße and Taubenstraße stands a striking design by Pei Cobb Freed & Partners: its sharply angled projections and its black and white façade hark back to the rich tradition of German Expressionism. Known as

Quartier 206, this building is a mini-mall of luxury stores and recalls the handsome shopping arcades built in cities like Paris and Milan in the late nineteenth and early twentieth centuries. A visit to Quartier 206 is a must, even for visitors who do not intend to buy—the splendid shops and mosaic flooring are well worth a look. And a ride on the escalators is a good way of appreciating the charm of the Art Deco-inspired interior.

Just a stone's throw away, French architect Jean Nouvel created a sensation with his Berlin branch of the Paris department store, the Galeries Lafayette, on the corner of Friedrichstraße and Französische Straße. The rounded corner harks back to the curves favored by Berlin modernist architects of the 1920s, the suggestion of a dome alludes to the city's classical architecture, while the sleek glass façade is thoroughly contemporary. The interior startles visitors with its playful variation on the grand staircase typical of such department stores: two gigantic, transparent cones several stories high expand the space, allowing shoppers browsing in the circular galleries to have a view of the whole.

Many major newspapers have established their Berlin headquarters on Friedrichstraße. The people who work for them are naturally open to novelty, and flood Friedrichstraße in search of original items or a *café au lait* in the Galeries Lafayette.

The glass cone in the Galeries Lafayette unites all the floors of the department store. With its mosaic flooring, spectacular stairways, and Art Deco-style décor, Quartier 206 has become a popular attraction for shoppers and sightseers.

Courtyards, such as this one at Prenzlauer Berg, are blossoming with foliage that residents maintain with patience and imagination (above). The group of courtyards known as Hackesche Höfe in Charlottenburg is perhaps the most spectacular example of renovation, housing small businesses, apartments, art galleries, and cafés.

Life in Berlin's Courtyards. In Berlin, an intimate link between work and home, between housing and business premises, has long been part of the urban landscape. The manufacturer August Borsig himself built his legendary villa (where he invited the Kaiser) in the middle of a property occupied by his machine factory in the Moabit neighborhood. More modest entrepreneurs opted for the "courtyard" solution: they lived in a fine house facing the street, then set up a firm (printshop, photo lab, sewing-machine factory, fur trade) in a side wing or building in a rear courtyard. Thus a whole series of premises were divided into living spaces and workshops, especially in the Kreuzberg neighborhood where this system of lively courtyards spread extensively, which is why people still refer to a "Kreuzberg mix." Yet such courtyards also exist in Mitte, Schöneberg, Neukölln, and Prenzlauer Berg—in fact wherever small firms flourished. Sometimes, a building might contain three or more courtyards in a row. Some of them were completely devoted to housing. Even today, the wings overlooking renovated courtyards are highly sought after for their quietness. More and more Berliners are turning them into little gardens or playgrounds, or opening galleries or bistros there.

In recent decades, many small factories have closed. Service industries have taken their place. There where hammers were heard, where machines puffed and panted, people now draw, study their computer screens, or perspire: fitness clubs, dance schools, tiny theaters, language schools and software developers have moved into the courtyards, allowing them to survive. Strollers in Berlin should not hesitate to venture inside when passing the large entrance to a building. There will surely be something or other to discover: a fashion-design workshop, a second-hand store, an art school, or at the very least a picturesque bench alongside a flowering shrub.

One particularly successful restoration has drawn attention to these courtyards. The Hackesche Höfe, located in Hackescher Markt, is a vast series of eight courtyards which, like many other sites of the same type, were in a dilapidated

state in the early 1990s. Initially occupied by young squatters, they were subsequently renovated by smart investors who turned them into mixed premises that became a magnet for art lovers and the night crowd. Those who enjoy traditional coffee houses, fine restaurants, music-hall shows, specialized art galleries, or underground movie theaters come to Hackesche Höfe. Once tourists have seen it, they realize that a truly new Berlin exists, where it is possible to hang out and have fun. Built in 1906–7 by architect Kurt Bernd, these courtyards were renovated by August Endell; they created a sensation by showing how the old can be made new thanks to an alliance

The three linked courtyards bounded by Sophiestraße and Gipsstraße are known as Sophie-Gips-Höfe, and are devoted to the visual arts. The text on the wall at the left is an artwork by Thomas Locher, Wunsch und Wirklichkeit *(Desire and Reality); next to it is the entrance to the Hoffmann collection.*

Trompe-l'oeil paintings on the façades and walls of Berlin are becoming increasingly common. Permanent residents and visitors alike can enjoy a surreal image on Wilhelmstraße in Kreuzberg, a giant zipper in Charlottenburg, or a wall painting not far from Potsdamer Platz (above).

between courageous investors, imaginative architects, a shrewd town council, and an enthusiastic population. There are twelve houses flanking the courtyard, in addition to a theater dedicated to Jewish culture, and stores selling jewelry, clothing, shoes, and bicycles. The Aedes architecture gallery, which has a branch on Savignyplatz, is also located here. The whole complex covers 100,000 square feet and is the largest of its kind in Europe. The façade of the building on Rosenthaler Straße, together with the one on the first courtyard, have been wonderfully restored, and for good reason: a delight to the eye, they are late examples of Art Nouveau, incorporating Art Deco features and a play of forms and bright colors that notably include a touch of cobalt blue.

The neighborhood to the northwest of Hackescher Markt is an extension of Spandau. Here there once stood a city gate leading from Berlin to Spandau. It was a poor neighborhood, and many Jews lived here. Forced to the edge of the city, they maintained their own culture there. These days, Jewish immigrants are particularly drawn to this district, and they are beginning to set their seal on the neighborhood once again. Now renovated, it has lost its shabby appearance; the gold dome of the synagogue sparkles, and the many courtyards lend charm to the area. The success of Hackesche Höfe has sparked other projects. Sophie-Gips-Höfe, for instance, houses a new building designed by architects Hilmer and Sattler. The Kunstsammlung Hoffmann (Hoffmann Art Collection) has moved in and can be visited on Saturdays (reservation required); visitors are greeted by a surprising monochrome electric installation. Also worth mentioning is the Kurt-Bernd Höfe, a fine restoration of buildings dating from 1912 that now house offices. Not far from the Hackesche Höfe, these two complexes can be seen on a single tour. Somewhat further west, near the Oranienburger Straße station, is the Kunsthof, which has a similar history. It was also highly dilapidated, but has now been carefully modernized. It offers charming galleries and several restaurants, including the Café

Silverstein, founded in 1910, with a delightfully authentic ambiance. Nearby, in the Heckmann Höfe between Oranienburger Straße and Auguststraße, are a number of off-beat little galleries. Such courtyards are an irresistible invitation to shop or stop for a coffee. Also nearby is the Kunsthaus Tacheles (Arts Center), where the Berlin's new off-Broadway theater scene emerged. Shortly after the Wall fell, this former department store was slated for demolition, but it was rescued by a group of young artists, musicians, and kindred spirits who were determined to turn the place into their "arts center." With its graffiti-covered walls, Kunsthaus Tacheles is the venue for a range of provocative and stimulating concerts and productions.

Two of Berlin's most famous wall paintings are the bow of a ship done in sophisticated perspective on a building in Charlottenburg, and the teeming imagery on the Kunsthaus Tacheles (left and above). The latter, in particular, encapsulates the spirit of Berlin's underground scene.

The word Kiez is used when talking of a neighborhood with a pleasant "village" atmosphere that is more than just an address (top). The Kulturbrauerei is part of the Kiez of Prenzlauer Berg; residents are proud of the friendly atmosphere and visitors are made to feel at home (above). In the new Berlin district of Mitte, early twentieth-century buildings have been completely renovated, their top floors being converted into superb lofts. Modern buildings have also sprung from the ground (right).

Neighborhood Cultures. To really get to know Berlin, it is essential to explore a *Kiez*. *Kiez* is an old Slav word that means "quarter" and is now used with reference to neighborhoods with a highly mixed population, where there is a strong feeling of social cohesion and where the concept of neighborhood still means something. Such neighborhoods attract young people, immigrants of all nationalities, large families, artists—people who cannot pay high rents and who like living in places that are old, sometimes poorly maintained but always dynamic. Many residents fall in love with their neighborhood and remain there all their lives, because they have come to know it and watch it change, sometimes with curiosity, sometimes with melancholy. In short, a *Kiez* is a friendly place where people feel at home in the middle of a large, throbbing, anonymous city. Not all neighborhoods, of course, can become a *Kiez*. The Dahlem district is not one, nor is the delightful Lichterfelde with its affluent population and beautiful villas. In contrast, the old town on the southern tip of Spree Island, where a large number of very poor Berliners once lived, was called *Fischerkiez* (fishermen's quarter). And in Kreuzberg or Prenzlauer Berg, residents still speak with pride and affection of "their" *Kiez*.

Neighborhood cultures are thus local, varying greatly from one *Kiez* to another. In Kreuzberg, a district in the west of the city that is once again benefiting from its proximity to Mitte now the Wall is gone, has a culture strongly marked by squatters who, in the 1970s and 1980s, saved the old buildings from destruction. Many students, artists, and young dropouts live here, but there are also Turks, asylum-seekers from all over, and retired folk who have never left the neighborhood. The district is bounded by the River Spree, by Viktoriapark to the south, and by the remains of a station, the Anhalter Bahnhof. Most of the old streets are well equipped and decorated, and the houses have sometimes been restored by the owners themselves, attracting attention because they form little oases or even rural villages nestling in the heart of the city. They are easy to identify from the gardens in front or on the rooftop. Many such houses are located around Oranienstraße, a multi-ethnic shopping street in the middle of the *Kiez*, between the U-Bahn stations Görlitzerbahnhof and Moritzplatz (not to be confused with Oranienburger Straße, another unusual if somewhat disreputable street). Music and the scent of barbecues from courtyards spill into the street. Here, street parties are highly popular and last a long time. And since Kreuzberg is one of the poorer neighborhoods, it is the residents themselves who play the music and perform theatrical improvisations. They also hang out in the area's smoky coffee houses, strange bars, tiny taverns, Indian restaurants, and microscopic theaters.

The southern edge of the quarter is marked by Viktoriapark, the oldest public park in Berlin. It embodies three typically Romantic features: closeness to the people, a dash of patriotism, and love of nature in its wild state. The hill on which the park is perched was originally called Mount Tempelhof, and is the highest mount in the city, offering a splendid view. The Gothic cross raised in remembrance of the "Wars of Liberation" (against Napoleonic domination) was the work of Schinkel, and gave the hill and surrounding neighborhood the new name of Kreuzberg ("cross mount"). The park was laid out later, in the nineteenth century, and was named after the crown princess of the day, Victoria. It was designed in a Romantic spirit, that is to say as a landscape garden yet retaining the vistas overlooking the city. In the early twentieth century, Viktoriapark was further enlarged in order to provide the growing population with a place of leisure. Even today, many Kreuzberg residents are drawn to this highly picturesque site, spending hours in front of a beer at the Golgotha Biergarten. From the top of the hill, looking toward Großbeerenstraße, you can see the former newspaper district along Kochstraße. You can also see "Checkpoint Charlie," the famous point of passage into East Berlin for the Allies; on the left is the ruined entrance to the Anhalter Bahnhof station, preserved as a memorial. In the foreground is the Hebbel Theater, a surprising Art

The Maybachufer market, between Kreuzberg and Neukölln, is called the "Turkish market" or "Little Istanbul," which is hardly surprising given the high percentage of Turkish residents in both neighborhoods (above).

The word Destille
(distillery) refers to
a place where schnapps
is made. These days,
the sign indicates a bar
where strong spirits are
served. The Henne (The
Hen) on Leuschnerdamm
in Kreuzberg is a typical
Berlin tavern with a
typical interior: a long
bar, strong shelves to hold
the bottles of alcohol,
a chandelier hanging from
the ceiling, and a warm,
friendly atmosphere. This
establishment dates from
1907. There is only one
dish on the menu—
chicken. Which should be
washed down with beer.

The easiest way to get around Berlin is by bicycle. Even gourmet restaurants are aware of this, and provide bike racks (above). Tourists who wish to see the city in a peaceful fashion can hire motorless rickshaws at the Rikscha cycle service in the Mitte district (above right). A beer garden in Mitte, where the benches quickly fill up when the weather is fine (right).

Nouveau building that hosts performances of avant-garde dance. With Berlin booming once again, Kreuzberg is redeveloping its business activities without, however, sacrificing its dynamism and multi-ethnic population.

In both Prenzlauer Berg and Mitte, it is easy to see the extent to which the city has been transformed on the social, practical, and architectural levels. This old working-class neighborhood was relatively unscathed during the war. It came under East German control and was never renovated. After 1989, the barracks-like buildings were severely dilapidated. But buyers and tenants were drawn to the area, charmed by the Art Nouveau tiling and colored glass. A number of writers moved in. Time seemed to have stopped here, and the layers of dust concealed a love of detail on the part of the area's original working-class inhabitants. The housing was not luxurious, of course, but nor was it just a series of rabbit hutches.

After the fall of the Wall, the structure of the population changed radically in just a few years. As before, artists and creative people the world over have been fascinated by the atmosphere of rebirth that is occurring here. Many young business people in new sectors of the economy have set up their headquarters here, along with their apartments. They spend their evenings in one of the many cafés in the *Kiez*, for example the Prater on Kastanienallee, the oldest

Biergarten (beer garden) in Berlin. Just around the corner, down the unusually broad Oderbergerstraße, there is a series of bars, galleries, and restaurants that have retained their charm. For three days each year, Oderbergerstraße becomes "the street of art," and is lit by thousands of candles at night. Those seeking a meal between two exhibitions sometimes stop off at the Rosenbaum, a restaurant featuring excellent regional cuisine.

Back up Kastanienallee to the north is Knaackstraße with its Kulturbrauerei, a magnificent red brick building—not unlike a medieval fortress—where beer was once brewed. Today, however, it features a brew of art and theater. The cultural center in the building offers various types of entertainment: concerts, exhibitions, flea markets, theater, movies, plus coffee shops and restaurants. Just across the street, meanwhile, is the secret heart of Prenzlauer Berg—Kollwitzplatz. This is where you will find such well-known spots as the Café Westphal, Restauration 1900, and the Russian restaurant Pasternak. This *Kiez* has all the makings of an artists' neighborhood.

The Fascination of Berlin. The big city on the banks of the Spree and Havel Rivers has always attracted foreigners, due to its rapid growth and its modernity. In the second half of the twentieth century, the fascination of Berlin was a

*Checkpoint Charlie
on Friedrichstraße was
once the only gateway
between East and West
for Allied troops and
foreigners (left).*

fascination with horror. People came to see the Wall, the
ruins, the remains of Nazi buildings. They came to have a
fright. Now a new era has dawned. Berlin can revel in its
unification and its freedom—it can indulge in leisure, cultural,
and artistic activities. A great sigh of relief can be heard all
across a city that can now win the hearts of visitors for
qualities other than the morbid appeal of devastation. Berlin
is seizing this opportunity, creating new construction sites
even as it preserves older buildings that testify to past
grandeur. The world looks on with enthusiasm and
curiosity at what is happening on the banks of the Spree.
And everyone is buying tickets for Berlin.

At the start of its history, the town of Berlin was just a watering spot for livestock on the route from the Rhine to regions east. This seclusion is still perceptible today: as though placed in the wilds of Brandenburg by two powerful hands, Berlin rises amid fields and forests like some roaring Moloch. Luxuriant nature is now creeping back into the city, although the growth of housing has always been contained by a green ring of parks and meadows. And had some giant founded the city by letting Berlin fall from the sky, there would have been a hell of a splash, because the area flows and gurgles with a skein of rivers and lakes that give a maritime feel to things, even though the sea is far away.

Lakes cover an area of 4,800 acres, while the rivers and canals run for 125 miles. Germany's capital can be completely crossed and visited by boat. Almost no other city boasts so many bridges: there are 1,195, of which 560 span water.

The abundance of bridges stems not only from the size of Berlin and the number of meanders taken by the River Spree. It is also due to the fact that Berliners neglected to build streets, lanes, banks, parks, and façades parallel to the river. Such development would have allowed people to explore the town by following the waterway, as can be done in Paris, for instance.

In the days when Berlin was being developed, residents viewed the River Spree as both an advantage (which permitted navigation) and an obstacle (which had to be spanned). But they never considered it as a potential treat for the eyes.

The Baroque palace of Charlottenburg stands majestically in the grounds overlooking the Spree. It can be reached by water from Potsdam (previous double page). In summer, the Tiergarten is a favorite spot for Berliners, young or old, native or newcomer (left). The Wannsee links Berlin with Potsdam (facing page).

58

The Landwehrkanal (above). A view of the entire city can be had from the top of the TV broadcasting tower on Alexanderplatz. Here we see the River Spree running through Berlin's industrial center. (right)

THE RIVER SPREE

The Spree permits waterside strolls only at certain spots, for example at Kronprinzenufer or Reichstagufer in the Tiergarten and Mitte neighborhoods, or on Schiffbauerdamm near the Friedrichstraße S-Bahn station downtown (where Kupfergraben also follows the Spree). But quayside paths are never very long and always terminate in a dead-end. Visitors are thus obliged to take a boat if they want to discover the full length of the Spree, or at least its central section from Charlottenburg Park to Rummelsburger See.

Central Berlin's second most famous body of water is the Landwehrkanal. In a way, the canal is a southern pendant to the Spree, giving a special feel to the Kreuzberg and Schöneberg neighborhoods in the heart of the city. Narrower than the Spree, the canal was clearly designed for work and not pleasure, but it provides some of Berlin's rare waterside strolls, notably along Paul-Linck Ufer and Maybachufer.

Attitudes are now changing and people are beginning to realize that a river is a visual asset as well as an economic one. Indeed, waterways have become synonymous with leisure. In the past, the banks of the Spree were occupied primarily by barges that noisily transported coal and gravel. Nowadays, these vessels have new dockside neighbors: on terra firma, a growing crowd of strollers in search of fresh air, and on the water itself an ever-increasing flotilla of excursion launches. People are acquiring a new taste for the beauty of the riverbank with its flora and fauna; they enjoy the sight of swans gliding along the water, of seagulls flapping their wings, of froth rimming the waves.

Where should the conquest of Berlin's waterways commence? On the Spree. Nearly 250 miles long, it rises in Saxony, runs through Spremberg and Cottbus,

A fleet of white barges takes tourists through the city on the Spree and the Landwehrkanal. This one is cruising down the Spree through the Nikolaiviertel. In Charlottenburg, houses that overlook the river are highly prized (left).

The Oberbaum Bridge is an emblem of East Berlin, because the Wall crossed the Spree over it. It was built in 1894–96 to resemble a fortified medieval bridge (right). The Treptowers office building (1995–98) rises some 400 feet above the Spree. To the left is Molecule Man, a 100-foot sculpture by Jonathan Borofsky (above).

crosses the Spreewald (a separate region to the south of Berlin) and Müggelsee, then meanders through Berlin before flowing into the Havel.

It is a major thoroughfare running from east to west, capricious yet navigable, often marked by bends but sometimes providing straight, smooth stretches, as at the eastern docks. Here, in the inner city, one bridge after another throws its path of stone over the water; everywhere, pedestrians wave to passengers on board the boats. If you reserve a seat on an excursion boat that leaves the Spree at Kreuzberg to head down the Landwehrkanal toward Wannsee and the Havel, you will see that Berlin is an island in the midst of waterways that periodically widen to form lakes.

The joys of bathing
in the Wannsee are
legendary. The beach
of white sand, which is
dotted with wicker huts,
has a distinct seaside feel.

WANNSEE AND GRUNEWALD

In the days when Berlin was emerging from the Brandenburg plain, when the rivers flowed around the town, protecting and fertilizing it, both east and west were endowed with broad freshwater rivers and lakes. The Wannsee to the west is nevertheless the Berliners' favorite lake. This wide stretch of water—nearly two-thirds of a mile across—is a bay of the River Havel (itself a tributary of the Elbe), on the western outskirts of town. Its wooded shores have been perennially popular. As soon as people arrive at the Wannsee, they forget the city. The eastern shore of the lake surprises visitors with its Mediterranean-style beach—the longest inland beach in Europe. In summer, city dwellers stream to this large expanse of fine white sand, relaxing in beach chairs, under umbrellas, in beach huts. From there they can watch children splashing in the water, sailboats, and the graceful strip of trees on the opposite shore. At the Wannseeterrassen Restaurant, customers can enjoy a meal on the terrace as they watch bathers in Europe's largest inland lake.

After a swim and a meal, pleasure-seekers head into the neighboring green woods, or Grunewald, that surround the Wannsee and the Havel with beech, birch, oak, and pine. Despite the large number of strollers, the woods still abound with game, including wild boar. In the heart of the dense forest, one suddenly glimpses the shimmering waters of the Schlactensee, Krumme Lanke, and Grunewaldsee (where concerts are held in the summer). They form a chain, a group whose dappled, fragrant clearings give the dark wood its appealing, peaceful nature. On the shores of these magical little lakes people loiter, fish, and swim; nearby are inns with terraces, boats for hire, flirting couples, and chirping birds (not to mention the

mosquitoes). All these lakes—for there are still others, such as Hundekehlesee and Teufelsee—are so many gaps riddling the gigantic Grunewald, like windows shedding light in a dark vaulted ceiling. In summer, Berliners flock to them in large numbers.

Heading east through the woods, in the direction of the Havel, sooner or later the stroller arrives at Grunewald Tower, which offers both a wonderful view and a good cup of coffee. Opposite, on the edge of the Grunewaldsee, is another point of interest, the Jagdschloß. This little "hunting lodge" was built in 1524 for Elector Joachim II. Heavily altered in the seventeenth and eighteenth centuries, it is now an amalgam of styles. Inside are displayed paintings by Dutch and German masters from the sixteenth and seventeenth centuries, including works by Cranach the Elder and Rubens.

The Wannsee is also very popular with sailors. There are even Berliners who believe that yachting was invented in their city.

The Grunewald "hunting lodge" was built in 1542 and lent its name to the area: "Zum grünen Walde" (in the green woods) (left).
The Königsee is slightly to the north of the Grunewaldsee, in Wilmersdorf, and is thus within Berlin city limits (above).
The inner courtyard of the Grunewald hunting lodge is a bucolic sight (right).

THE MÜGGELSEE

The top of the Müggelsee tower offers a wonderful view of the lakes to the east of Berlin, including the Müggelsee, Seddinsee, Krampe, and Langer See. The network of streams and canals between Erkner and the Müggelsee has been dubbed "New Venice." Along its leafy banks (right), East Berliners formerly installed little summer homes with gardens, called Datschen *(right).*

To continue our tour of Berlin's lakes, we must cross the city or travel down the Spree in order to get from the Wannsee in the southwest to the Müggelsee in the southeast. This lake is an eastern replica of the Havel and Wannsee, and makes for an equally pleasant outing by boat. Its surface area of nearly 1,800 acres makes it the largest lake in Berlin. It also has a beach. Leaving from Jannowitz Bridge, you can go as far as Rübezahl dock, halting at an inn of the same name. This trip has the added charm of a little journey back through time. Indeed, East Berlin, having remained behind its wall for decades, was spared all forms of modernization and mass tourism, and thereby preserved a bucolic simplicity perfectly suited to the green city of Berlin. Residents and tourists alike can breathe clean air and contemplate waterfowl. The Romantic peacefulness of the spot draws visitors seeking still, deep waters, hoping to hear the hum of a dragonfly's wings from time to time.

What the Wannsee is
to the west of the city,
the Müggelsee is to the
east. Locals simply call
it "the swimming hole."

It is not as developed
as the Wannsee,
however, and is the ideal
place to relax or take
a peaceful stroll.

At the Kalksee in Woltersdorf, you can take a boat trip through New (or Little) Venice, via the Flakensee and the Dämeritzsee, and then across the Müggelspree. Lining the banks, which are so close you can nearly touch them, are the tiny Datschen *built by Berliners. For avid paddlers, canoes can also be rented. The journey ends at the Müggelsee where, by crossing the lake itself, you reach the Köpenick district of Berlin (above left and left).*

A villa at Rahnsdorf by the Müggelsee (left). Also on the banks of this lake is the Museum im Wasserwerk, a waterworks museum based in a nineteenth-century pump house now listed as a historic monument.

ISLANDS IN THE HAVEL

landscape architect, Peter Joseph Lenné (1789–1866). Like his fellow architect Friedrich Schinkel, Lenné resisted the craze for Rococo splendor, preferring instead to meditate on the mute grandeur of the ancient Greeks and the noble diversity of the somewhat less ancient Italians. Lenné adopted the fertile ideas of English landscape gardening, which had emerged in the previous century, and created a second, falsely primal nature from raw materials. Horace Walpole pointed out at the time that gardeners henceforth displayed their talent by hiding their art. Lenné had that kind of talent. And this part of the Havel, with its islands, its vistas, its copses, and its parks, still bears the traces of his genius.

Pfaueninsel. "Peacock Island" is Germany's purest surviving example of an early landscape garden. Visitors arrive by ferry, because cars are forbidden. They then follow paths to the palace, in the footsteps of Frederick William II's mistress (for whom the park was designed). Although the paths seem naturally overgrown with vegetation, nothing is a product of chance. Here and there a glimpse can be had of an imitation ruin or charming fountain and then suddenly you arrive at the magnificent Kavalierhaus. Such surprises are a traditional part of landscape gardens, designed to imitate reality almost to the extent of including wild animals to frighten strollers—indeed, there was once a menagerie on the island. Waterfowl can still be seen on the pond, however. A temple can be glimpsed through the bushes, venerable trees stoop overhead, and to the south a rose garden perfumes the isle. Buildings, benches, flowerbeds, and fountains echo one another like rhymes in a poem or episodes in a story, welcoming and guiding visitors with ceremonious zeal. Art is not only hidden here, it plays hide-and-seek, crouching beneath the mask of

Pfaueninsel (Peacock Isle) is one of the most magical spots on the Havel, and its hidden nooks conceal amusing surprises. These include the artificial ruins of a castle with a Gothic footbridge, and a dairy in the form of a medieval tower (above and facing page).

The Wannsee, as we have seen, is a lake hollowed from the River Havel. It is impossible to miss, for it dominates the southwest edge of town, where it sparkles vast and blue under the sun (or bubbles nervously under a silver-gray rain). But the Havel also keeps a few little secrets—its islands. Not only do they have Romantic names—Schwanenwerder, Lindwerder, and Pfaueninsel (Peacock Island)—but they host Romantic retreats featuring a little palace surrounded by lanes, grounds, and animals. Pfaueninsel boasts some sixty peacocks, which wander around in complete freedom, uttering their distinctive cries. Was nature the architect of all this beauty? Not at all. The part of the Havel that so charms us today, running from Potsdam to Spandau and including Grunewald and the plain and forests of Glienicke and Zehlendorf, was largely the work of a brilliant Prussian

The palace on Pfaueninsel was also called the "Roman House." The décor includes allegorical reliefs, such as these in the tea room, that are based on antique models. Queen Luise's favorite room in the palace was this bedroom with its elaborate floral decoration (right).

chance and random vegetation. It is best to visit the island on a weekday during the off-season, so that you encounter the fewest possible tourists when discovering this idyllic setting.

The king who began the palace and grounds died very young. He was succeeded by Frederick William III, whose famous queen, Luise, had asked Napoleon to spare Prussia. Frederick William III enjoyed spending his summers months here, and it is worth taking time to see the charming interior of the palace. The rooms, with their strange mixture of styles in the Romantic manner, have been well preserved and maintained.

In the palace on Pfaueninsel, lavish dinners and chamber music concerts were held in the large reception room upstairs. It is almost entirely paneled in wood of various kinds. The walls and floors were worked in the classical style, as was the relief over the doorway. Most of the palace is made of wood (far left). This spiral staircase leads to the top of the south tower. Following the well-known axiom of English landscape gardening—to unite art and nature—the stress was placed on organic forms (left).

The octagonal room in
the north tower gives
the illusion of a little
bamboo hut. It was
designed to create a
meditative atmosphere.
Real windows alternate
with painted ones,
stressing the play between
dream and reality.
The painted window
above offers a view of
Pfaueninsel itself, set in
an imaginary tropical
landscape complete
with parrots and
pineapples (left and
above).

KLEIN-GLIENICKE

Among the royal palaces and parks, Klein-Glienicke (located to the south, just opposite Pfaueninsel), holds the promise of even greater pleasure. Also designed by Lenné and Schinkel, it might be considered the very model of a *locus amoenus*, or pleasant spot, thanks to the delightful harmony between palace, garden, river, and grounds, between domesticated nature and exuberant fountains, between nostalgia for antiquity and the Romantic spirit. This magnificent setting is one of Berlin's most appealing attractions. Here, Prince Karl of Prussia (son of Frederick William III and Luise) joined Schinkel and Lenné to form a felicitous triumvirate that created a veritable gem of a palace set in a pleasurable décor with monumental entrance, fountains, pavilions, and belvederes. Here, everything is lightness, allusion, quotation, flirtation. The belvederes, offering fine vistas, are called the "Great Curiosity" and "Little Curiosity," while the gilded lions stationed in front of the *Schloß*, or palace, are copied from those at the Villa Medici in Rome; the third "curiosity," known as the Stibadium, was based on a semi-circular bench originally unearthed in Pompeii. When Prince Karl acquired the property in 1824 it had already been developed, so Lenné and Schinkel merely had to modify things. Karl and his designers saw eye to eye on everything, combining to create a very esoteric garden.

To the south of the "Curiosities" is the Glienicke bridge spanning the Havel. Here, 150 years later, things were not so funny. Along with the Wall, this bridge was the major symbol of the division of Germany and of Berlin as a front-line city. The bridge separated East from West, and it was here that the United States and the Soviet Union regularly exchanged their captured spies (many films show the bridge cloaked in gray mist).

The palace of Klein-Glienicke harbors belvederes and pavilions, and has now been transformed into a restaurant and an elegant casino over-looking the Havel.

Schinkel's veneration of antiquity is omni-present, from statue-filled niches and mosaic flooring to colonnades and porticos that imitate Roman villas (above and right).

*The "Great Curiosity,"
built by Schinkel on the
palace grounds in 1835,
is a belvedere that affords
an enchanting view of the
surroundings (left).
In 1824, Schinkel
transformed a billiard
room into an elegant
casino (right).
The large fountain
with lions at the palace
entrance is another work
by Schinkel (far right, top).
The pillars of the gate
are topped by gilded
griffins (far right, bottom).*

FROM CHARLOTTENBURG TO THE TIERGARTEN

Leaving the Havel and Grunewald behind us, heading north and then east along the Spree, we come to a remarkable site: the palace known as Schloß Charlottenburg and its grounds. The park is a successful blend of French-style formal layout with English-style landscaping. The palace was heavily damaged during the war but has been faithfully reconstructed, as have the surrounding grounds. Delightful flowerbeds, hedges, and downy lawns soothe the eye and lift the spirits. People seeking serenity can stroll the pebbled lanes; those who prefer stimulation can enjoy the sound of a fountain spouting in the middle of an octagonal basin. People drawn to the wild beauty of a landscape garden head for the carp pond (*Karpfenteich*). Fairly recently, the streams linking the pond to the Spree were cleared, having silted up a century ago; the palace can therefore now be reached from the river. To the west is the Mausoleum built for Queen Luise. Schinkel designed the building, with its antique grace and Prussian austerity, for the beautiful queen, while sculptor Christian Daniel Rauch immortalized her on the carved sarcophagus. At the north end of the grounds, near the river, is a belvedere hidden behind the trees; it houses a remarkable collection of porcelain.

If we leave Charlottenburg by the Spree and continue east along the river, we soon come to the largest and best-known park in Berlin—the Tiergarten. This local version of Central Park or Hyde Park extends across over 500 acres, and for a city like Berlin is already fairly ancient in a "historic" sense: the grand electors used to come here to hunt, until the Prussian rulers developed a sense of aesthetics and became more interested in the gardens than in the game. In the days of Frederick the Great, rectilinear

lanes were laid own for pedestrians and riders. Later, around 1790, the Bellevue Palace, currently the residence of the president of the republic, was built on the grounds. Lenné, in his day, also made a contribution by attenuating the formal austerity of the park, almost giving it the appearance of a wild landscape garden. These days, the grounds boast multiple features. There are charming, flower-dotted areas lined by little hedges, perfect for strolling, with curved wooden bridges that span idyllic lakes; but there are also fields for playing soccer, and restaurants for dining with the family. Particularly appreciated is Neuer See on the western edge of the Tiergarten. This particularly charming spot has a tree-shaded café right near the lake with its fish and birds. And yet we

The exuberant green decoration on the walls alludes to the four seasons and the four elements (facing page).
Sunlight enhances the splendor of the gallery (below).
The belvedere, or tea house, picturesquely set between the Spree and a pond, is an example of the successful transition between Baroque and early Neoclassicism (left).

at the top, who is popularly called *Goldelse*. The view from the top of the tower is definitely worth the trip (the steps are not too arduous): it overlooks the entire city, throwing into relief the highest buildings and greenest parks. In addition, Grosser Stern is where outdoor concerts and sound-and-light shows are held, and Berlin's newest mass event, the Love Parade, passes this way.

The Tiergarten with, in the distance, the Chancellery (above). The Spree runs through the Tiergarten, so the Victory Column serves as a landmark on water as well (right, top). Live-aboard boats manage to find a mooring on the Landwehrkanal, in front of a testing site for hydraulic and naval constructions (right, bottom).

are still in the heart of Berlin. For people who prefer pomp, the eastern part of Tiergarten boasts imposing memorials to composers Haydn, Mozart, and Beethoven, as well as a majestic statue of Richard Wagner done in 1903 (near Tiergartenstraße). In the southern part of the Tiergarten, the Luiseninsel (Luise Island), renovated in the 1980s, is another superb spot. The paths, trees, lawns, and even the gates and walls surrounding the flowerbeds, have all been restored in their original style. The result is extraordinary. The scent of flowers, the combination of colors, the silence, the play of water create an enchanting if melancholy atmosphere.

In the middle of the Tiergarten shines the Grosser Stern (Great Star), which is simultaneously intersection, panoramic tower, and memorial (to the war between France and Prussia, 1870–71). From far away you can see the gilded statue of winged victory

Every weekend, people flock to the Tiergarten for picnics and recreation (left). One of the park's most charming spots is the Luiseninsel (above). Victory spreads her wings at the top of her column (top). Berliners can even picnic next to Schloß Bellevue, the presidential residence.

Other Parks. For people who seek the calm and privacy of a garden in order to relax, but do not have the time to travel to the outskirts of town, Berlin offers an attractive selection of public gardens, parks, and green spaces located right in the city. Many such places exist, of greater or lesser size. Some, like Körnerpark in Neukölln, were laid out in a neo-Baroque style, while others, like Schillerpark in Wedding, are more relaxed in style. In a way, they have replaced the woods and meadows which were cleared to make way for the growing city. Hasenheide, between Kreuzberg and Neukölln, is another place where Berliners like to unwind. In 1586, when this green, hilly site was still attached to Cölln, Berlin's twin city, it was already an enclosed park or hunting ground. According to a decree issued by the Elector, the perimeter enclosure had to have holes large enough "so that rabbits can get through it." These days, Hasenheide is a lively garden where families come to picnic, play games, and make music. People seeking greater peace and quiet should head for the Botanical Gardens (Botanischer Garten). These splendid grounds, covering some 100 acres, are known for their colonial architecture and 18,000 rare plants, most of them from exotic lands. On weekdays, when the weather is damp, the gardens are almost empty; yet they are invaded by heavy, shifting scents evoking the garden of some oriental harem. Built over 100 years ago, the gardens employ the natural hills and dales with their ponds to capture the rays of the sun required by trees and bushes from foreign climes. Elsewhere, artificial banks were built to recreate the conditions of wind, humidity, and heat similar to those found in Asian regions. Strollers who come here are inevitably struck with a strong yearning for points south—the same kind of nostalgia that Lenné and Schinkel once fostered so skillfully.

Berlin's Green Belt. One final word on Berlin's wonderful outskirts: the lakes in Märkische Schweiz and Wandlitz are marvels of light and beauty, preserved in their wild state. Here, no one has developed the banks or laid out pathways. The occasional visitor can gambol like deer or hare through the woods; trees even grow in the lakes. The lake is pure as spring water, and is dense with water-lilies and strange fish. Only in rare places does a skiff or landing indicate that people have passed this way. Although this description is most accurate during the off-season, even on summer weekends crowds are rare in the countryside surrounding Berlin. The country is too big, too spacious, and above all too underpopulated for throngs to form. And every Berliner sufficiently interested to explore "his" or "her" parcel of countryside knows a secret place no one else does, apart from a few squirrels. A place where you merely have to stoop to gather up all the plums you can eat.

Given its vastness, the green belt around Berlin will remain wild and pleasant for a long time to come. A new generation will be able to appreciate and preserve the splendid serenity of Brandenburg's marshes, meadows, and lakes. Berlin, that fundamentally pragmatic, assertive, down-to-earth metropolis has a true need for bucolic poetry—the city needs to be reminded that life is not all hustle and bustle, that at the gates of the city, beyond the gardens that attract strollers, there lies nature in all her mystery, so gentle and inviting.

In summer, the neo-Baroque Körnerpark is the principal attraction in Neukölln (facing page). The clear waters of countless little lakes just outside Berlin inspire peace and calm (top left). For nearly one hundred years, an annual tree-blossom festival draws visitors to Werder, south of Berlin (above).

A dream garden in Berlin: these narrow little plots in a Gartenkolonie allow Berliners to enjoy the pleasures of gardening. They are often adorned with little wooden chalets (above right).

INTERIORS

Berlin has always had its heart in several places, which means that one homogeneous style of interior decoration has never been embraced by all. During the Gründerzeit, or "foundation years" (1871–1913), affluent burghers had a heightened source of self-importance and adopted the William II style. In terms of interior decoration, this meant that ceremony was more important than comfort, appearances more important than practicalities. Living rooms had to project an imperial image, with ostentatious, majestic overtones. The predilection for pomp was also reflected in decorative accessories, such as lace tablecloths, fabrics of plush cotton or wool, and curios. Furniture was arranged in each room more to define space than to serve a practical purpose. An apartment was a stage set on which important families played out their lives.

Although most of bourgeois Berlin adhered to this general spirit, it was implemented in widely differing ways—William II style was characterized by a wealth of ornamentation that encouraged a casual approach to decoration. No strict guidelines existed, everyone had the right to combine or contrast whatever seemed appropriate: Rococo and Biedermeier, Classicism and Art Nouveau.

The twentieth century tore asunder what William II had brought together and the diverse fragments were amalgamated with the products of modern art, from Bauhaus to Postmodernism via Art Deco, "New Objectivity" and strict functionalism. Today Berlin serves as an experimental field for all those who combine and invent styles. Massive sideboards, little dressing tables, imposing wardrobes, ethereal glass cabinets, and magnificent sofas of the nineteenth century are still around (at least in drawings and photographs). But they have been rearranged and modified according to the new, sober lines of the twentieth century. Thus we arrive at an eclecticism that is somehow typical of Berlin.

Berlin interiors often blend the old and the new. This spare, modern living room in a listed historic building was designed by Arne Sterf (previous double page). This elegant pavilion was inspired by Schinkel's Pomona Temple in Potsdam. The wooden deck is ideal for sunbathing (right), while the interior has been made comfortable for days when the weather is not good (left).

WOLFGANG JOOP'S
FIRST HOME

The garden invades the home as fresh flowers adorn tables and furnishings. The screen hides a Biedermeier-style bed which reminds us that 150 years ago the average height of people was somewhat shorter than it is today.

Once upon a time there was a very old farm right next to the gardens of the palace of Sanssouci. The king's gardener bought the farm for his son. And the son moved in with his wife. This occurred in the early twentieth century, and it was a great stroke of luck for the fine old house and property.

Today, the royal gardener's granddaughter, Ulla Ebert, occupies this property on Ribbeckstraße, near Potsdam. She was born in the house eighty-three years ago. She shared a happy childhood with her sisters, but it ended suddenly with the outbreak of war. In the torment of the final days of the conflict, one of her sisters had a child by a man whose name—Joop—was already famous at the time. So on November 18, 1944, little Wolfgang Joop entered the world in the old family house, surrounded by his loving mother and aunts. And while bombs were pounding in the night and Russian troops were marching on Potsdam, Wolfgang's life began in the care of the three sisters (his father had been taken prisoner and would not come home for nine years).

This education, initially provided solely by women, certainly marked little Wolfgang as much as the architecture and beautiful gardens and interiors that were part of Potsdam's tradition. But once the country was divided, Potsdam found itself in the East German sector, and the Joop family left for the West. Ulla Ebert, however, could not bring herself to abandon the old property.

Perpetuating family tradition by constantly perfecting the magnificent garden became her one goal in life. "I was always trying to create new impressions and landscapes. People are right when they say a garden is never finished." Absorbed by this long-term project, Ebert remains very active. Her nephew, who not long ago was swinging in the garden, has now become Germany's leading fashion designer. He began making a worldwide name for himself in the 1980s, which was a boon to his aunt back in East Germany— she won the right to travel. And Wolfgang Joop would visit her on Ribbeckstraße, bringing his friends from the world of art and fashion. "The house was always in an uproar." In the dining room decorated with fine marquetry furniture from Florence, they "pushed back the tables in order to dance."

Then came the watershed of 1989. It was a long time coming, but not so long that Ulla Ebert missed it. The Joop family home was completely modernized with a great deal of finesse. Frau Ebert has lived through some dramatic times in the handsome old dwelling: "Sometimes it was very trying, but you have to know what you want in life. What I wanted was this house and garden."

The old kitchen has been modernized in a charming way. The rustic doors on the cupboards conceal state-of-the-art kitchen appliances. Although Frau Ebert appreciates such luxury, her main goal was to recreate the atmosphere of a traditional kitchen (right). She is also very proud of her Biedermeier furniture, some of which are family heirlooms, others being gifts or bargains discovered at flea markets (above).

HEINZ BERGGRUEN
IN CHARLOTTENBURG

The Stüler barracks (1859) were named after its architect, a student of Schinkel. Standing opposite the main façade of Schloß Charlottenburg, it has two wings, one to the east and the other to the west, and was built to house the king's personal guard. It was never imagined that this late Neoclassical edifice would house a bourgeois interior with kitchen and bedroom, yet that is what has happened. The person living in the west wing of the barracks is not just any old body, of course: he's Heinz Berggruen, a native Berliner forced to flee his home town due to his Jewish background. He became an art connoisseur, collector, and dealer, first in California and later in Paris, returning to Berlin just a few years ago with his outstanding collection. This act of reconciliation generated relief and admiration in Berlin and throughout the rest of the world.

Berggruen placed his collection of 175 works of modern art at the disposal of the city of Berlin, which suggested displaying it in the Stüler barracks. At the same time, the collector was given an apartment above the exhibition rooms. That means that Heinz and Bettina Berggruen not only live opposite Schloß Charlottenburg in the heart of west Berlin, they also live among their treasures, which include eighty-five works by Picasso. Berggruen was a friend and admirer of the Spanish artist. Yet his neighbors also include—via their paintings—Paul Klee, Henri Matisse, Paul Cézanne, Georges Braque, Alberto Giacometti, and Vincent van Gogh. Berggruen is surprised by the crowds who throng to the gallery. Although the hubbub from the galleries can be heard in the upstairs apartment, he is delighted by the popularity, because he does not like to keep art hidden in private places, away from the public. "The paintings are there to be seen and appreciated."

The apartment of art dealer Heinz Berggruen is reached by ascending this graceful spiral staircase (facing page).

He and his wife live in an apartment above his extraordinary collection of modern art (above).

A LITERARY SALON IN WILMERSDORF

If the hints of a renaissance of Berlin's "salon" culture turn out to be true, then all future gatherings of the city's best minds will have a single forebear: Nicolaus Sombart. The writer and sociologist, who is nearly ninety years old, taught at Ulm, Freiburg, and Wuppertal, but his greatest achievement has been the salon he has hosted in Berlin since the 1980s.

Those years were not propitious to such an initiative. It was felt that the days of intellectual salons had passed. The semi-private, semi-public gatherings known as salons were invented in France by high society women such as Juliette Récamier and Germaine de Staël. Later, well-known salons were organized in Germany, especially Berlin, where the one held by the legendary Rahel Varnhagen is still remembered. Hosting a salon means receiving a variety of guests, introducing them to one another, and encouraging them to discuss music, painting, literature, politics, and current events. It is an art in its own right, one in which women excelled. Sombart has now proven that a man can also achieve success in the field, and he has inspired the hope that the remarkable institution of salons still has a future.

A salon should take place in a handsome interior and Sombart's dwelling in Wilmersdorf provides a perfect setting. The typical Wilhelm II décor, with its stucco-edged ceilings, parquet floors, and glazed, ornamental doors, goes perfectly with the furniture of velvet settees, heavy carpets, and divans covered with brocade throws. It is clearly an intellectual's home—the shelves of a large bookcase stretch across every wall in the room, and almost all the souvenirs (pictures, figurines, photographs) are related to the host's intellectual career. The furniture is not costly,

Nicolaus Sombart's life is guided by three main drives: mental stimulation, eroticism, and intellectual debate among guests. His comfortable home provides a perfect setting for such things. The columns flanking the entrance to the salon are typical of large, bourgeois apartments of the imperial period.

just friendly and comfortable. There is no superfluous decoration to distract the proceedings that begin every Sunday at noon, which involve making contacts, launching ideas, exchanging opinions, sharing witty conversation. The standards are high—there is constant debate, occasional gossip—and Sombart, as host of the salon, makes sure that no guest leaves without having learned something new.

It is not a public salon. An invitation is required. Every guest is entitled, however, to bring one other person who can contribute to the conversation. Some guests appear regularly, others are invited at intervals of several years The food and drink are unimportant—Sombart serves tea and cake for those who may have skipped breakfast. What really counts is the food for thought, which the host carefully prepares, seasons, and serves to his guests. Without Sombart, these Sunday gatherings would not be what they are. Yet he is seeking successors, young people who, like him, possess the gift of spurring intelligent minds to converse. More particularly, he is encouraging young women to revive the grand salon tradition.

Some of the fine architectural models owned by Ernst von Loesch (top), who also collects miniature obelisks as souvenirs of his travels to southern climes (above). A view of the apartment from the bedroom. The wrought-iron chandelier lights the passage between the rooms (right).

CLEAN-CUT CLUTTER
IN FASANENSTRAßE

Bronze, Sienna marble, alabaster—these were the kinds of souvenirs brought back from a grand voyage in the eighteenth and nineteenth centuries, when people toured southern Europe and northern Africa. Ernst von Loesch sells these old mementos and model monuments, which he also collects. He lives surrounded by them in a wing of a grand building on Fasanenstraße in Charlottenburg.

The colors of those treasures are echoed in two apartments situated one above the other. Von Loesch inherited the lower floor from his grandmother, Susanne Gropp, a well-known interior decorator. She left behind vestiges of the 1950s, such as a built-in kitchen and mirrored doors. "When kids used to visit," recalls Loesch, "they found it fun and very original." He has managed to integrate his favorite pieces of furniture not only with eighteenth- and nineteenth-century works, but also with contemporary designs, a blend that has seeped into every room of the home. "This is what I call clean-cut clutter," he says with a smile. Von Loesch and his wife have applied some witty touches; when they found an old nineteenth-century wooden lotto game at an antique shop, they brought it home and placed it on an inlay Biedermeier commode, next to everyday objects such as an iron device used to wind wool.

In addition to miniature monuments, Herr von Loesch also collects and sells old architectural drawings to collectors. "I rarely see professional architects," he says. What fascinates him about these sketches and drawings is the contrast between the technical depiction of abstract cross-sections and the attractive views of the buildings themselves.

In the upstairs apartment, a sketch for the design of a mosaic floor in Berlin hangs above a red sofa. The

table in the middle of the room is also reddish, but with black legs—it is in fact a Chinese chest made in the 1850s. The exotic effect is deliberate. Of lacquered leather, at one time it was a veritable luxury item. Boldly, von Loesch has added everyday objects in red iron from northern Germany. In the downstairs apartment, a counterpart to the one upstairs, decorated in much the same fashion, a touch of red recurs in the sitting room. An old Chinese children's bathtub sits next to the fireplace, above which is an old mirror made at the royal glassworks near Potsdam. Both interiors brilliantly demonstrate how to marry the old to the new, the useful to the playful, the professional to the personal. The couple have created a world built on miniatures, one that is nevertheless expansive. Von Loesch comments: "I often wander through the rooms and leaf through objects the way you'd leaf through a good book."

The bedroom creates a feeling of spaciousness and peace. Hanging over the bed are precious nineteenth-century Chinese scrolls that accompanied books of poetry.

MIXING STYLES
IN MOABIT

Moabit is a typical Berlin neighborhood. The buildings in the southern part, bounded by the Spree, are grand and imposing. To the north, near the working-class district of Wedding, the exteriors are sometimes in a sorry state, and the living conditions of the inhabitants are not always the most comfortable. Nevertheless, you can still find apartment houses there with fine, decorated facades. One of them is home to an artist who is especially fond of old-fashioned Berlin interiors. He lives in a surprisingly well preserved turn-of-the-century apartment building and has succeeded in giving his home the same aura as it must have had in 1900, when it was originally built. The result is simply stunning.

The apartment is composed of three superb salons, divided by double doors. Close inspection reveals that these lavishly decorated, comfortably appointed rooms combine several styles. The combination is successful, if a little unsettling. In the bedroom with balcony, cherry wood Biedermeier furniture cheers the room, lit by a light fixture of Murano glass; a stone-incrusted Indian table sits in a corner opposite the balcony. The sitting room, meanwhile, features three large sofas covered in rasberry-colored fabric. Above one of them hangs a reproduction of Van Dyck's *Rest on the Flight to Egypt*. The owner admits that the quality of the print is less than perfect, but he wanted this harmonious painting in this very spot. The dining room is endowed with a long table, palm trees, and frescoes painted by Viennese artist Stefan Riedl in pastel shades of yellow, showing antique-style porticos. A door to the kitchen is masked by wallpaper. The paintings on the walls belong to various periods, schools, and countries.

Everything is different, yet unity emerges. The secret of that unity lies in the period being recreated—the "foundation years" from the end of the nineteenth-century to the beginning of the twentieth-century, a period of bourgeois affluence and opulent architecture and decoration.

"I like that period," admits the owner with a smile. It is a somewhat risky confession, because those years under the German empire, marked by a taste for pomp, are not very fashionable today and held by some in low esteem. Is such an attitude still justified? That is the question that comes to mind on seeing these rooms so full of charm and sensuality. True enough, the Berlin of the past did tend toward pomposity and heaviness, but that is hardly the case here. It was and evidently still is possible to combine eclectic styles in a very pleasing way. Gilded stucco for a Rococo touch? Why not? Biedermeier comfort in the sitting room? Naturally. Not to mention nostalgia for Mediterranean climes in the dining room and Henri Chapu's bust of Joan of Arc in the entrance hall. Collectively, all these elements create a curious but playful atmosphere, staging a witty, stylistic tribute to Berlin's former heyday.

A bedroom in the working-class neighborhood of Moabit. The wood floor and frame bed create a wonderful contrast with the refined detailing on the chandelier and door handles (left).

The dining room is enlivened by murals and luxuriant plants and flowers. The sitting room, meanwhile, is marked by the imposing presence of venerable furniture in cherry wood (right).

This little Swedish table in the "blue room" features lamps from Nany Wiegand-Hoffman's collection (top). In the larger, mainly "red" sitting room, this mirror creates a striking presence. It is flanked by nineteenth-century Italian engravings. The narrow marble-topped table is French Empire style (bottom). The Gustav-period settees in the "blue room" surround a classic pedestal table with legs in the form of dolphin heads. In the left foreground is a table with legs in the shape of bird's feet by Meret Oppenheim (facing page).

CLASSICAL AND MODERN

On entering Nany Wiegand-Hoffmann's apartment, visitors suddenly feel as though they have arrived in the grandiose rooms of a Prussian palace in the days of Karl Friedrich Schinkel.

Just before the Wall came down, Wiegand-Hoffmann, a professional architect, moved here with her husband and two children. At the time, she was already familiar with Schinkel's work. She had learned to appreciate the value of tradition during four years of school in England, yet had also discovered the modern architectural idiom by studying under Finnish master Alvar Aalto in Helsinki.

She herself designed the modern furnishings such as the table, lamps, and white marble dishes that make up her Berlin collection. Her trademark approach involves reducing classical shapes and proportions to their essence. Although she combines modern objects and furniture with antique ones, there is no rupture—everything seems to form a whole. In the silk-screens composing her "Berlin cycle," she borrowed and revived classical motifs that symbolized the advent of a new Berlin. Above a console table, a dancing Victory is affixed to the wall; in the Pompeii-like sitting room you can see the Quadriga and the Reichstag. This mixture of classical and modern elements is typical of her new "Berlin style."

The main, Pompeii-style room near the entrance is used as a reception and meeting room. The color red dominates and Wiegand-Hoffmann herself painted the walls. Furniture from various periods is present here: the chairs along the wall are Regency (which might be considered a British variant of Schinkel's style), whereas other pieces—a commode, a console table, a set of shelves—are Empire style. The eighteenth-century gilded sphinxes come from France.

A narrow, typical Berlin hallway lined with showcases of porcelain and glassware leads to the kitchen. It has retained its original blue and white Meissen tiling, which goes perfectly with porcelain from the same factory. Blue also dominates the bathroom, and the marble decoration is once again the work of the mistress of the house. It is hardly surprising to learn that she painted the walls herself—it was in Salzburg, with artist Oskar Kokoschka, that she learned to handle colors.

THE ELEGANT STYLE OF THE 1920S

In a quiet part of Halensee, a sober white building hides behind a curtain of foliage. People walking down the street hardly notice it. But anyone invited to enter will be fascinated to discover an interior that has all the charm of period decoration. The four ground-floor rooms (dining room, living room, conservatory, and bedroom) feature the elegant style associated with the 1920s, with its discreet ornamentation and clean lines. Such pure examples of this period are rare in Berlin. In the dining room, two built-in Art Deco commodes immediately evoke the days when this lavish villa was built. In the room leading to the bedroom (originally intended to serve as a study), connoisseurs are delighted to recognize a humidor set into the wall, designed to prevent cigars from dying out. In the living room, meanwhile, indirect lighting creates a discreet atmosphere conducive to reverie. The paintings on the walls and ceilings, by artist Wilhelm Blanke, also date from the 1920s and reflect Art Deco taste, as do a delightful chinoiserie in the living room and seascape in the dining room.

No home, however, can thrive on the past alone. New elements must be added to the old treasures, blending into the whole. The fairy godmother of the premises is Manuela Alexejew, an interior decorator and connoisseur of objets d'art who has lived here for three years. She brought the villa's original beauty back to life, because part of it had been altered (such as the honey-colored parquet hidden by carpeting). Alexejew enhanced these elements by adding all kinds of objects that have nothing to do with Art Deco yet go with it perfectly, such as three large theater figurines made in Bologna during the Baroque period, and a tiled table placed in the dining room (designed by herself with tiles from old Berlin buildings). In the

The painting over the bed is a portrait of Frederick the Great's sister. The bedspread matches the color of her dress. The left wall is almost completely covered by The Whip, *a painting by Pop artist Allen Jones (left). The figurines lined up on a sideboard in the dining room were unearthed by Frau Alexejew (right).*

living room there is also a commode with gilded bronze decoration from a Berlin palace, which accords surprisingly well with a modern painting by Ernst Wilhelm Nay. A set of chairs inlaid with fine wood and mother-of-pearl, also from the Art Deco period, is another of the villa's treasures.

Alexejew feels obliged to respect the character of her home. So she cares for it and maintains it while enriching it by adding other features. Despite her devotion to style and decoration, this interior remains a highly pleasant place to live. It could hardly be otherwise, for the strong-willed designer has a knack for placing a telling detail here and there: a flower pot from Japan, a designer candelabra that can be transformed into a vase, a multicolored cushion, a side-table of wrought iron. Alexejew blends, combines, associates, and contrasts diverse elements while respecting the individuality of each object and each room.

ANNE MARIA JAGDFELD

Quartier 206 on Friedrichstraße is one of Berlin's most impressive new buildings. Natural colors—blacks, browns, and creams—predominate there and visitors are sometimes surprised to find these same shades when they enter the Quartier 206 design boutique. Anne Maria Jagdfeld's boutique on Friedrichstraße has become the place where Berliners learn to make naturalness rhyme with refinement, simplicity with luxury.

Jagdfeld has employed the same colors in her own penthouse apartment, where light brown sometimes tends toward gold, black may become slate gray, and a light-struck cream may turn silvery gray. The decorator has made sure that daylight floods into her rooms. She designed some of the furnishings herself; they are simple and geometric yet remain comfortable, for Jagdfeld is no fan of strict functionalism. Clarity should not be allowed to get the better of comfort. For her, a bedroom should project distinct, palpable sensuality. And yet when it comes to decorative details, Jagdfeld cultivates restraint and elegance—a few light fixtures placed judiciously, African-style vases and dishes, plus black-and-white photos set in black frames to create a graphic effect. Anne Maria Jagdfeld tries to create timeless interiors, ones that provoke an irresistible desire to touch the fabrics and materials—velvet, cedar, sandstone, iron. Everything can be stroked with the fingertips, everything makes a visitor feel comfortable and peaceful, like some park on a Sunday afternoon: the pale floors recall gravel pathways, the beige surfaces of tables and chairs are veined like flowers and fruit, while the dark table legs, picture-frames, and vases seem like sturdy trees.

Sliding panels stretched
with translucent animal
skin add lightness to
the room (left).
The way the pictures are
hung is typical of Anne
Marie Jagdfeld's style.
She manages to create
a feeling of harmony
and well-being despite
the presence of a sloping
roof (right).

The bathroom is given
a touch of extravagance
by the old-style tub
placed beneath a photo
of rock singer Patti Smith
(below).

Jagdfeld owns a major
collection of art
photography, which
she employs judiciously
in the decoration of her
apartment (left and top).

ROOFTOP VIEW OF BERLIN

On arriving at Gisela von Schenk's place, visitors are greeted by tropical plants in large terracotta pots set on zinc-gray pilasters. Here, in this former sixth-floor attic, streams of light allow the magnificent floral décor to bloom continuously. In the dining room (the first room on entering the apartment), in the kitchen, and in the double living room further along, visitors are struck by grand floral compositions. On the terrace extending from the bedroom, which overlooks the rooftops of Berlin, there are grasses, boxwood, and hydrangeas arranged with an attention to detail which immediately suggests that the woman living here is passionate about flowers.

Von Schenk, who has extensive experience in journalism and advertising, now runs her own business. Along with Frank Stüve, a gardener by training who doubles as a designer, she offers a range of high-quality services: parties for the jet set, gala evenings, grand openings, balls, and weddings. The pair create original floral settings of great elegance, supplying not only pots, statuary, and other decorative accessories, but also chairs, linen, lighting, and everything else that makes an evening so special. Not everyone is able to create an ambiance. In addition to experience, it requires some expert magic in the art of matching colors, scents, and fabrics. And that is the rare expertise offered by Gisela von Schenk and Frank Stüve. It was they who created the décor for the opening of the Adlon Hotel. They not only provide decorative elements, they seek them out, frequenting trade shows and undiscovered designers in an effort to forge a refined yet unaffected style. This style is reflected, it goes without saying, in Frau von Schenk's apartment in Charlottenburg. The color white

dominates, instantly lifting the spirits. The delightful sofas, in pale fabric, are by a surprising young French designer, Henri Becq, as are the tables and chairs with slightly bowed legs.

Von Schenk is equally enthusiastic about fabrics: the weight of taffetas, the rustle of certain synthetic materials, the delicacy of silk embroidered with roses in matching tones. With such fabrics she dresses windows and beds both at home and in her boutique, the Villa Harteneck. When presenting flowers, bouquets, and compositions of foliage, she employs innovative materials such as lead which, combined with terracotta, is becoming increasingly fashionable. She uses not only wicker but also polished aluminum and zinc, which resemble unburnished silver. Ultimately, what von Schenk continually produces, presents, and forges at Villa Harteneck is nothing other than pure beauty itself. Which is just what she has always wanted to do. "I've made my life's dream come true."

The set of champagne-colored chairs beneath the sloping roof includes components by Paris designer Henri Becq. The atmosphere of the room changes with the light over the course of the day, yet always produces an impression of freshness (facing page). From the little desk in the bedroom, you can see the greenery on the balcony and get an idea of the day's weather in the morning (above).

SOBRIETY AND MODERNITY

This apartment is entered via the kitchen, a friendly space that is perfect for welcoming visitors. The kitchen is also practical, the table being just a step away from the working and cooking surfaces.

For the past three years, Kiki and Jan Bassenge have lived next to the Villa Grisebach auction house on Fasanenstraße, one of the city's most elegant shopping streets. Their garden, meanwhile, borders the Literaturhaus (a charming café-cum-literary center). When the couple first became interested in the neighborhood in the 1980s, the villa was dilapidated and the Literaturhaus housed a brothel; the street was slated to be revamped for modern traffic, pierced by a tunnel. It is hard to imagine the street back then.

The building in which the Bassenges live dates from 1887 and was originally an apostolic nunciature. "This is just the most recent renovation," comments

Jan Bassenge. Taking an elevator with doors on both sides, visitors enter directly into a vestibule connected to the kitchen by a sliding, mirrored door. The building was designed as an *Einspänner*, that is to say with just one apartment per floor. A long hallway links the large rooms overlooking the street to those in the back. The Bassenges have redesigned everything to their own taste. Ceilings have been raised, partitions have been demolished, and doors have been eliminated. This vast apartment now looks like a loft, just as the new owners intended. The white-walled rooms are lit by tall windows that face east and west, allowing light to enter all day long.

The Bassenge family is a good illustration of Prussia's venerable policy of encouraging immigrants. French Huguenots arrived in 1648, attracted to Berlin by the Great Elector. Ever since, the Bassenges have been in the art business; the Gerda Bassenge Gallery is one of Berlin's most reputable auction houses for objets d'art and rare books.

Kiki and Jan like sobriety and modernity. This is reflected in their choice of art: paintings by Fernand Léger, Pablo Picasso, and Henr Matisse decorate the walls. The apartment has been custom-designed: the bed has been placed somewhat precariously on a mezzanine, below which is a wardrobe and dressing space; the bathroom next to the bedroom has been completely tiled in a sumptuous green marble from Guatemala, a marble of extraordinary softness and amazing appeal, contrasting with the sparse decoration of the other rooms.

When visitors leave this fine old apartment that has been given a new lease on life and plunge back into the crowd of shoppers on Fasanenstraße, they suddenly realize that it is thanks to the artistic initiatives of people like Kiki and Jan Bassenge that Berlin has retained its charm.

This may be the wildest bedroom in Berlin: the stairs lead to a mezzanine for the bed, just below which are large and easily accessible closets. The door in the background leads to a wonderful bathroom whose marble walls and color counteract the coldness usually associated with such places (left and above).

A COURTYARD
IN MITTE

The renovated courtyards known as Sophie-Gips-Höfe were once part of a district of workshops and housing whose buildings are now being refurbished and transformed. Erika and Rolf Hoffmann have contributed a great deal to the rebirth of this historic neighborhood. On a former factory site they set up an art gallery which also serves as their home, thus demonstrating that an old building could be carefully restored and brought back to life in the form of a wonderful interior. The Hoffmanns have 18,000 square feet on two floors, enabling them to display a large number of contemporary artworks. Their outstandingly rich collection includes works by Sigmar Polke, Felix Gonzalez-Torrez, Ernest Neto, Katharina Sieverding, Andy Warhol, and Frank Stella.

People sometimes exhibit paintings in their homes, but they rarely live in the exhibition space. The Hoffmanns feel passionately that art should not be confined and restricted to museums, so living in their gallery was natural for them. They wanted to prove that art can be brought back to the center of people's lives, and has a place in the everyday world. Art lovers cannot just drop by any time of the day or night, however; guided tours are available on Saturdays by appointment only.

The couple's career demonstrates the importance they place on reincorporating art into life. They formerly owned a shirt factory in Rheinland-Westfalen. After selling it, they devoted themselves totally to their passion for contemporary art. When the Wall came down, they felt drawn to Berlin because their love of art is related to the "present" in the strongest sense of the term—they wanted to show how developments in modern life are expressed

in and through artworks. When great changes occur, art changes too. The couple therefore felt compelled to move its collection to Berlin.

On entering Sophie-Gips-Höfe (so named because it is bordered by Sophienstraße and Gipsstraße), visitors discover art in architecture: Thomas Locher has covered one wall with an artwork, *Entweder/Oder* (Either/Or) made up of words that designate opposites. Two of these opposites correspond exactly to the Hoffmann collection: "public or private" and "alive or frozen."

The Hoffmanns feel that art should be removed from the stuffy environment of the museum and incorporated into everyday life, which is why they change the artworks in their home at regular intervals.

The air was cold. A casual passerby could have heard disconnected words spoken from the phonebooth: 1. forget 2. Twilight 3. darling. From the first syllable of each word a white vapour formed, the visual manifestation of her breath. This is not to imply that connecting words could not be heard by persons whose number she dialed. A train whistled in the night.

The gallery is thoroughly alive. The works on show change, yet the nature of the large, light-drenched rooms never varies. The couple work, eat, and live among the installations, paintings, and sculptures, and some of their furnishings are precious design objects. Does that mean public and private spheres are never separate? Never on Saturdays. It is worth sacrificing some personal privacy for art. Especially since visitors who want to know what a "living collection" looks like, or who want to view a specific piece such as a Frank Stella, represent a limited public of connoisseurs.

The Hoffmanns have mastered the art and technique of living among rare paintings and sculptures to perfection. Tea is taken beneath a collection of old ceiling lamps. The stairs lead to the children's bedrooms and the guest room. A rooftop terrace makes it possible to take advantage of fine weather and affords a view of the Sophie-Gips courtyards below.

OPPOSITE THE BRANDENBURG GATE

The apartment of art dealer Paul Maenz has one of the best locations in Berlin. It is situated on the Pariser Platz right opposite the Brandenburg Gate and occupies the two top floors of the building. A narrow terrace runs the entire length, providing an outdoor platform for the extraordinary view. Not only can you see Victory in her four-horse chariot (Quadriga) on top of the Brandenburg Gate, you also discover that she has a sister: from this angle, you can see the statue on the Siegessäule (Victory Column), which seems surprisingly close. The green and silver roofs of the Adlon Hotel and Frank Gehry's DG Bank building glimmer in the sun. The Berlin sky bathes all 2,500 square feet of this lofty haven in a light that changes according to the time of day and the season.

It is usually fairly difficult to appreciate Berlin's amazing sunsets. At this height, though, they can be admired every day, for they render the interior both majestic and warm. In particular, a wall tiled in tiny mirrors casts a pinkish or golden veil over the rooms and works of art in the apartment. This wall was specially designed for the living room by John Armleder. The veil effect was not exactly what Paul Maenz had expected, but it perfectly fits his conception of art, namely that it should surprise. Also surprised was the estate agent employee who handed over the finished apartment: a little shrub of cables was still sticking out of the wall. "I'll have the wires removed right away," he said blushing with embarrassment. Paul Maenz had to explain to him that the cables were a work of art.

A bicycle rests against the mirror-tiled wall as though someone had just left it there. Artist Maurizio Cattelan was asked to produce an artwork for a recent Venice Biennale; without further ado, he

showed up with three stolen bicycles and insisted that they be exhibited by being placed against another work of art. His wish has come true in this interior, to the satisfaction of both Armleder and Cattelan.

A tour of the apartment provides further evidence of the owner's desire to live surrounded by art. The "official" route leads directly into the living room with its skylight, fireplace, and large table. The unofficial route goes through the bedroom, with its fine wardrobe. Walking by the tall windows, you then cross through the bathroom, office, and kitchen before returning to the living room. When the sliding doors dividing them all are opened, the entire sequence of rooms comes into view.

The bicycle here is not a means of locomotion, but rather a work of art (facing page). The large, light-filled living room, which overlooks the rooftops of Berlin, is decorated with a sober fireplace and furniture by the likes of Gerrit Rietveld and Charles and Ray Eames (above).

COURTYARD COLORS

Large apartments sometimes resemble galleries, but a small, 500-square-foot apartment overlooking a back courtyard has a hard time creating an impression of artistic space. Art student Iris Both and gallery owner Edzard Brahms nevertheless proved that it can be done. The knowing visitor probably wonders what fine bottle of wine the couple will uncork as he or she crosses a vast courtyard located in the western, middle-class part of Kreuzberg. One wing of the building, destroyed by bombs, has been replaced by a garden with wild roses and grasses; a woman who has lived in the building for many years planted it and tends it.

The apartment, reached by ascending several flights of stairs, creates an immediate impression of cheerfulness. The hallway is painted bright red and has the feel of being an additional room rather than merely a space to be passed through; rushing through it would mean arriving too soon at the living room, truncating the "gallery visit" that begins at the entranceway. Various works of art encourage pause. As thoughts return to the bottle of wine, however, the gaze wanders toward the kitchen, which is where the occupants of the house are often to be found. Maybe that is because Edzard Brahms likes to cook, and his second profession entails advising people on their wine purchases. Several chairs surround a small, old table—the first indication that this couple has a soft spot for elegant, minimalist seats. Their faces light up as they describe them and, in fact, a comfortable stool turns out to be a little library stepladder. The other chairs are the work of great designers such as Jasper Morrison and Charles and Ray Eames.

The multicolor squares on the wall caused a few nights of insomnia for the couple, who were unable to decide which colors to include in the scheme. Once they finally agreed, everything happened very quickly—the exact placing of the hues was left to chance.

In the living room, another masterpiece sits in front of the couch—Sori Yanagi's Butterfly Stool (1954). It is hardly surprising that this chair was designed by a Japanese designer: the form focuses on essentials, and is vaguely reminiscent of Japanese rock gardens. Brahms and Both attach great importance to a meditative atmosphere. "It's all a question of organization," declares Brahms with a smile. "And you should keep only what you need." In a small apartment like this one, space can thus be granted to art without compromising comfort. There is neither television, nor radio, nor even a desk—"I'd fill it up much too fast," he says. Brahms and Both need clean lines in order to survive in the clutter of a big city. Ideally, they had intended to leave one wall entirely blank—and they nearly managed it. But they could not resist installing an amazing electrical composition by Swetlana Heger and Plamen Dejanov entitled *Space Pearls in Red, Purple and Jade Falling Down.*

As modern as the apartment may feel, its owners nevertheless respect tradition. Most of the vases belonged to Both's grandfather. The sofa, wardrobe, and table were also commissioned by the family: Brahms's grandparents had them made in the 1930s by a village carpenter in eastern Frisia, based on Bauhaus models. Clearly, the love of clean, clear lines runs in the family.

The bright red hallway gives onto an intriguing light installation in the entranceway of the apartment (facing page). The kitchen is well equipped (above). The owners have managed to create a feeling of space despite limited surface area; the famous Butterfly Stool sits in front of the sofa (left).

WORKS OF ART

The small balcony overlooks the Ringbahn (above). The living room combines the personal touch of an apartment with the majesty of an art gallery (facing page). Collectors who visit the artists are usually invited to sit in the Le Corbusier armchair or Bauhaus sofa.

At the entrance to a quiet, leafy street in Halensee, stands an old Berlin building. The entrance hall greets visitors with a fireplace. The nineteenth-century elevator shakes as it rises slowly past four floors to the top of the building. There is only one apartment on the top floor, so it might be expected to be fairly large. Yet once past the door marked with a B (for Buechler), the effect is so disorienting that the visitor almost wishes for a floor plan: a string of rooms seems to run as far as the eye can see. "There are around nine rooms in all," says Annette Buechler.

To the right of the entrance hall is a studio with work surfaces and a great deal of equipment, tools, sketches, and finished paintings. Obviously inspiration is no problem in this wonderfully light space, because the storage room next door seems pretty full. Creativity is apparent in every aspect of Peter Buechler's place, whether in the artwork or the décor.

After the studio comes the living space. A light-filled room adorned with gilded stuccowork serves as sitting room, which can be described in one word: vast. The TV is set like a fireplace into a steel cabinet designed by Buechler. There is a deliberate contrast between this archaic altar dedicated to the media and the walls covered with handsome cream wallpaper, a contrast that recurs throughout the home. The three paintings that dominate the room are by Peter Buechler. Just above the television, a photomontage has been hung on the wall, showing two women leaning over an intense light source. Meanwhile, two large paintings opposite the windows echo one another, one being primarily golden, the other silvery. These works play on reflections, changing before the viewer's eye as the light changes. "These three painting are not for sale," states Buechler.

From the sitting room, a sliding door opens directly into a showroom, behind which is an office. Thus the sitting room is part of what Buechler calls a "trail" that stretches from one end of the apartment to the other. Along the way, art-loving or art-collecting visitors are confronted with ever changing artworks. Annette says, "Sometimes I come home in the evening and almost trip over some new creation." She is also an artist, but that is not her main profession. Every morning she commutes half an hour to the advertising agency where she works, in Berlin's new center.

With all these art objects exposed for admiration and sale, in a space where visitors are welcome, it is difficult to imagine where private life can be lived. "In the bedroom," answers Annette, to which Peter adds, "and the kitchen." With its dark paneling and black ceiling, the kitchen merits special mention. It creates an instant sense of ease, and its enormous burgundy table is an invitation to sit and watch the small kitchen TV by the window.

When night falls in Berlin and the lamp hanging low over the table is the only one alight, it seems as though the room has no ceiling, that the night sky is the sole roof. As Buechler admits, "It's a little out of the ordinary." He adds, "There are very few good solutions when it comes to kitchens," which is why he had to work at devising this one. "I always make many plans, and then think a lot: I first explore one possibility, then another. And if it doesn't work out, I don't hesitate to rip it all out."

Which is just what the artist had to do when designing the bathroom. There he undertook a task worthy of Sisyphus, sticking thousands of tiny Chinese "good luck" papers to the ceiling in order to obtain a smooth surface with golden reflections. After several weeks, however, the glue lost its adhesiveness in the constant humidity, and the little papers began swirling down. Armed with a water-resistant starch glue, Buechler started all over again. It was worth the effort. The bathroom resembles an oriental harem and harmonizes with the rest of the interior marvelously.

Peter and Annette Buechler live among their artworks even as they fashion their home—here, the living space itself has become an artwork.

The showrooms, where paintings and objects are regularly changed, also feature animals placed there by Peter Buechler, who says he is fascinated by the "contrast between civilization and nature," between technology and fauna.

AT THE TOP OF "THE SNAKE"

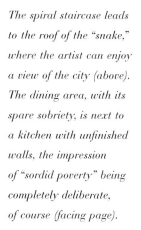

The spiral staircase leads to the roof of the "snake," where the artist can enjoy a view of the city (above). The dining area, with its spare sobriety, is next to a kitchen with unfinished walls, the impression of "sordid poverty" being completely deliberate, of course (facing page).

Artist Erik Schmidt lives at the Platz der Vereinten Nationen (United Nations Square). Just a few years ago, it was still called Leninplatz but, like many other places in East Berlin, it was renamed after the Wall came down. Both the old name and the new attest to the ambitious scale of the two large buildings opposite one another. Berliners are quick to pin nicknames on their monuments (the airlift memorial near Tempelhof Airport is dubbed "the rake of hunger," while the World Culture Center is "the pregnant oyster") and these two huge apartment blocks are called "the boomerang" and "the snake" respectively.

Schmidt lives in "the snake." Both buildings were erected hastily, in the days when cheap high-rises sprang up like mushrooms. The cost of such an approach was thin walls and noisy living conditions. And yet these edifices are now listed as historic monuments, which means that they cannot be altered, not even painted a different color. Many of the original residents still live there, for the apartments were in great demand. Life there was not anonymous, because people met regularly and everyone knew everyone else. From the outside, "the boomerang" and "the snake" are pretty unappealing; they turn their backs to the street and their entrances are concealed, accessible only via narrow passageways. Schmidt lives at the top, on the eleventh floor, in one of the apartments reserved, right from the start, for "workers in the cultural sphere." Which is why it has a large studio with tall windows.

Light spills into the apartment. As if all that sunlight were still not enough, a spiral staircase leads to a roof terrace that extends for practically the full length of the building. Since other "cultural workers" occupying the other studios were the only people with access to this terrific view overlooking a tall TV transmitter, the artists would get together to swap ideas during roof parties. Such convivial gatherings still take place today, also attended by creative types from advertising agencies who come to shoot commercials or music videos on the terrace.

Schmidt has furnished his apartment very simply. Most of the objects in it were bought at street markets. Since the media have become interested in this type of housing, he launched a vogue among young people for the cheap furniture formerly—and hastily—manufactured in East Germany.

The kitchen contains only the bare necessities; it is open and practical, like an American kitchen. The

roughcast prefabricated elements underscore the simplicity of the room, perfectly matching the wickerwork chairs. No one is bothered by the patches of paint peeking from behind the tiles.

Next door is a kind of living room. The table is an old IKEA model (now displayed in the IKEA museum), the chairs are imitation leather. Another throwback to the 1960s are the stackable, orange chairs by Verner Panton—at the time, they could be seen in every ad that tried to look modern. On the balcony, Schmidt has planted pink geraniums. The artist is not attached to things, and gives many of them away. Maybe his apartment will soon have a completely different look, or maybe he will decide to leave Berlin—who knows?

Everything finds a place in this setting, whether old or new, bric-a-brac or prototype. The plastic lettering over the doorway—haben—was a present from an art dealer.

CRAFTING AND SALVAGING

Martin Schacht and Hermann Weizenegger lived in the Schöneberg district before the Wall fell. Three years ago, they moved into an apartment on Linienstraße in the Mitte neighborhood of east Berlin, which has become the ideal place to meet people working in the arts, media, or design.

Schacht makes television documentaries and is also working on a novel about Berlin, based on a biography of the famous transvestite Romy Haag. Weizenegger is a designer specializing in new media and the design of telecommuting workspaces. In collaboration with Oliver Vogt, he developed the "Imaginary Factory" project. At the time, his office was on Oranienstraße in Kreuzberg, opposite a home for the blind where people with visual impairment and other handicaps were still making brushes and brooms that nobody wanted anymore. The home was under threat of closure. Weizenegger crossed the street and suggested a new concept, which worked like a charm. The distribution network and, above all, the products manufactured by the visually impaired in Berlin were completely revamped: the home began to produce solely to special order, and offered exclusively objects made out of natural materials such as horse hair, goat hair, coconut fiber, or wicker. Such items were more satisfying to the people who made them, and also to the people who bought them. And the founders of "Imaginary Factory," Vogt and Weizenegger, are delighted to have given the home a new lease on life.

For some time already, Weizenegger had been reflecting on ways to offer individuals high-quality design at affordable prices. "We're living in a Disney-ized era," he says. "That's why we have to save as much of our tradition as we can." He procures

manufacturing plans for his clients "so that they can build their own furniture." In the apartment he shares with Martin Schacht, there are many examples of this new craftwork to be seen. The 1,000 square feet of open-plan space—many doors have been removed—presents a strange combination of bric-a-brac, prototype furniture, and family objects. The upshot is a highly personal atmosphere that is original without being in any way pretentious. A head of the goddess Juno, now in the dining room, was salvaged from a house undergoing demolition. The palm tree in the bedroom, meanwhile, was rescued from a street dump by Schacht's mother.

The modular sofa designed by Vogt-Weizenegger consists of three elements on coasters that can be moved at will. Another simple and practical touch: four piles of magazines and a sheet of glass make a table.

LIVING AND WORKING SPACE IN DAHLEM

This modern house in Dahlem, with its echoes of Bauhaus design and 1920s architecture, is both a home and a creative studio. Thanks to extensive glazing, indoor and outdoor space interpenetrate. Natural materials such as wood and slate are used throughout (above and facing page).

It all began with a "nightmare construction site" in the quiet Dahlem neighborhood. Abandoned by the bankrupt architect and construction company, the building remained in a half-finished state for a year until the young architectural firm of Beyer & Schubert came to the owners' rescue.

The latter wanted a modern, timeless house that would be functional along Bauhaus lines. The initial plan called for two cubes topped by a hovering roof; the two blocks were originally designed to be separate, but a passage was eventually added. Many other, similarly unresolved issues afforded the new team a good deal of maneuvering room.

The autonomy of the two blocks has been preserved by a glazed entrance hall. The magnificent hovering roofs were eventually built: larch-wood beams decorated in a fishbone pattern were set on a glass structure. In contrast, the designs for the garden, façade, and interiors were changed by the new

architects, in close collaboration with the owners. The simple plaster façade was replaced with tougher Wittmund brick (these fine, dark red, peat-fired bricks are a traditional Berlin building material). In order to divide the high, outer façade and reduce it to more human dimensions, various decorative bands were introduced, employing patterns reminiscent of the 1930s. The house thereby harmonizes perfectly with its neighbor, which dates from just that period—so much so that some visitors think the new house is a recently refurbished old one.

The interior features maple and teak, mosaics and slate. The architects used only natural materials and these were deliberately left untreated and unadorned. The sobriety and beauty of the house, already visible on the outside, thus extends indoors. A silvery slate, dotted with tiny fossilized plants, was used in the bathrooms, on the walls, on the floors, and also outside. With its naturally changing hues, this material is a delight to the eyes.

A particularly successfully wardrobe is set in the middle of the bedroom, with the bathroom to the left and the bed to the right, near a large window. The wardrobe can be opened from both sides, so that husband and wife can each access their own things.

The "nightmare construction site" ultimately became a dream site for living and working. According to the architects, the family is perfectly comfortable living in a house that harks back to the early days of modern architecture. Thus when a building company goes bust and an architect abandons his clients, the outcome is not always an unhappy one. In this instance, the replacement architect was able to transform the foundations into a dream house, generating harmony by incorporating local materials and local styles.

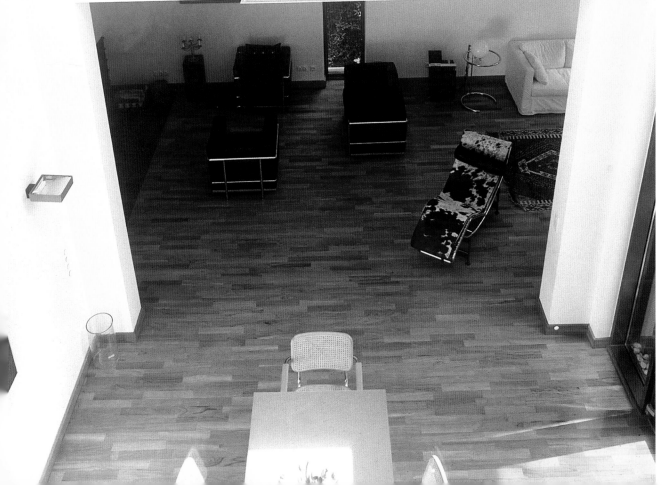

A LOFT IN A FORMER FACTORY

In the Kreuzberg neighborhood, which suffered greatly from the division of Berlin, there was an old factory where telephones were manufactured. It included several inner courtyards flanked by what used to be workshops and dwellings, all abandoned and dilapidated. As with all disused industrial buildings, the question was whether to demolish it or refurbish it. Architect Elke Knöß felt strongly that in this case the buildings should be given a new life, so together with her architectural partner Wolfgang Grillitsch (their firm is called called Peanutz), she set about turning the factory into housing. They even decided to convert the old, 22-foot-high stairwell, with its steel steps and impeccable brickwork, into accommodation. Although some people might have felt this part of the scheme was over-ambitious or unworkable, Knöß and her partner enthusiastically drew up plans with the owner, who works in the advertising business.

"He wanted spaces within the space, that is to say a composed and arranged landscape," explains Knöß. When working on the design for this home, the architects set out to create something truly spectacular: a steel structure perched in the air like the prow of a ship, above the kitchen but reachable by a staircase. This panoramic tower extends over three floors, so it is the kitchen that anchors everything to the ground. A specially designed staircase climbs over the kitchen cabinets and leads to a cabin that serves as a guest room. Higher still, the living room has a multimedia screen, which provides entertainment without disturbing others. From there, a bridge of glass leads to the bedroom, which also serves as office and bathroom. Like the gallery, it is fitted with walls of industrial glass that provide indirect lighting. Natural light can thus filter right throughout the apartment.

Luminosity varies from hour to hour; as the architect points out, with a beaming expression: "The apartment wakes up fresh and eager in the morning, and dresses up for the evening."

Bookshelves of imitation mahogany line the walls of the bedroom. "When they were delivered, the truck driver asked if we were opening a Chinese restaurant, says Knöß with a smile. The blend of materials is unconventional but deliberate—the flooring of fine, dark oak contrasts with decorated plasterboard and doors padded with imitation leather. But since all these materials are used in several places and form an ensemble, the result appears thoroughly

The bathroom is used as a source of indirect lighting, since light passes through the frosted industrial glass into the kitchen (left).
The kitchen is filled with eye-catching features, such as the table and chairs, and the kitchen cupboards. The latter form a highly original staircase, which simultaneously saves space, economizes on materials, and provides access to the little guest rooms. The unit projecting above the kitchen looks like the command post of a rocket ship. All the storage space is camouflaged, hidden in every nook of this strange apartment—the leather-topped stools in the foreground, for example, are used to store CDs and DVDs (facing page).

coherent and modern. So successful is the final result that the owner rents out his magnificent loft for shooting commercials. "He leaves the house in the morning, and when he comes home at night he's made a lot of money," jokes Knöß. She and her partner became friends with the owner during construction, and even enjoyed the privilege of living in the loft for a two-week trial period. And they were delighted. "We created exactly the type of interior I'd like to live in myself some day," comments Grillitsch.

This is clearly the loft of a bachelor who likes his creature comforts—the glass gallery, reached by a staircase, it is equipped with an inviting hammock for contemplating the bustle in the courtyard below. The biggest surprise of all, however, comes in the bedroom (above), where the adjoining bathroom suddenly appears from behind the sliding bookshelves.

Colored film on the windowpanes alter the daylight, giving it a warm glow. What better way to see life through rose-tinted glasses (right). This light-filled interior is relatively spare yet welcoming and bright (facing page). The simple décor enhances the decorative objects hanging on the walls, which were chosen by the owner's friends. Functional rooms such as the kitchen (top) and the bathroom (bottom) are also very luminous—the oppressive darkness that was typical of homes in this neighborhood has given way to light, simplicity, spaciousness, and improvisation.

AN OLD INDUSTRIAL WORKSHOP

Spandauer Vorstadt was a treeless street in the heart of new Berlin, where buildings are narrower than elsewhere in the city. It was once Berlin's poorest neighborhood. Nowadays, it is lined with attractive, albeit rather strange and surprising, renovated houses. Nearby, small businesses have moved in. Several of these homes used to be workshops, where small industry and housing were grouped together in a series of courtyards. Safety deposit boxes were once made in the apartment under discussion; in the Kunst-Werken (art workshops) next door, margarine used to be made.

Having become a star of raucous German "new wave" rock music, a female vocalist decided to move into the top floor of this old factory, which had been "occupied" for a while following the fall of the Wall.

The unusual nature of the neighborhood is reflected in the apartment.

Although she has lived in the city for over twenty years and was familiar with neighborhoods in East Berlin, the singer moved into these premises just three years ago. Prior to that, it was impossible to live here because the building was a ruin. Berlin architect Hans Düttmann refurbished and modified it, raising the height of the building by 15 feet to admit more light. The daylight coming through the windows, meanwhile, is multicolored. "Since winters in Berlin can be gray, I put colored film on the panes." As to the rest of the apartment, the rock singer and producer simply asked her friends to furnish and decorate it. Not everyone is so easygoing!

One of her friends was Bernhard Coenen, "Berlin's last nomad." Since he is always moving around and has no need of a home of his own, Coenen likes to design interiors for other people. Perhaps he has the detachment required for the job. Coenen is the one who sought and found the mirror, the many paintings, and the piece of wood decorated with flowers. The works hanging over the side table were made by homeless people. For a handsome fee, Coenen also had an artist paint two plates of Meissen porcelain: two mythological animals represent the loft's two inhabitants, the rock singer and her husband. The staircase, with its somewhat strange banister, had to remain very narrow, so the solution was to create a "samba stairway": each foot has its individual step, linked to the next. Such steps produce a swaying gait that is not hard to picture. If in a hurry to descend, you can always slide down the "tabledance" pole, like a firefighter in a rush. Thus an aspect of city life of old—the somewhat harsh and hurried life that once characterized the Spandau neighborhood—continues to survive in this intriguing loft.

BOLD CONTRASTS

Light, air, and sun are the building blocks of architecture, according to Stefan Arne Sterf. It is therefore hardly surprising that this well-known architect is a specialist in creating attic apartments. Initially, he designed one for himself, respecting two guidelines: dynamism and an optimum use of space within the constraints of the building. In 1998, German television broadcast a program on his efforts. Half an hour later, Sterf had two enthusiastic clients who wanted an apartment just like the one they had seen on television. The couple, a writer and a woman who runs a well-known Berlin restaurant, had fallen in love with the architect's bold style, so rich in contrasts yet pleasant to live in. "I need contrasts in order to work," he says. As with music, tension plays an important role here—uniformity leads to boredom.

The contrast between shiny floor and flocked wall, between sharp angles and curved lines, is what adds interest to a home. Sterf's clients wanted to renovate a building listed as a historic monument, so the architect had to respect a series of guidelines, and the street façade had to remain unchanged. In the courtyard, however, the Historic Monuments Commission was more accommodating: Sterf was allowed to cut a large oval in the sloping roof. A terrace then projected from the gap like the prow of a ship. "The effect was intentional. We decked the terrace with planks from a ship." The Fernsehturm (broadcasting tower) that blinks in the distance could even be taken for a lighthouse in the midst of this sea of rooftops.

In addition to the requirements of the Historic Monuments Commission, Sterf had to respect his clients' special wishes. The architect devised convex and concave walls pierced by niche-like passageways, and

even gratified the writer with a narrow little bedroom of 80 square feet under the eaves. He used frosted glass between the bedroom and bathroom, which allowed light to enter while preserving privacy. Here again, Sterf took dynamics into account: in the middle of the room he set a piece of round sculpture which forms a stairway on one side, ending in a gallery. This whirling form, underscored by combinations of colors and contrasts, has earned this apartment the nickname of "spring roll."

The owners' family grew during construction—the baby needed a room and additional closets had to be included. A dressing room and storage space were hidden beneath the gallery. Thanks to Sterf, this very modern interior is well adapted to family life.

A clever and practical idea was to paint the kitchen cabinets so they could serve as blackboards: little messages, memos or lists can thus be written and erased, without leaving a trace. Unsurprisingly, given their common vision, the architect and the delighted family became fast friends during construction.

The plain, curved walls of this extraordinary attic apartment create a modern look combined with a feeling of comfort. The hallway, with its contrasting colors and niche-like doorways, leads to an airy kitchen.

Some streets in the heart of Potsdam have retained their Baroque façades, either in their original state or after sensitive restoration.

Berlin and Potsdam might be called adjoining cities, because their buildings, bridges, and waterways touch. Potsdam begins on the southwest edge of Berlin, where the outlines of the capital begin to blur on the shores of the Havel. The Glienicker Brücke, a bridge that was a royal way for two hundred years, both separates and joins the two towns. After World War II, it became the Bridge of Unity, but once the Wall went up it became the border crossing where the two sides swapped secret agents. These days, it once again brings people and places together.

Despite their proximity, the twins differ radically in appearance and temperament. Berlin is a big city, Potsdam a small town, Berlin is a young city, Potsdam an old one. Berlin bustles, Potsdam unwinds. Berlin is the capital of the entire nation, Potsdam of the *Land*, or state, of Brandenburg. Berlin was built along the Spree and was shaped by that river's meanders, while Potsdam is located on the Havel, at a spot where the river resembles a vast inland lake, dotted in several places with islands and spits of land.

Berlin grew along with industry, Potsdam remained a quiet little town. It is that very tranquility which Berlin's high society now seeks, in the footsteps of the kings of Prussia. Just as many Potsdamers willingly do their business in the great city, many Berliners dream of retiring to Potsdam at the end of their lives.

Potsdam is a rare gem surrounded by a series of lakes and parks. It is the "Eden of Brandenburg," or "Little Amsterdam on the Havel." Although no major architect came to exercise his talent here—apart from those who designed the palaces—the best artisans in the land worked in Potsdam. The town itself is a masterpiece, the incarnation of a garden as the Prussians imagined it. Its architecture has only one goal: beauty.

Russian writer Nicolai Mikhailovich Karamzin visited Potsdam in 1789: "We rode toward Sanssouci. This pleasure palace is situated at the top of a vineyard from which you can see the town—a picture of extraordinary beauty! The palace is small and low, but whoever sees it will agree that it is exquisite" (previous double page). Inside the grounds, the Hauptallee links the summer residence of Sanssouci with the much larger and more imposing Neues Palais, the tall dome and entrance of which can be seen here.

SANSSOUCI: PARK AND PALACE

Let us first stroll through the grounds. They are vast, extending over 700 acres, and were landscaped in the eighteenth century. In addition to the palace, the park features the Ruinenberg (Mount of Ruins) to the north and the Neues Palais (New Palace) to the west. A century later, the Rococo style of Frederic the Great was joined by Italian-influenced Romantic Classicism when Frederick William IV built the Schloß Charlottenhof to the south and an Orangery to the north.

There are many splendors for visitors to admire, but it takes time: the various circuits through the grounds last several hours, and it takes two days to explore it completely. In this quiet, pleasant setting, it is possible to walk through vast lawns and groves of poplars, oaks, plane trees, and cypresses; or to stroll along ponds, watercourses, and fountains, encountering paths that open onto magnificent vistas on all sides. The southern part of the garden, around Charlottenhof, is unforgettable—it projects a majesty recalling ancient Rome. The park's main center of attraction nevertheless remains Sanssouci Palace to the north, nearer the town.

At the round ornamental basin called Franz Rondell (French Circle, because some of the sculptures surrounding it were given to Prussia by the king of France), a series of staircases begins to climb the terraced vineyards leading to Schloß Sanssouci. From below, the palace is more sensed than seen, not only because it is a single-story building, but also because it has been set back, endowing it with all the charm of a refuge nestling in nature. It almost seems as though the palace is putting on airs or playing hide-and-seek, a game encouraged by the caryatids supporting the cornice, the warm tones of the quince-

yellow façade, and the flat crown on the dome.

Sanssouci, an architectural marvel, will forever remain associated with the personality of one king, Frederick II of Prussia. The palace was his undertaking and it reflected his goals. "Old Fritz" was an aesthete who preferred an idyllic retreat to pomp and show. His idea of beauty was influenced by French art and culture. The predominant Rococo style (from "rocaille," or rock- and shell-work), was above all a style of interior design. It accorded perfectly with Old Fritz's natural inclination to withdraw inside, into his shell. That is probably why he refined the style to a point where it became know as "Frederick Rococo."

The Musenrondell (Circle of the Muses) on the Hauptallee at Sanssouci features statues of the daughters of Zeus, the goddesses of the arts and sciences (facing page). Unusual "French doors" open onto the vegetation decorating the six terraces leading to the palace. This part of the park is dedicated to the theme of Bacchus and pleasure (above).

Trellised pavilions on each side of Schloß Sanssouci add a touch of refined elegance. The statue of the praying child is a bronze copy of an antique work.

In Potsdam, Frederick II the Great hoped to enjoy an insouciant—or carefree—life. So the palace he built on Wüster Berg (Arid Mount) was named Sanssouci ("without a care" in French). He designed the six terraces covered with grapevines, curved in the middle to exploit the modest sunshine to a maximum. On these terraces, glass niches made it possible to grow fig trees. Even today, delicious figs can be enjoyed in September. Between the niches grew grapes from Italy,

France, and Lake Neuruppin (where, as a young man, Frederick had already laid out his own garden). Trellised fruit trees were also planted—apricot, plum, and cherry trees. Numerous garden parts of the grounds featured greenhouses for cultivating peaches, oranges, and bananas. Today, everything remains just as it was.

Once the visitor arrives at the stop of the stairs, overlooking the terraces, fountain, and grounds, the harmony of the site becomes apparent: palace and

Rheinsberg Castle, full of music, festivities, and philosophy. As an elegant summer palace, Sanssouci truly corresponds to an art lover's ideal. It has only twelve rooms, and was therefore smaller than many bourgeois dwellings found in Hanseatic and imperial cities. The interior nevertheless boasted one of the finest Rococo décors found anywhere, as exemplified by the white-walled Concert Room. Frederick himself played the flute, composed music, and wrote libretti; his music stand can still be seen by a *hammerflügel* (predecessor of the grand piano). Fanciful ornamentation, like some lavish virgin forest, covers the walls and ceiling of the room, almost giving it the feel of a vine-covered arbor. Two large windows are set opposite two large mirrors which enlarge the room to an almost infinite degree, making this room a masterpiece in its own right.

The façade of Sanssouci overlooking the garden— from here, Frederick the Great could admire his grounds beyond the vineyard (left). Tendrils and vine shoots adorn the ceiling of the Concert Room (below). The theme of grapes and Bacchus recurs in the caryatids and nymphs supporting the roof of Sanssouci (following double page).

vineyard are part of an ensemble. The landscape is particularly beautiful early in the morning, when iridescent light enhances the nobility of the setting.

Georg Wenzeslaus von Knobelsdorff (1699–1753), the most famous northern German architect of his day, took only three years—from 1745 to 1747—to build this "pleasure house." It had to reflect Frederick's love of nature and art. The Rococo residence was designed to recreate the atmosphere of the king's youth at

The grounds are dotted at regular intervals with circles populated by statues—their white marble forms a wonderful contrast with the dark greenery of the trees (below). The Chinese Teahouse (1754) is one of the finest examples of this eighteenth-century architectural vogue (right).

The roof of the teahouse's round gallery is held up by gilded palm trees. Sculptors Johann Gottlieb Heymüller and Johann Peter Benckert invented all kinds of life-sized characters, covered with gold leaf, playing music or drinking tea (far right).

The Grounds in the Days of Frederick the Great.

On the north side of the palace, through the semi-circular colonnade, can be glimpsed the Ruinenberg just opposite, where Knobelsdorff and a theatrical set designer arranged highly picturesque artificial ruins. From the entranceway, Frederick's guests received this symbolic salute from Antiquity.

The grounds are traversed from east to west by a lane approximately one and a half miles long. At certain places, it widens to form round intersections where green arcades head into various parts of the gardens. One of these intersections, called the Musenrondell (Circle of the Muses), was designed by Knobelsdorff. Its eight marble statues representing the divinities of art and science were sculpted by Friedrich Christian Glume (1714–1752). In 1748, a French-style orangery was added to the grounds. Following Knobelsdorff's plans, it was endowed with large windows and a heating system. The orange trees were planted in large boxes, and ramps made it possible to

The painted copper roof is crowned by a pot-bellied mandarin, also gilded (above). After Sanssouci, this teahouse is the best-known and best-loved building in the entire park.

move them outdoors; in summer months, when the Orangery was empty of trees, it was used for concerts, dances, and performances of Italian operas. Twenty years later, it was transformed into guest accommodation and renamed the Neue Kammern (New Chambers). Each room was decorated in a late "Frederick Rococo" style, and each had its own color, echoed in the furnishings, marble floor, and decorative panels on the walls. Various canvases illustrated themes from Ovid's *Metamorphoses*, a motif that recurs in the Ovid Gallery, a magnificent reception hall based on the model of a French-style hall of mirrors.

The park contains another outstanding structure: the Chinesiches Teehaus (Chinese Teahouse). Its dainty form perfectly accords with Rococo taste. Although Old Fritz had hoped to build the teahouse quickly, construction dragged on due to the Seven Years War (1756–63). The pavilion now houses an exhibition of eighteenth-century porcelain from China, Japan, and Meißen. In the summer, weekend concerts are given in front of the glimmering green and gold building.

The eighteenth-century vogue for chinoiseries can also be seen in the Drachenhaus (Dragon House), built by Carl von Gontard (1731–1791). Located next to a vineyard on the northwest edge of the park, it served as accommodation for the head of the vineyard. The gold dragons perched on the roof of the pagoda keep watch over the customers of the café now found inside.

The paintings on the ceiling of the teahouse were based on sketches by French artist Nicolas Le Sueur, who taught drawing in Berlin (left).

Fine stucco decoration adorns the walls and ornate consoles hold precious porcelain from China (right).

The New Palace.

The Neues Palais (1763–69) was Frederick the Great's largest palace. Four architects worked on its design: Büring, Gontard, Manger, and Legeay. It is a vast building over 240 yards long. More than four hundred sculptures adorn its façade. This "royal backdrop" was originally supposed to be built in town. But no location could be found in Potsdam itself, so the palace was given a country setting. The palace is composed of three wings plus nearby

The Neues Palais is an imposing late Baroque edifice, built shortly after the Seven Years War. Such architectural projects were an expression of Prussia's political power (above). The gilded brocading and woodwork in the various rooms once again evoke Rococo exuberance (right).

outbuildings, linked by a colonnade. During the rapid construction of the palace, the king intervened several times to soften the grandiose appearance it was assuming. He dismissed the building as a *fanfaronnade* ("piece of braggadocio") and rarely stayed there.

In the summer, when the royal family's relatives were staying in Potsdam, they would be housed in the Neues Palais. The interiors were thus designed and furnished for that purpose. The magnificent, princely apartments (each with its own décor) are next to four state reception rooms. The supernatural, dark, cool ambiance of the Grottensaal (Grotto Hall), its walls adorned with strange sea creatures concocted from coral, shells, and semi-precious stones, made it possible to remain cool on very hot days. Just next door is its counterpart, the Marmorgalerie (Marble Gallery), a light, imposing hall decorated in red jasper and Carrara marble. Upstairs, the largest room in the palace is the two-story Marmorsaal (Marble Hall), whose walls are covered with the most precious stone available; its inlay floor is particularly impressive. Next door, the upstairs gallery boasts the most surprising décor in the Neues Palais, one that combines Classical features with Baroque ones. Meanwhile, the Schloßtheater (Palace Theater) in the southern wing is one of the most marvelous eighteenth-century theaters still extant. With its majestic red, white, and gold decoration lit from a sun carved into the ceiling, it provides a ravishing setting for concerts and plays even today.

The Grounds in the Romantic Period: Charlottenhof and the Roman Baths.

The southern part of Park Sanssouci breathes peace and quiet. Here strollers are rare and silence reigns. The

*The Grottensaal gives
visitors the strange
and wonderful feeling of
entering an undersea
world. The vast hall
is tiled with marble
of various colors, while
the stucco and shellwork
exploit various marine
motifs.*

Neoclassical palace known as Charlottenhof, with its fine, tall-columned façade, is set in a landscape garden that has retained its original, artificially wild appearance. Small copses alternate with lawns and ponds—visitors have the impression of reliving a bygone era, even as the scent of beech, poplars, and birch call them back to the present.

The palace and grounds were designed by Karl Friedrich Schinkel and Peter Joseph Lenné, who must have enjoyed working together, for they were perfectly complementary. The famous architect and the landscape gardener had been hired by Crown Prince Frederick William, who had received the property from his father as a Christmas present in 1825. Lenné apparently wanted to completely transform the Baroque park into a landscape garden, just then coming into fashion. But he had to proceed patiently, step by step. He began by creating a Romantic setting just around Charlottenhof, taking care to incorporate alleys that opened onto vistas (which he called "lines of sight"), notably including the Neues Palais and Sanssouci. Even today, it demonstrates that nature must be fashioned the way a painting is composed, so that observers do not notice the artifice right away. On the occasion of the 2001 Bundesgartenschau (Federal Garden Show), the garden was enhanced by a small copse of chestnut trees, to a design by Lenné.

With great economy of means, Schinkel transformed an existing house into a small, classical palace worthy of the crown prince. Perhaps one of the finest buildings in Park Sanssouci, this summer palace is now considered to be one of Schinkel's most striking works. By simplifying his architecture to an extreme, he created a radically new edifice whose modest proportions obliged him to come up with

From the top of her column, a bust of Princess Elisabeth, wife of future king Frederick William IV, gazes like a sentinel upon Schloß Charlottenhof, where the key word is simplicity (left). Ladies-in-waiting were housed in a tent that was somewhat small but elegantly appointed (above).

ingenious solutions. A room reserved for ladies of the court, beneath a tent, was equipped with folding furniture; a service stairway had a hidden closet built into it. Unlike the main palace, the living quarters were furnished simply, like a bourgeois interior. The silvered wood furniture in the bedroom and study was designed specially by Schinkel. The vestibule, meanwhile, is one of the finest rooms in the palace, with star-patterned glass in the windows bathing the space in an unreal, bluish light.

On the eastern edge of the garden, visitors will discover the Römische Bäder (Roman Baths). Never intended for bathing, they are there mainly to evoke Italy. A good view of them can be had from the island in the Maschinenteich (Machine Pond, so called because the water pumping mechanisms were formerly located there). Eight pale-colored buildings in the style of Roman villas dotted the area to give the perfect illusion of an Italian landscape. In fact, there were so many examples of Italian architecture in Potsdam that

At Charlottenhof, Schinkel himself designed many of the furnishings and everyday objects, the sphinx being one of his favorite decorative motifs (above and far right, top). The mahogany divan in the red corner study probably comes from the Stadtschloß in Berlin (right).

The royal bedroom is a perfect concord of green, gold, and honey (above). Schinkel endowed this room with French doors that overlooked the greenery of the grounds.

The vestibule at
Charlottenhof receives
little light, and the large
basin and medallions on
the balustrade lend it a
certain solemnity (right).
In the rooms, on the other
hand, the gaily colored
décor and furnishings
create a more relaxed,
less ceremonious
atmosphere (above).

These sphinx heads
adorn a dining table and
a stone bench in the park
at Charlottenhof (top).
Blue windows in
the vestibule face west,
filtering light from
the setting sun (above).

The Roman Baths evoke an idealized Italy whose architecture perfectly suits the landscape (far left). This group of statues is found in the caldarium (left). Neptune is part of a wall frieze ringing the impluvium (below). The wall of the baths' Pompeii-style atrium is decorated with an imaginary landscape evoking the Bay of Naples (following double page).

Frederick the Great, on visiting Palermo in Sicily, sighed in disappointment: "In the end, this town resembles Potsdam in every way."

A cluster of several buildings recalls antique villas—the gardener's house, the assistant gardener's house, an arbor, tower, and guest house. The group is linked by an arcaded passageway to the teahouse, whose spare interior contains only two chairs, designed by Schinkel.

To the north of the grounds, the Romantic era produced another remarkable piece of architecture in the form of the Orangery. It was built in the reign of Frederick William IV on the model of Italian Renaissance villas. Along with a water pump in the guise of a mosque, it is the second technical outbuilding preserved in Park Sanssouci. In summer months, the nearby terraced gardens take on a Mediterranean air, especially the Sicilian Garden and Paradise Garden.

POTSDAM, A JEWEL ON THE BANKS OF THE HAVEL

The Baroque Marstall (royal stables) was part of the old palace in Potsdam. The building was converted into an orangery in 1685. Under Frederick William I, it was transformed into a riding school—hence the equestrian statues over the door (above). In the old town of Potsdam, many streets have retained their Baroque façades (facing page).

Frederick the Great once said that Potsdam would seduce everyone who laid eyes on it. Each feature contributes to the harmony of the whole, with the exception perhaps of the Neues Palais and Schinkel's majestic Charlottenhof in Park Sanssouci. Nowhere else can the history of eighteenth- and nineteenth-century art be so appreciated, as for example in Charlottenstraße, one of the longest streets in Europe still lined entirely with Baroque façades. Although it was seriously damaged in the final days of World War II, Potsdam remains a delight to the eye. Visitors can enjoy the charm of its parks and palaces, its houses of affluent burghers and craftsmen, and its Roman-style villas built for aristocrats, senior civil servants, officers, and industrialists who valued the atmosphere of a small city so close to Berlin.

Potsdam being of modest size, everything is within convenient distance. Coming from the station, visitors can stroll west and then cross Lange Brücke (Long Bridge), arriving at the Filmmuseum im Marstall (not to be confused with the Film Studios in Babelsberg), which displays items formerly used in the UFA film studios. It is housed in Frederick William I's former royal stables, or Marstall, the oldest edifice in downtown Potsdam, opposite the Alter Markt (Old Market). This fine Baroque edifice with its long façade is the sole vestige of Potsdam's old palace. It is a building worth seeing, as is the "cinema café" next to the museum.

Dutch Quarter. Potsdam and Amsterdam have certain things in common. Both were built on swampy land. Furthermore, Prussia's royal family was related to the Dutch dynasty. King Frederick William I stayed several times in the handsome city of Amsterdam and did all he could to build Potsdam on the Dutch model. He had lateral canals dug around the town's main canal in order to make travel by boat possible. His successor enlarged the town by adding lots arranged in a regular plan, as can still be seen in Gutenbergstraße and Brandenburgerstraße. On four such lots, a Dutch quarter was erected between 1737 and 1742. Like the Great Elector who had welcomed 20,000 French Huguenots to Prussia, this soldier-king brought Dutch craftsmen to Potsdam. He hoped that their arrival would spark a new boom in the country, which was falling behind. Into town came weavers of velvet and damask, carpenters, locksmiths, masons, goldsmiths, and court painters. In order to make the craftsmen and artists feel at home in Potsdam, Frederick William I appointed a Dutch architect to build the famous quarter allocated to them. It was this same architect

who designed the Baroque town hall in 1753. At first sight, the houses give an impression of great uniformity. The king had taken care to establish a certain homogeneity by personally dictating the size of the bricks to be used; but in fact, almost every house has its special feature, as demonstrated by the varied decoration of doors and other details. All houses had a garden on the street side, and windows were—and still are—glazed with small panes and equipped with typical half shutters and white frames. In order to maintain their bright red color, the houses were plastered with a blood-red finish known as *sang-de-bœuf*. The attic windows, the relatively modest height of the houses, and the alternation of pinnacle gables with stepped gables all lend delightful charm to these homes.

After the war, when Potsdam became part of East Germany, the Dutch quarter was stigmatized as a symbol of Prussian militarism; the little houses were not maintained and fell into ruin. Now the neighborhood has been restored, and today it is a fancy address for investors who wish to provide the perfect setting for ambitious art galleries, fashion designers, refined coffee shops, and little antique dealers. Berlin's leading hairdresser, Udo Walz, has set up here, and France's Maison du Chocolat on Benketstraße now sells delicious chocolate, something hard to find in Berlin itself.

Artists and craftspeople are once again offering goods and services in the picturesque buildings of the Dutch quarter (facing page).

The wooden houses in the Russian settlement are still delightfully maintained with floral decoration (right).

The number of sumptuous houses from the past is amazing. From the outset, they belonged to Berlin's

The Russian Colony. Another unusual neighborhood in Potsdam is the Russian colony, a long row of detached wooden houses seemingly transported there from a distant land. Unlike other town houses, these homes are incredibly far apart. Formerly, the families who lived here needed space for the sheep and fruit trees that provided their income, since the homes were built on the Russian model for twelve military choristers who arrived as prisoners of war in 1812. Frederick William III, fascinated by their sad, moving music, did not want them to go back. So once a military alliance was signed with Russia, the czar offered to let his new ally keep his army chorus—he even dispatched replacements when wounds and homesickness decimated the original corps. Although uprooted, the singers were provided with suitable accommodation. The eldest son in each family had the right to inherit the home, and now three direct descendants of those Russian immigrants still live here. Wooden plaques in black list the deceased members of each family, white plaques identify the living. To the north of the settlement is a Russian church that Schinkel designed so that the singers could feel at home and make their fine voices heard.

To the east, not far from colony, is Neuer Garten, which extends along the shore of the Heiliger See. The best way to get there is along Alleestraße.

senior civil servants and businessmen, and that is still the case today (above and left).

NEW GARDEN

Neuer Garten is a Romantic park whose Marble Palace extends out into the lake due to the narrowness of the shore. The view across the water delighted Crown Prince William, who moved into the palace with his wife Cecilie in 1880. It was turned into a museum in 1997.

To the north of Potsdam, the Havel widens to form the Jungfernsee. A narrow canal, the Hasengraben, connects the Jungfernsee to the Heiliger See, west of the Neuer Garten. This "new garden" is not comparable to Park Sanssouci in scope, yet it too is dotted with splendid buildings. It derives its own special charm from its extensive lake-side shore.

In 1786, on the death of Old Fritz, as Frederick the Great was known, the reign of Frederick William II began. The new king was an enthusiastic advocate of Neoclassicism and English landscape gardens. One year later, he commissioned Johann August Eyserbeck (1762–1801) to lay out a new park to the north of the city, between the Jungfernsee and the Heiliger See. On this land were successively built the Marmorpalais (Marble Palace), which has recently been restored, the Dutch porter's lodge, the Orangery, and the Pyramid. This summer estate, with its belvedere topped by an ornate roof, were located at the water's edge. It was one of the first Neoclassical buildings in the region and

the main attraction of the grounds. Due to lack of materials, several marble columns from Sanssouci were reused. At the end of the main lane are the lodgings built for the staff, which recall Potsdam's Dutch quarter.

The palace also had its own tree-lined Orangery and a very fine, wood-paneled palm court, ideal for concerts. To the east of the Orangery sits a mysterious sphinx. As to the Pyramid, standing alone in the middle of the grounds, it was in fact a cold store for the king's butter and meat (every winter, ice from the lake would be stacked inside it). Certain parts of the park are now used for botany classes at the University of Potsdam. Strollers are free to admire this unusual architectural ensemble that marks the transition from Rococo exuberance to Classical solemnity.

Cecilienhof. At the north end of the New Garden is Cecilienhof Schloß, the most recent dwelling on the grounds. It is now used as lodging for official guests. It was designed in 1911 for Princess Cecilie von Mecklenburg-Schwerin and her husband, Crown Prince William, in a mock-Tudor style. The architect, Paul Schultze-Naumburg, was a disciple of Hermann Muthesius. With its half-timbered façade and low roof, the palace resembles a comfortable, if particularly spacious, country home—it was the last residence to be built for the Hohenzollern dynasty. The rooms are charmingly elegant and simple, especially the bathrooms and the smoking room with its fine woodwork. The private study is unusual, having been organized like a ship's cabin. The Potsdam Conference at the end of World War II took place in the main hall, which is reached by a monumental staircase in the Gdansk Baroque style.

The interior of the
Marmorpalais boasts
floors of precious marble
and walls with exquisite
paintings on exotic
themes. From time to
time, the king would
have certain items
from Sanssouci brought
to this palace.

The Pyramid (above), designed by Carl Gotthard Langhans (who also designed Berlin's Brandenburg Gate), was intended to serve as an architectural counterpoint to the Marmorpalais. The Neo-Gothic library on the southern tip of the lake was commissioned by Frederick William II in 1794 (right). The king used the charming two-story pavilion as a place of rest, a belvedere, and a private library.

It was only in the mid-nineteenth century that Park Sanssouci was provided with a regular water supply, when a steam pump was built in the form of a mosque, its minaret masking the smokestack. The Moorish decorative motif was even pursued inside, making this steam engine one of the finest hydraulic pumps in Europe.

BABELSBERG

Schloß Babelsberg was built in an English Gothic Revival style on a hill facing Potsdam. Its many towers and turrets give it a fairy-tale charm. It offers splendid views of the Tiefer See, a branch of the River Havel.

Park Babelsberg, flanked by two branches of the Havel, the Tiefer See and the Glienicker See, is located to the east of Potsdam. The most recent of Potsdam's parks and gardens, it was suitably named "Babel Mount" because it occupies the heights. To reach it, a high hill must be climbed. The trek is worth it, however, for once on top visitors discover a grandiose view and a delightful park with an enchanting palace. The Prussian prince who ordered construction of the palace chose the sight for its wonderful view.

That prince was named William. At the time, Glienicke and Charlottenhof were the fashionable accomplishments of the Arcadia being built around Potsdam, and William wanted an estate of comparable beauty for himself. Lenné drew the crown prince's attention to Babelsberg, given to the prince in 1833, which was on the shores of the Tiefer See. Thanks to its relief, this was a perfect spot for creating a park with sweeping views. Somewhat overshadowed by its

neighbor Sanssouci, this vast park draws less visitors and is a peaceful place all year around.

The palace itself, Schloß Babelsberg, lies to the north. It features Gothic Revival turrets and castellation, with interior furnishings in the same style. Nestling in its vast grounds, the palace looks rather like a medieval English castle. It was built by architects Schinkel, Persius, and Strack. The site also includes a smaller palace (the Kleine Palais) built specially for the ladies-in-waiting, and lodgings for the mariners who crewed the royal yachts and manned the gondoliers.

The project was ill fated, however. Lack of money and constant interference by the prince's wife irritated Schinkel, who did not include the building in his list of accomplishments. The clarity and unity of the façade, along with the harmony between façade and interior, were destroyed by the later addition of corbelling, towers, and windows of various sizes. To cap that, the plants chosen by Lenné lacked water; in 1839, the prince of Pückler-Muskau, an inveterate traveler and playboy, took over the landscaping. He designed a delightful English-style esplanade, composed of twenty-seven flower beds. Since the plants flowered at different times, the grounds dazzled with delicate colors from spring to autumn. Some of the patterns imitated the motifs decorating the tapestry in the bedroom of Augusta, the capricious princess. Pückler-Muskau was a ladies' man and he knew how to beguile the princess, who gave him a free hand. He then redesigned the lanes devised by Lenné and completed the network so successfully that Babelsberg was henceforth recognized as the garden in Potsdam with the most varied vistas.

In 1840, William became King Frederick William IV and the situation changed. "The duke of Dessau turned his land into one single garden. I cannot do likewise because my land is far too vast. But, little by little, I can transform the environs of Berlin and Potsdam into a

The summit of Babelsberg
is crowned by the
Flatowturm (150 feet
high), built by architect
Johann Heinrich Strack
in 1856. It was named
after a domain in east
Prussia, whose revenues
financed construction.
It was graced inside
with precious objects
and furniture; the tower
is now a museum open
to the public.

grand garden. I have perhaps another twenty years to live, and that should be sufficient time to accomplish the project. I authorize all improvements!''

To provide the gardens with water, industrialist August Borsig was commissioned to build a *Dampfmaschinenhaus* (steam engine house); Ludwig von Persius designed the exterior of the building in a "Burgundian Romanesque" style. Two years later, the engines were pumping water from the Glienicker See with sufficient power to send the jets of the fountains some 40 yards high. Henceforth, all the plants could be watered. A second pump, designed to supply Sanssouci with water, was built at Neustadt on Havel Bay. The exterior of this building imitated a mosque and its Moorish architecture was so perfect, inside and out, that Muslims would come to the door to pray. The Flatowturm, a lookout tower located near the middle of the park, is a counterpart to the belvedere perched on Pfingstberg at the top of the Neuer Garten. This picturesque site with its two towers can be seen from quite a distance, and offers one of the most beautiful views of Potsdam, the Havel, and the surrounding woods. One could stay in this park forever.

Movie Town. Visitors who prefer action and movement to peace and quiet should head south of the enchanted garden for the Filmpark Babelsberg. If heading there from Schloß Babelsberg, it is worth taking the time to stroll along Rosa-Luxemburg-Straße or, better, along Griebnitzsee, to admire the villas once belonging to the movie stars who naturally lived near the studios, in lavish houses overlooking the lake. A strange atmosphere reigns here: the status of certain properties has still not been resolved, and the villas seem to be sleeping, bewitched. In the 1930s, the area was called UFA-Stadt (after the giant UFA film corporation). Now dubbed Medienstadt Babelsberg (Media City), it was founded in

1912 and soon became Europe's largest film studio. In 1929, the famous Tonkreuz was built here—four sound sets in the shape of a cross, where silent movies learned to talk. The tourist train that wends through the studios retraces ninety years of film production, evoking the likes of such important figures as Fritz Lang, Ernst Lubitsch, Marlene Dietrich, and Greta Garbo. In addition to modern production studios, visitors can see historic buildings used in the shooting of Lang's masterpiece *Metropolis,* as well as the oldest and largest European studio, built especially for that film. Exhibits include other original sets and décors. It is also possible to see modern films or stunts being shot, as TV channels and film production companies, as well as radio stations, now operate on the premises.

Thus even in the twenty-first century, Potsdam remains a town where people dream, create, and invent. In Medienstadt Babelsberg today, dreamweavers the world over continue to invent a kind of Arcadia, an earthly paradise formerly imagined by the kings of Prussia, taken to its zenith by Frederick the Great and recreated by Schinkel and Lenné.

A tour through Babelsberg film studio park takes visitors past the Wall in former East Berlin, here recreated as a film set (above). The Einstein Tower, built by Erich Mendelsohn in the 1920s, is one of the finest examples of German Expressionist architecture. It was built to house practical experiments on Albert Einstein's theories and is still home to scientific research today (facing page).

RENDEZVOUS

People who think Berliners are unsociable are only half right. It is true that Berliners can be rushed and rather reserved much of the time. And yet that does not prevent them from loving their neighborhood bars, cafés, and businesses, or from sitting for hours in an outdoor *Biergarten* in the shade of chestnut trees, letting the day draw quietly to a close or partying all Saturday night until dawn. Spurred, since reunification, by a growing sense of pride, they know they must avoid disappointing the countless curious visitors now besieging the city. Berliners have invested much courage, imagination, and money in developing their infrastructure. They have created more pleasant streets, more luxurious hotels, and a wide variety of better, more elegant restaurants. The influx of a new population group—the notorious politicians with their cortege of reporters, diplomats, and artists—is now making a permanent impact on everyday life in Berlin. It has sparked fertile competition among good restaurants, fine hotels, charming old cafés, and sophisticated stores. In Berlin, going out on the town is becoming more and more fun, while shopping offers ever more surprises. A stroller may stumble upon a little-known museum, an idyllic *Biergarten* or, in the evening, an old tavern that provides a unique experience. In daytime, on the other hand, tourists seek above all cultural experiences and outstanding artworks, and therefore head toward small museums and collections as remarkable as they are unusual.

The Riva bar (previous double page).
1 *The marzipan store.*
2 *Café Am Steinplatz.*

3 *Zwölf Apostel Hotel.*
4 *KPM casts.*
The Dorint Hotel (facing page).

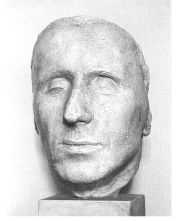

*The rooms in the Brecht-Haus on Chausseestraße have remained
unchanged since the days when Bertolt Brecht and his wife lived here.
The playwright liked modest, indeed spare, surroundings, and preferred
raw materials such as wood and leather in their natural state. The
windows overlook a cemetery whose peacefulness appealed to the couple.*

LITTLE-KNOWN MUSEUMS

Alongside the major, prestigious institutions on Museum Island, there exist more obscure museums of a different kind. They are harder to find but can be explored in a single visit. One such discovery is the Georg-Kolbe-Museum, installed in the sculptor's former home and workshop at 25 Sensburger Allee, not far from Theodor Heuss Platz. The villa was built in the Bauhaus style, and is protected from the bustle of the street by a stand of pine trees. Prior to his death, Kolbe (1877–1947) had bequeathed his house and works to the city on condition that it be turned into a museum. Once the museum opened in 1950, it became a dynamic sculpture center. Most of the works on show date from the first half of the twentieth century. The foundation displays some 200 sculptures and 1,500 drawings by Kolbe, as well as his personal sculpting tools, furniture, and everyday objects. The collection also includes work by famous contemporaries of Kolbe, such as Ludwig Kirchner, Aristide Maillol, and Wilhelm Lehmbruck.

It is easy to walk straight past the simple façade at 125 Chausseestraße, for people who do not realize that here, too, a site of human creativity has been turned into a museum. This is the house where poet and playwright Bertolt Brecht lived with his wife, actress Helene Weigel. The Brecht-Weigel Gedenkstätte displays the couple's work and living spaces. In the basement, it is possible to enjoy a cup of coffee and something to eat, the dishes on the menu having been taken from "Helle" Weigel's cookbook.

The Filmmuseum is somewhat better known, yet is unique of its kind and reminds us that Berlin was once a temple of the silver screen. In September 2000, the Filmhaus opened in new premises on Potsdamer Platz. Right in downtown Berlin, at 2 Potsdamer Straße, it boasts two art film theaters on the ground floor, a film school on the top floor, and the museum with its amazing collection in between the two. In addition to movie history, stars, and techniques, the museum captures the intangible side of movies, the aura and mythology. Its sixteen rooms display a permanent collection featuring, among others, Marlene Dietrich, Fritz Lang, and Heinz Rühmann.

Among the wealth of Berlin's museums, there exists a true gem out in Mahlsdorf: the Gründerzeitmuseum. It all began when someone

1

2

1 *Georg-Kolbe-Museum.*

2 *Filmmuseum.*

3

4

3 *Jewish Museum.*

4 *Panke Museum.*

decided that the aesthetics of Germany's "Gründerzeit" (foundation years), from 1871 to World War I, were worthy of a museum. That someone was Charlotte von Mahlsdorf, whose real name was Lothar Berfelde, a collector of furniture from this period. It was a time when the bourgeoisie was highly conscious of its importance, as reflected in the objects on display: the amazing variety of styles, from Renaissance revival to Prussian pseudo-Baroque, lend these artifacts an air simultaneously pompous and comfortable. In 1960, when the Mahlsdorf neighborhood was still part of East Berlin, "Charlotte," an iconoclast who broke down the barriers between sexes as well as styles, founded "his" museum, initially limited to two rooms in a middle-class house slated for demolition. This initiative led to a running battle with the authorities but guaranteed him support from an interested public, especially among the gay and lesbian scene. Charlotte's museum long remained a little-known affair. In 1991, "she" was awarded the Cross of Merit and her house became an attraction. Shortly thereafter, Charlotte emigrated to Sweden, where she founded a museum devoted the turn-of-the-century era. The Mahlsdorf house was closed and part of the collection was sold. Then a solution was found and the museum reopened; luckily, its most famous room had been preserved, namely the Mulackritze, a complete interior of a 1920s tavern from the Scheunenviertel (Barn Quarter).

The Ephraim-Palais, located on the edge of the Nikolaiviertel (Saint Nicholas quarter), also boasts an unusual history. The four-story Rococo building was one of the city's oldest and most beautiful residences, having been built in 1766 by architect Friedrich Wilhelm Dieterich for Veitel Heine Ephraïm, jeweler to Frederick the Great. Its round façade, on the corner of Mühlendamm, was notable for its gilded balustrades and rich ornamentation. In 1936, when the street was widened, it was dismantled piece by piece. Every column and stone—all 2,493 of them—had to be numbered and stored in a warehouse. Once the street was widened, Ephraim's palace was to have been reconstructed sixteen yards back. But the project was delayed, and then the war came, followed by division: the dismantled palace was in a warehouse in the West, while Mühlendamm was located in the East. Following difficult negotiations, the pieces were finally transported across the Wall, and the palace was rebuilt in the Nikolaiviertel, not far from its original location.

1

2

1 *Ephraim-Palais.*
2 *The old Hamburger Bahnhof on Invalidenstraße has been transformed into a museum of contemporary art.*

3

4

3 *The Kunstgewerbemuseum in the Tiergarten.*
4 *Bauhaus Archives on Klingelhöferstraße in the Tiergarten.*

In the museum devoted to the Gründerzeit (foundation years), Charlotte von Mahlsdorf collected furniture typical of the imperial period. The chairs, sideboard, and other items go together perfectly, as do the twin beds and mirrored wardrobe in the bedroom. The museum also boasts a fully equipped kitchen.

The Deutsches Technikmuseum. The airplane mounted plane on the roof participated in the Berlin airlift during the Cold War (left).
The Vitra Design Museum (below).

Most people consider the results to be a great success. The wrought iron banister on the stairway in the entrance hall alone is worth a visit. Nowadays, the palace houses a fine museum devoted to the history and art of Berlin. A charming café is located on the ground floor.

The Vitra Design Museum, meanwhile, is brand new—the institution that is, not the building. The Vitra opened in June 2001 in Prenzlauer Berg as the Berlin branch of a museum that Frank O. Gehry had designed in Weil am Rhein. The branch moved into surprising premises, namely the Humboldt power plant, an austerely beautiful monument of industrial architecture that was built in 1925. Here, in the main hall where high-power transformers were once installed, people now discuss fashion, style, design, and architecture. Often those issues are raised in the context of interdisciplinary exhibitions. To remain informed about the forms, colors, and materials out of which the man-made world is fashioned, it is worth asking for the program of this highly original museum.

In Charlottenburg, one little-known museum is even called the "Hidden Museum" (Das Verborgene Museum). It is entirely devoted to documenting and exhibiting work by women artists. Its name is a reminder that female artistic creativity, especially in the early twentieth century, took place in the shadows and was overlooked—but that women's art should not remain oblivion. The term "hidden," however, also refers to the fact that this little museum is set in a courtyard, invisible from the street.

The Sammlung Berggruen (Berggruen Collection) is a must for anyone interested in modern art. It includes eighty-eight works by Picasso (a long-time friend of the collector), plus works by Paul Klee, Paul Cézanne, and Vincent van Gogh, all in a pleasant setting. These paintings and sculptures are on show opposite Schloß Charlottenburg, in one of the royal barracks designed by Stüler—which is also where art dealer Heinz Berggruen, founder of the collection, now lives.

|

2

3

4

1 *Käthe-Kollwitz-Museum.*
2 *The Berggruen Collection.*

3 *The exhibition space on Lützowplatz.*
4 *The Lapidarium in the Köllnischen Park.*

HOTELS

Ever since Berlin was named the capital of united Germany, tourism has boomed, spurring the establishment of new hotels. Today there are 450, providing some 50,000 beds for visitors. For a long while already, hotels have been concerned not only to make a guest's stay pleasant and comfortable, but also to improve his or her health, savor each moment, and stimulate artistic appreciation. Many of the new hotels provide sophisticated accommodation, offering good design, atmosphere, special services, and sometimes even exhibitions of artworks.

Take the example of the Art'Otel Ermelerhaus on Wallstraße in the center of town. This hotel has been designed—or "staged"—by the great contemporary painter Georg Baselitz. The works on display interact with the architecture, which presented the architects with a particularly difficult challenge because they had to incorporate the Ermelerhaus—one of the few surviving late-eighteenth-century aristocratic mansions—into the hotel.

Equally ambitious is the Grand Hotel Esplanade (not to be confused with the house of the same name on Potsdamer Platz, now just a ruin). This building, located on Lützowplatz near the Landwehrkanal, was built in 1988. The triangular building embodies the spare, glass-walled aesthetic typical of modern architecture. Inside, hotel guests can enjoy an exhibition of work produced by German artists in the 1980s and a library specializing in art books boasting some 2,000 volumes. The hotel offers such luxury services as the rental of a private restaurant barge for exploring Berlin's waterways while enjoying a meal. It is also home to the highly popular Harry's New York Bar, where an impressive canvas by Rainer Fetting hangs.

A stay at the Schloßhotel Ritz Carlton (formerly Schloßhotel Vier Jahreszeiten, and before that Schloßhotel Gehrus) is more than a simple hotel experience: it is a veritable adventure combining nostalgia, design, art, and landscape gardening. The Schloßhotel occupies a mansion dating from 1912, which fashion designer Karl Lagerfeld renovated from top to bottom in 1991. Lagerfeld managed to recreate the delightful style of a 1920s interior, complete with light fixtures and coffered ceilings, counterbalanced and complemented by

1

2

3

4

1 *The Art'Otel occupies a historic eighteenth-century building.*
2 *The Art'Otel's dining room.*

3 *Hotel Künstlerheim Luise.*
4 *The hotel's "royal suite."*

The Ritz Carlton in Grunewald is probably Berlin's most elegant address. The palace has been completely transformed into a luxury hotel that exudes grandeur. It is the favorite meeting spot of successful television producers. The dinnerware, like everything else, is signed Karl Lagerfeld. On the right is Lagerfeld's private room in the hotel.

1

2

1 *Adlon Hotel, Unter den Linden.*
2 *Riehmers Hofgarten Hotel.*

his own ideas of what makes a fine hotel. The design is total Lagerfeld, from dinnerware and mirrors to rugs, fabrics, and tablecloths. By way of fee, a suite has been placed at Lagerfeld's disposal.

The Am Gendarmenmarkt Hotel can justly claim to satisfy the most demanding tastes. Located on Charlottenstraße, not far from the famous square whose name it bears, the hotel charms visitors with its fresh colors and simple, clean-cut approach to design. Its second name, Royal Dorint, betrays the fact that the hotel belongs to the Dorint chain, which applies to the letter the dictum expressed by the famous French writer, Stendhal: "I know of only one rule: style can never be too clear nor too spare."

Just a stone's throw away is the Four Seasons Hotel. Here again, many of the rooms overlook the monumental Gendarmenmarkt. But the hotel has adopted a decorative scheme completely different from the Royal Dorint. Luxury is the main theme and marble is the main means. This extraordinary natural stone, imported from Italy, glows and shimmers in all its hues, ranging from shell pink to pigeon blue. Behind this grand hotel is another chain, this time Canadian. The style of the foyer and salons tends toward a nineteenth-century Biedermeier Classicism—a range of furniture from that period rests on the marble floors. In the restaurant, a fireplace and walls with fine woodwork create the warm atmosphere so appreciated by clients in search of relief from the hectic pace of the big city.

Any list of "grand" hotels in Berlin must of course include the Adlon. More than a hotel, it is a veritable legend located "under the linden trees." The original Adlon enjoyed an ideal location on Pariser Platz, near the Brandenburg Gate, and opened its doors with the blessings of the Kaiser. It welcomed the cream of high society (and everyone who passed for such). The Hotel Adlon was famous for its huge parties, its illustrious guests, and endless succession of grand ceremonies. Toward the end of World War II, this magnificent edifice was damaged in a fire. The building was eventually torn down in 1984 and it was not until reunification that its reconstruction was envisaged. Although one story taller, the new hotel—completed in 1997—closely resembles the original one thanks to its old-style façade and green copper roof. Even before the hotel opened, it was

3

4

3 *Dorint Hotel.*
4 *Hotel-Pension Funk.*

the talk of the town. It provides today's Berlin with a touch of tradition and refinement. The five-star hotel is run by the Kempinski corporation, and is used to lodge foreign heads of state when on official visits—which is why Germany's president attended the inauguration in person.

Not everyone, however, wants to stay in a grand hotel. Turning to less prestigious establishments, there is a range of charming addresses to choose from, starting with the Riehmers Hofgarten at 83 Yorckstraße in Kreuzberg. Bordered by Yorckstraße, Grossbeeren-straße, and Habelberger Straße, the building that houses this hotel was built as an apartment complex at the end of the nineteenth century. There are three wings, each with its own entrance. The interior has been decorated in a style that is modern but far from bland or austere. Thanks to its location, visitors can make the most of the lively Kreuzberg neighborhood while enjoying a quiet retreat. The hotel has twenty rooms in all. Its restaurant, the E.T.A. Hoffmann, is a further asset, as its refined cuisine is praised throughout the city.

Those who wish to flee the commotion of the great city should head for the Fortshaus Paulsborn. This bucolic little hotel on the edge of the Grunewaldsee, near the delightful Jagdschloß (hunting lodge), has just ten rooms. Here you can take advantage of rustic Berlin without being too far from the modern city center. A pleasant restaurant enhances your stay.

Downtown, in the ever-popular middle-class neighborhoods of west Berlin, the Hotel-Pension Funk is a useful address, although some may find the decoration slightly pompous. The establishment dates from the 1930s and features fourteen rooms with typical Berlin dimensions—that is to say, large with high ceilings—guaranteeing privacy and comfort.

5 *Four Seasons Hotel.*
6 *Bleibtreu Hotel.*

BISTROTS, BIERGARTENS, CAFÉS AND BARS

The boom period of the Gründerzeit, straddling the late nineteenth and early twentieth centuries, saw the development of a Berlin specialty, the *Destille*. The term "distillery" referred to the manufacture of schnapps, yet was also used to refer to a tavern where people could drink to their heart's content among friendly company in a pleasant atmosphere. In those days, poverty was such that bars functioned as a kind of second living room—home was crowded and cold, but the distillery was warm and conducive to a comfortable doze. This venerable tradition has survived into the present. Since the nights are long, breakfast is sometimes served as late as 4 P.M., sometimes non-stop. In the days of the Wall, Berlin claimed to be the capital of taverns, since there was at least one distillery on every street corner; now that the two parts of the city have been reunited, its preeminence in this field goes unquestioned. Since these bars dotting the entire capital are a traditional part of city life, the clientele is composed of locals. And in a living room where everything is already comfortable, there seems little point in changing anything. Which is why many taverns have retained their original decoration. That is the case of Leydicke in Schöneberg, where East German spirits and orange liqueurs are still distilled according to a traditional, homemade recipe. The walls of this distillery, founded in 1877, are covered in paneling that dates from 1898, and the old cash register is still in service. Only the staff has changed.

The Henne ("The Hen") in Kreuzberg is another of Berlin's old-fashioned joints. As its name suggests, the beer on tap often washes down a house specialty for which the tavern is famous: young game hens. The décor is somewhat more modern than the Leydicke—it dates from 1907.

Max und Moritz is another Kreuzberg tavern. Five years older than the Henne, its wood interior and pretty blue wall tiles mark it out as a truly authentic old Berlin bar.

The nearby Neukölln neighborhood seems like an entirely different world: a solemn atmosphere reigns at the Café Rix, originally frequented by modest folk. In the large, early-twentieth-century main room, decorated with gilding and a stucco ceiling, customers enjoy

1 *Leydicke tavern in Schöneberg.*
2 *Beer garden at the Café Rix.*

subtle regional cooking and homemade cakes. The café opens onto a courtyard sheltered from Karl Marx Straße and the relaxed atmosphere in summer, beneath sturdy chestnut trees, gives it the feel of a *Biergarten*.

The Stäv (an abbreviation of Ständige Vertretung, or "permanent representation") would not have existed if Germany had never been divided. Its name is a reminder of the fact that, although the two German nations maintained diplomatic relations, the West German "embassy" could not call itself such; hence the term "permanent representation" for its diplomatic presence. The owner of the Stäv, a large café full of reporters and politicians, previously ran a restaurant in Bonn, the former capital of West Germany. When Berlin regained that status, he was the first move to the banks of the Spree—literally, as the Stäv is located on Schiffbauerdamm, perfectly placed between the Brecht theater and the Friedrichstraße station. It met a clear need for a "home away from home" for Bonn natives exiled to Berlin, as reflected in its Rhineland traditions of food and beer: *Himmel und Erde* ("Heaven and Earth," apple sauce and mashed potatoes served with sausage) and *Pittermänchen* (a small cask of beer set on the table). Although the food and photographs of the old days of the Bonn republic are indeed nostalgic for exiles, Berliners feel right at home here, too.

Intellectuals and artists can be found at the Diener, a traditional tavern in Charlottenburg. The rooms are somewhat dark, the tables wobbly, and the benches worn. Yet regulars constantly bring their foreign friends to this "second living room," which they present as a typical Berlin tavern. Photos of famous customers—actors, comics, and directors—line the walls. The Diener occupies the ground floor of an old red brick building whose façade features the word "Tattersall" in large, Art Nouveau letters. Tattersall was the name for riding schools for women, popular in the early twentieth century; a certain Lord Tattersall spearheaded this innovation against the reigning prudery. He was amply rewarded, because in German his name is now permanently linked with the relaxed morals associated with the equestrian crowd.

3

4

3 *The Stäv, in the heart of Mitte.*
4 *The old-fashioned décor of the Diener.*

Beer Gardens. Berlin is the capital of tenants—in no other German city do so few people own the home they occupy. Most of them have no garden, either, so to compensate for that lack, they can opt for a little park along Berlin's green belt, or go to a *Biergarten*. The term "garden" is a little misleading, because there are neither flowers nor bushes. But there are trees (usually chestnut trees in the middle of a yard), and sometimes, not far away, a pond shimmers in the sun. The first part of the term, "beer," should not be misunderstood either; the list of drinks in a *Biergarten* ranges from wine to coffee and usually includes a wide choice of tasty dishes. Beer is nevertheless highly appreciated in summer, and tastes even better when enjoyed outdoors. The atmosphere is less exuberant and deafening than in Bavaria or in Berlin's own dive bars, and can vary from lively to melancholy depending on the neighborhood and weather.

Berlin's oldest *Biergarten* is the Prater on Kastanienallee in the Prenzlauer Berg neighborhood, the heart of the brewing district. Since 1837, in the shade of hardy chestnut and linden trees, the Prater has been serving beer and coffee (families used to arrive with their own coffeepot, which they would fill on the spot). These days, the Prater is also a venue for shows, simultaneously functioning as a restaurant, an outdoor theater, and a nightclub. Within the neighborhood, it is almost considered an institution—the most unlikely celebrations and concerts are held there.

The spacious and idyllic Café am Neuen See can be found in the middle of the Tiergarten, by the Landwehrkanal, right near the zoo. This is a traditional and therefore popular establishment. Light beer is often accompanied by rustic specialties, such as white sausage or fresh pretzels. The vast garden has recently become a haunt for the nearby embassy staff. One special feature of the café is the possibility of a little outing in a boat on the lake before or after having a drink.

In contrast, the Golgotha in Kreuzberg is frequented almost entirely by locals. The tables are packed on two floors. Whereas people go to the Café am Neuen See in the afternoon to enjoy the lake in sunshine, they head to the Golgotha at night, with the intention of staying late. As night falls, the landscape darkens into blackness all around, because this *Biergarten* is located right in the middle of Viktoriapark. No one, therefore, will be disturbed by the noisier customers.

1

2

1 *Berlin's popular* Weisse
(light beer).
2 *The Alter Krug* Biergarten
in Zehlendorf.

3

4

3 *A terrace on the banks
of the Müggelsee.*
4 *Prater, a famous* Biergarten
in Prenzlauer Berg.

The Café Einstein on Kurfürstenstraße brings Viennese charm to Berlin. The waiters still display the pleasant deference typical of imperial days, retaining a certain haughtiness while doing everything they can to satisfy customers (above).

The Tadschikische Teestube is a tearoom set in a palace that invites customers to sit on cushions on the floor (right).

The Luise, in Dahlem, nestles in the most peaceful scenery imaginable, namely the Grunewald. The customers fit right into this setting, for they come from the surrounding—very refined—neighborhood. In summer, when the weather is hot, it is wonderfully cool in the shade of the chestnut trees. Throughout the warm months, barbecues are lit and crusty *Flammkuchen* (a kind of savory crepe) are eaten. In the event of rain, customers can sit indoors in the restaurant with its retro decoration.

Cafés. In addition to bars and taverns, Berliners are fond of cafés. Two cafés, both named Einstein, have Austrian roots, but have long been part of the local landscape. The first moved into a villa formerly owned by Henny Porten, an actress with the UFA film studios. This magnificent residence was built in the Tiergarten. The interior matches its façade: customers enter an imposing main hall with little tables of marble and a high, Viennese-style ceiling. Waiters are dressed in livery, and the menu lists all the mysteriously named specialties of the Austro-Hungarian empire, such as *Einspänner* (coffee with whipped

cream, served in a glass), *Mélange* (equal portions of coffee and milk), *Großer Brauner* ("brown" coffee, that is to say served with just a drop of milk). The café has a large garden with fruit trees, a spot that is always full in summer. The atmosphere is both lively and relaxed. It should be mentioned that the man who bequeathed his name to the café was not the discoverer of the theory of relativity, but rather the writer Carl Einstein: "Rare are people with the courage to spew forth nonsense. Nonsense, when oft-repeated, stimulates reflection; at a certain level of intelligence, you lose interest in everything reasonable and correct." True enough, after having tasted the café's delicious apple strudel, you begin to lose interest in being reasonable.

The Café Einstein on Unter der Linden is much smaller, and therefore quieter and more private. A customer can remain sitting on one of its red leather benches for hours, reading a newspaper, watching the other customers, or sipping a *Großer Brauner*. In summer, the Einstein sets up tables and chairs on the sidewalk down the middle of the avenue, its customers thereby enlivening the boulevard atmosphere.

A stone's throw away, the Manzini is popular for its inner courtyard with arbor, flanked on each side by two red-brick buildings typical of Berlin. The size of this large terrace is surprising, and behind it is a garden of wild grasses—a haven of peace right near Friedrichstraße. In the evening, the café becomes a restaurant, featuring international cuisine and delicious fresh bread.

Bars. Just as in the 1920s, many photographs these days feature Berlin after dark. The borderless city suddenly appears larger and still more mysterious. Yet is that really the case? Is there truly a night life here? In the days of the Wall, bars were not obliged to respect a legal closing time, yet night creatures in search of interesting spots still had a hard time. Things are now changing. New bars based on ingenious concepts are opening all over the place.

The tastefully decorated Zucca is a light, roomy bar topped by a vaulted ceiling—in fact, it is located under the arches of the elevated urban train, in Hackescher Markt station. And since these arcades with their shops, pubs, and bars are exclusive to Berlin, they are well worth a visit.

1

2

*1 Zucca's is located beneath
the elevated train.
2 The famous Paris Bar.*

3

4

*3 Bar Am Lützowplatz.
4 La Casa del Habano
in the Savoy Hotel.*

The Paris Bar is veritable institution. Located in Charlottenburg, it has been a hangout for celebrities since the 1950s. Actors, artists, writers, TV celebrities, and politicians come regularly to enjoy its cosmopolitan atmosphere. As in Parisian bars, the tables and chairs are packed together, making it difficult to forge a path to admire one of the fine paintings hanging on the walls. It is the perfect place for nighthawks, who come here just to drink and watch.

The Bar am Lützowplatz (near the Grand Hotel Esplanade) boasts one of the longest bars in the world (52 feet). Inside you will find the bar, bottles, bar stools, a few armchairs, and nothing else—except for a huge poster of Mao, which occupies the back wall and gives the place a strange atmosphere. Drinks are expensive here, which is why happy hour lasts for several hours.

The Kaffee Burger functions as bar, café, and performance venue. The public readings given here are highly popular with young book lovers and talent scouts. The establishment is located on Torstraße in a part of Mitte that still projects the grim and oppressive ambiance of East Germany, giving it a slightly surreal air. You can sit at the round, socialist-made tables lit by lamps with wicker shades and listen to droll, wacky texts. This slightly bizarre place offers a slice of the underground scene, but without sinking into *Ostalgie* (nostalgia for *Ost*, or East, Germany).

The Oxymoron in Hackesche Höfe is a sensual bar, with light fixtures like the ones seen in Wim Wender's film *Wings of Desire*. In the morning, you can have your breakfast and listen to debates, in the evening you can drink a glass of wine and watch a dance performance. The joint's special ambiance comes from its mixture of somewhat shabby colonial style with cozy English interior. Visitors should take advantage of a visit there to look around the main courtyards, each forming its own nook. Near the entrance, the walls are decorated with the glazed tiles typical of Berlin.

The Casa del Habano, the restaurant in the Hotel Savoy in Charlottenburg, generates the pleasant atmosphere required to savor exotic drinks and cigars. The parquet floor, the pillars, the expensively paneled walls, and the deliciously deep yellow leather armchairs give the bar the refined feel of an up-market consultancy.

5

6

5 *Oxymoron, a restaurant and nightclub.*
6 *The restaurant at the Literaturhaus.*

7

8

7 *Bar 925 on Gendarmenmarkt.*
8 *Café Odeon in Mitte.*

RESTAURANTS

Berlin has always been known for its quick snacks, such as curry sausage or meatballs. In recent decades, the whole world has become familiar with sausages chopped into pieces and drenched in ketchup, a dish Berlin is proud to have invented. In West Berlin, obviously, there always existed a few havens of gastronomy, but connoisseurs of fine cuisine remained a minority for a very long time. Now things seem to be changing. Demanding business leaders, politicians, and journalists are swamping the city, followed by great chefs. The tastes of local residents are becoming refined, and restaurant owners now rival one another in offering gastronomical taste experiences, aware that the competition is only just getting underway. That is why both famous chefs and young prodigies are moving to the metropolis. Furthermore, great masters of cuisine now have access to fresh produce from the city's green outskirts. When it comes to raw materials, they can get the deer and boar hunted in the countryside around Berlin, as well as the perch and pike caught in the clear Brandenburg waters. Meanwhile, high-quality traditional ingredients such as lard and knuckle of pork are enjoying renewed popularity.

The Aigner restaurant on Gendarmenmarkt is known for its regional cuisine. Its specialties include a delicious roast duck from the nearby countryside. The wine list offers a good selection from German and Austrian vineyards. The Art Nouveau furnishings— including a stove—come from the Aigner café in Vienna. Also brought over was a billiard table, converted into a table for birthday parties or business dinners: the balls are still there, like colorful eyes watching the guests celebrate. It is a warm, welcoming place, with soft light dappling the marble tiles and people clustered comfortably in booths.

Maxwell, in the Mitte district, is reached by crossing an inner courtyard that leads to a Gothic Revival façade. Although the building was once the Josty brewery, it now seems more like a holy sanctuary. The remarkable cuisine is composed almost exclusively of products from Brandenburg. In a room that functions as a gallery, you can admire top-quality art, including work by British enfant terrible Damien Hirst, who enjoys dropping in, especially since one of the duck dishes has been named after him.

1 *Maxwell's in Mitte.*
2 *Barconi's in the Sophie-Gips-Höfe.*

3 *"Twelve Apostles" in Mitte.*
4 *Café de France-Peugeot on Unter den Linden.*

Many restaurants are located in hotels,
such as the Wintergarten in the Hotel
Brandenburger Hof (left).
The Aigner restaurant is part of the
Dorint Hotel on Gendarmenmarkt.
The interior decoration and furniture—
including the piano—come from an
authentic Viennese café (below).

*Sale e Tabacchi, a restaurant in
Kreuzberg, also serves customers
in its pretty garden (above).
The Tucher on Pariser Platz not
only offers find food, but also food
for thought in the form of a
library (above left).
Borchardt is one of Berlin's most
highly rated restaurants (left).*

The house of August Friedrich Wilhelm Borchardt, a former royal counselor for trade, is located on Französische Straße. For over 150 years it has been making rare and delicious specialties available to Berliners; originally, the entrepreneur supplied the most affluent residents with wines and delicacies. Nowadays, the Borchardt restaurant is delighting Berliners with sophisticated cuisine. The main room, boasting four columns with gilded capitals, has been very carefully restored.

In the middle of Kreuzberg, the classic residence of master mason Wilhelm Riehmer is now home to a top-notch gourmet restaurant: E.T.A. Hoffmann. The setting is elegant yet sober; the tables are placed comfortably apart, creating a relaxed atmosphere. Tim Raue, the eccentric young chef, celebrates the great art of inventive cooking with his wife, Marie-Anne. "Eccentric," of course, here means a chef who likes to experiment.

The Schloßhotel Ritz-Carlton houses the magnificent Vivaldi restaurant with its impressive wood ceiling. The Vivaldi is a gourmet restaurant par excellence, proving that the new capital will stop at nothing to draw the best chefs in the country. Paul Urch's superb, spirited cuisine is fresh, light, and refined, as demonstrated by dishes such as sweet-and-sour crayfish with anisette jelly, a parfait of foie gras and cherries, or a filet of venison in a frock-coat of pastry. Only a limited number of tables are available in this restaurant where food and atmosphere are perfectly matched.

Paris–Moskau is a typical Berlin restaurant. It is located right next to an old railway line, still in use today. When the Wall was still standing, the Paris–Moscow train ran past here (as it does today), reminding the encircled city that it was once open to the world. These days, the solitary, insolent restaurant stands like a leftover from the old days. The new chancery is just a stone's throw away. The little half-timbered house now offers some of the best food in the city, especially when it comes to fowl and desserts.

The oldest gourmet establishment in Berlin is Bamberger Reiter. Right next to beautiful Victoria-Luise Platz, it proposes a rich, rustic cuisine accompanied by fabulous sauces. Bamberger Reiter is one of Berlin's most elegant dining spots, enhanced by its Rococo interior and bottle-thick window panes.

1 *Lutter und Wegner.*
2 *Paris-Moskau.*

3 *Vau is a highly popular spot.*
4 *Pasternak.*

SHOPPING

Berlin is a wonderful place to go shopping. It offers something for every taste and every budget. Particularly appealing are the small, hidden shops where you can discover some unusual gem typical of Berlin. These Aladdin's caves exist here as they do in all large cities, but they are not always easy to find, for lack of advertising. Several of these little-known stores will be discussed below, but first we must mention the major shopping districts and describe the better known department stores. It is by spending time in such places that visitors can discover the real Berlin of today, the everyday Berlin of the middle classes with their hopes and desires, their likes and little pleasures.

The most unusual shopping street is still undoubtedly the Kurfürstendamm: along this broad, extravagant avenue, lively cafés alternate with luxury shops, friendly restaurants, old movie theaters, and department stores. On Wittenbergplatz stands the famous Kaufhaus des Westens (Western Department Store), generally called by its abbreviated nickname, KaDeWe. It was founded in 1906, at a time when the construction of large department stores inspired the finest architects. With a floor surface of some one million square feet, KaDeWe is one of Europe's major department stores—and one of the most chic. The items for sale are of high quality, as is the ambiance. The food department on the sixth floor offers every possible product imaginable, from exotic fruits (whose names remain a mystery) to truffles in jars (each costing a fortune). Naturally the store also boasts several bars, cafés, and restaurants.

Recently, Friedrichstraße in the Mitte neighborhood has become a fashionable place to go shopping. The French department store Galeries Lafayette (on block 207) and the Friedrichstadtpassagen (blocks 205 and 206) bring together the leading names in fashion and luxury goods. Here luxury boutiques are found next to interior designers and bespoke shoemakers. These three grandiose malls cover a vast area, offering a range of attractions from antique store to cafés. This stretch of Friedrichstraße demonstrates that Berlin is no longer just Berlin, it is an international phenomenon, a global city. Here is where you will find the products of the most famous companies in the world.

1

2

3

4

1 *The Peek & Cloppenburg store.*
2 *Galeries Lafayette.*

3 *Stilwerk shopping center.*
4 *Ruby in Mitte.*

Plaster casts in the National Museums cast workshop (above). The KPM porcelain works is one of the most traditional of firms, yet does not rely on pure nostalgia. In recent years, Italian designer Enzo Mari has headed the workshops (right).

Anyone seeking a refined shopping district typical of Berlin should head to the Fasanenpassage located between Fasanenstraße and Uhlandstraße, near the Kurfürstendamm in Charlottenburg. Here everything is worth its weight in gold—grand jewelers, designers, perfumeries, and fashion houses are gathered here. Fasanenpassage is considered Berlin's most expense and elegant shopping arcade. Here is where you will find not only Chanel and Cartier, but also the shoemaker Ludwig Reiter (since 1885), the men's ready-to-wear store Hellmann and Sabine Anton's made-to-measure clothing boutique. The entrance at numbers 28 and 29 Fasanenstraße is superb, and runs between two splendid old houses from the Gründerzeit period, decorated with wrought-iron banisters and boasting impeccable, flowery courtyards.

The specialty stores described below are secret places scattered all across town. Beginning in Wilmersdorf, an affluent neighborhood in the west, there is an amazing chocolate store called Hamann on Brandenburgische Straße, not far from Fehrbellinner Platz. Founded in 1912, Hamann is now being run by the family's third generation. The elegantly simple interior, dating from 1928, is a mixture of Bauhaus and Art Deco styles. On entering to the scent of chocolate, visitors immediately note the wonderful displays and the honey-colored maple paneling. The house specialty is little sheets of bitter chocolate, thin as cigarette paper, made in traditional fashion in the workshop next to the store.

The nearby neighborhood of Charlottenburg also has a great little sweet shop. Located on Pestalozzistraße, it is run by eighty-eight-year-old Irmgard Wald and her granddaughter Gina. Called Marzipan Wald, it specializes in that irresistibly sweet almond paste known as marzipan, the finest being Königsberger Marzipan. Irmgard Wald was originally from east Prussia and brought the recipe with her. She has been making her marzipan-filled chocolates here on a daily basis since 1947. She still waits on customers in the store. Inside, the pink-striped wallpaper and the little light fixtures are straight out of some fairy tale. The Wald ladies have won several prizes for their marzipan and receive orders from all over the world.

But what is the point of the most delicious sweets in the world if you have nothing elegant on which to serve them? The finest and

1

2

1 *Bunzlauer pottery.*
2 *The KPM porcelain shop on Unter den Linden.*

3

4

3 *The refined décor at the Villa Harteneck.*
4 *An assortment of chocolates on Fasanenstraße.*

oldest German porcelain comes from Königlich-Preußischen Porzellanmanufaktur (Royal Porcelain Factory), abbreviated to KPM. It was in 1707 that Europe discovered the method for manufacturing "white gold," as true porcelain was known. In 1751, Wilhelm Caspar Wegely founded the first manufactory, which acquired its title of nobility in 1763 when Frederick the Great elevated it to the rank of royal manufactory. By way of coat of arms, it was entitled to display a blue scepter. Handsome traditional and contemporary porcelain can be admired and purchased at the showroom located on Wegelstraße in the Tiergarten. Every period is represented there, from stately vases with rose-shaped handles to the "Urania" setting, a product of the twentieth-century Neue Sachlichkeit (New Objectivity) movement. Remarkable designers such as Italy's Enzo Mari now produce their wares here.

Fans of more rustic porcelain, meanwhile, will be thrilled on entering the Bunzlauer Keramik store on Hohenzollerndamm in Wilmersdorf. Here is where the famous Bunzlau pottery is sold—blue and white coffeepots and teapots, cups, plates, cookie jars, and butter dishes, not to mention *Käsefrauen* (covered cheese dishes). All is available in abundance and at reasonable cost. The town of Bunzlau (Boleslawiec) is today part of Poland, and some connoisseurs go there to pick up their favorite items. But those who do not have the time for a trip to Poland can find what they want in this outlet on Hohenzollerndamm. Bunzlau ceramics perpetuate the tradition of the old Prussian school of pottery by retaining the same style and methods of manufacture. Artisans still work in traditional fashion there, hand-painting the decoration and firing the pieces at over 1300°C.

If you wish to pick up a souvenir of the former capital of Prussia, now the capital of reunited Germany, you should head to Charlottenburg. There, on Sophie-Charlotte-Straße, is a sober brick building dating from 1888, with a perfectly symmetrical alignment of windows. It is the Gipsformerei der Staatlichen Museen (National Museum Cast Workshop). Here, factory and showroom are one. As its name suggests, the workshop makes plaster casts of the objects found in national museums. It also makes some bronze casts. Art lovers can therefore buy busts of famous Prussians such as Frederick the Great, Emmanuel Kant, Wilhelm von Humboldt, and Queen Luise;

5

6

5 *Skoda.*
6 *Quarter 206 on Friedrichstraße.*

7

8

7 *KaDeWe department store.*
8 *Fiona Bennett's hat shop
in Mitte.*

certain models are painted in fine colors and are available in various sizes. A wide range of other museum pieces is also on offer, from antique graces to Aztec warriors.

Markets. Berliners love to dawdle in outdoor markets, exploring the diverse goods, perhaps observing the lively action while drinking a cup of coffee or glass of beer—or, more recently, a good glass of Riesling. Although Berlin is a flea market heaven, residents sometimes go for the fun and relaxation rather than to buy. Stressed-out city dwellers use the markets as an excuse to unwind. That explains why Berlin's markets are so numerous and so colorful. One of them, the Winterfeldmarkt, is located in Schöneberg. It is flanked by a good many cafés, from which you can admire the merchandise. The women here are radiant and even the men strive for elegance. They fish olives from wooden barrels, buy tiny carrots from Teltow, fresh asparagus or country bread. Even back in the early twentieth century, writer Kurt Tucholsky complained that Berliners were poor dressers; here, however, things are different. Attractive customers bustle everywhere—a bit like those marriage markets where people would meet the love of their life while buying one of the small loaves of bread Berliners call *Schrippen*.

The Maybachufer market is also very lively, though for different reasons. Almost all the merchants are Turks who sell their goods with loud cries. Because of the spices found there, the market feels like a bazaar in the center of Istanbul even though it is located on the banks of the Landwehrkanal. From bolts of cloth to chili peppers to delicious, flat Kreuzkümmel bread, buyers are exhorted to buy.

One of the most interesting and extensive markets—some two-thirds of a mile long—is the antique and flea market on Straße des 17 Juni. Here you will find an incredible variety of fine objects, from a Biedermeier wardrobe or a double bass to a feather boa or a chessboard. Some items are hand-made by craftsmen. The choice is vast, and the prices reasonable compared to the antique shops.

Finally, the Museuminsel market located on Museum Island is steeped in art and nostalgia. That is where to find original engravings of old Berlin, jewelry, or surprising souvenirs from the former East Germany, such as flags and Communist Party insignia. Furthermore, you can enjoy the pleasant atmosphere that reigns along Kupfergraben.

1 *Market, Karl-August-Platz.*
2 *The Turkish market.*
3 *A stall selling old luggage.*

4 *Scale-model Trabant cars.*
5 *Market on Straße des 17 Juni.*
6 *Flea market in Mitte.*

VISITOR'S GUIDE

This guide was produced by a team of contributors. It is subjective and is not intended to be comprehensive. In addition to a number of prestigious establishments, it lists a range of other excellent addresses, together with some personal favorites of the authors and their friends.

HOTELS

Berlin was ill prepared for the influx of tourists that hit the city during the 1990s. Like reunification, the tourist boom seemed to happen overnight. But the Berliners rallied round and welcomed their guests from both West and East with open arms. The upshot was a surge in the number of building projects, many of them based on highly creative and original designs; the growing stream of guests required ever more places to stay, eat, and be entertained. Many new hotels were built, where the new trend was to provide not just a place to sleep, have a shower, and eat a good breakfast, but a total cultural experience: art, music and cordon bleu cooking were also on offer to discerning guests. The following list of hotels provides a good starting point for your stay.

DESIGNER HOTELS

Art'otel ermelerhaus (Mitte)
Wallstraße 70-73
Tel.: 24 06-2
An impressive mixture of past and future, incorporating the grand old Ermelerhaus town house into a high-tech modern design. Art contemporary with the older building is on display, including some canvases by Georg Baselitz. Breakfast is available on a boat on the Spree, just in front of the hotel, for those who want to stretch their sea legs with their morning coffee.

Bleibtreu (Wilmersdorf)
Bleibtreustraße 31
Tel.: 88 47 40
This hotel was entirely renovated in 1995 to make it more environmentally friendly, creating an oasis of sensory and aesthetic pleasure through clever use of light and scent. It was fitted out by the local designer Herbert Jakob Weinand, using materials made exclusively to the hotel's requirements by Italian craftsmen. Every floor has its own personality. The entrance is scented with the hotel's own bewitching perfume.

Brandenburger Hof (Wilmersdorf)
Eislebener Straße 14
Tel.: 21 40 50

This luxurious hotel is in the Wilhelmine style on the outside, but the interior is totally modern. Its 86 rooms are in an understated Bauhaus style. Its most charming feature is its winter garden, based on a Mediterranean cloister design.

Grand Hotel Esplanade (Tiergarten)
Lützowufer 15
Tel.: 25 47 80
When this hotel opened shortly before the Wall came down, no one could have dreamed that it would become a magnet for Berlin's high society, thanks to its location on the border between East and West. The flamboyance of the mirrored complex attracted everybody who was anybody in the city, as well as crowds of wannabees. The crème de la crème came and drank exotic cocktails in the hotel's Harry's New York Bar. The hotel now even has its own river cruiser. Among its other attractions are exhibitions of contemporary painting: the hotel works closely with nearby galleries, and its exhibitions are constantly expanding. The Esplanade is very well placed for art lovers: it is directly opposite the Bauhaus Archives, and the Kulturforum is nearby.

Hotel-Pension Nürnberger Eck (Charlottenburg)
Nürnberger Straße 26a
Tel.: 235 17 80
With only eight rooms, this is really a family-run guesthouse, with a deliciously intimate atmosphere to match its small size. The 1920s- and 1930s-style decoration is entirely authentic. The clientele consists largely of painters, some of whom have decorated a room or two.

Künstlerheim Luise (Mitte)
Luisenstraße 19
Tel.: 28 44 80
The rooms of this very centrally situated hotel are all different, and every one is a work of art. Several artists, known and unknown, had a hand in the design. They are paid in kind, with free overnight stays. The building itself dates from 1825 and is classed a historic monument. The neighboring railway arches house restaurants and cafés

Maritim Pro Arte Hotel (Mitte)
Friedrichstraße 150-153
Tel.: 203 35
This designer hotel lies in the heart of Berlin's business district, just off Unter den Linden. It has 800 beds, and every floor is decorated with the work of a different artist, mostly from the "Jungen Wilden" school, who shocked German art circles in the 1980s with their insistence on content over form. Saporiti and Philippe Starck had a hand in designing the hotel.

mitART Pension (Mitte)
Friedrichstraße 127
Tel.: 28 39 04 30
Christiane Waszkoviak's hotel is more like an art gallery. Other hotels liven up their rooms and lobbies with artwork: she invites visitors to use the "gallery's guest bedrooms." Surrealism, Constructivism and Art Informel dominate. Works by the performance artist Barbara Heinisch and the Hungarian artist Imre Bak are also on display.

Ristorante & Albergo
Die Zwölf Apostel (Wilmersdorf)
Hohenzollerndamm 33
Tel.: 86 88 90
"The twelve apostles" in Wilmersdorf proposes a new culinary concept: a menu of Tuscan specialties accompanied by sausage, cheeses, and ham imported directly by the restaurant. There is also a good list of wines. The Italian ambience is accompanied by another, very fashionable theme: the Far East. The sushi bar is very popular. The restaurant is always full at midday for its main-dish-and-dessert menu, which changes every day, and its very reasonably priced sushis. In general, the first arrive soon after the last breakfast customers have left. A great deal of care also goes into the wine cellar and the cigar room, with its well-stocked humidor. The wine cellar can be rented for events with up to one hundred guests.

Ritz Carlton Schloßhotel Vier Jahreszeiten (Wilmersdorf)
Brahmsstraße 10
Tel.: 89 58 40
Karl Lagerfeld has taken this hotel in hand and redesigned it completely, recreating the atmosphere of the great hotels of the Belle Epoque, while managing to retain the intimacy of the hotel—or "hôtel particulier," as Lagerfeld calls it.

Sorat Art'otel Berlin (Wilmersdorf)
Joachimsthaler Straße 29
Tel.: 88 44 70
This hotel, right in the city center, showcases the works of Berlin artist Wolf Vostell. The interior is the work of designers Johanne and Gernot Nalbach, with contributions from Philippe Starck.

Sorat Hotel Gustavo (Prenzlauer Berg)
Prenzlauer Allee 169
Tel.: 44 66 10
This hotel is dedicated to the work of the Spanish artist Gustavo, who decorated the public spaces (lounge, reception, etc.) in his trademark light, bright colors. The reception desk is especially worth seeing.

HOTELS

Adlon Hotel (Mitte)
Unter den Linden 77
Tel.: 22 61-0
This legendary hotel, opened in 1907, today belongs to the Kempinski Group. It reopened recently, after a renovation that restored it to its former glory. Its unbeatable location, right by the Brandenburg Gate, means it is a meeting place for the great and good from the world of politics, the media, and showbusiness. The service is faultless. Even if you are not staying here, come and take a look at the luxury boutiques within the hotel.

Albrechtshof (Mitte)
Albrechtstraße 8
Tel.: 30 88 60
This hotel belongs to the Church. Its main pulling point is its handy location, near a number of theaters and museums, and a short walk from Unter den Linden.

Artemisia
Brandenburgische Straße 18
Tel.: 873 89 05
Among the number of Berlin's businesses, shops, and bars run by women for women is this hotel. The pleasant, relaxed atmosphere has assured its reputation. Children are welcome to stay in their mother's room at no extra cost.

City-Hotel Märkischer Hof (Mitte)
Linienstraße 133
Tel.: 282 71 55
A good, solid, middle-range hotel in the Scheunenviertel quarter.

Dorint Hotel am Gendarmenmarkt
Charlottenstraße 50–52
Tel.: 20 37 50
Close to the famous square whose name it bears, this hotel is entirely given over to cool, functional modernism. The facilities include a "wellness" area that includes a Roman steam bath and a fitness center. Both the location and the service are faultless. It belongs to the Dorint chain.

Dorint Hotel am Müggelsee (Köpenick)
Am Großen Müggelsee
Tel.: 65 88 20
This comfortable, family-friendly hotel is in a particularly enchanting and picturesque location. The restaurant terrace enjoys uninterrupted views over the lake, and specializes in typical Berlin fare like *Havelzander* (pike perch from the River Havel) and root vegetables.

Four Seasons Hotel (Mitte)
Charlottenstraße 49
Tel.: 203 38
This relatively recent hotel is one of the loveliest top-flight hotels in the eastern part of the city. The historic surroundings make evening strolls after a truly great meal in the hotel restaurant a tempting prospect. The 204 rooms are fitted out to the highest standards, including marble baths and open fireplaces.

Grand Hyatt (Mitte)
Marlene-Dietrich-Platz 2
Tel.: 25 53 12 34
Only the best is on offer in this luxurious hotel. It has truly earned its five-star status, with its 325 splendid rooms and its private fitness studio. It is near the new Sony Center and all the favorite Berlin stamping grounds, which makes it especially popular with media types.

Heckers Hotel (Charlottenburg)
Grolmanstraße 35
Tel.: 88 90-0
The down-to-earth, simple, yet welcoming ambience of this hotel is due to the furniture, from designs by Frank Lloyd Wright and Unger. Works of art are on display in the lobby and throughout the hotel.

Hotel Alexander (Charlottenburg)
Pariser Straße 37
Tel.: 881 60 91
The Hotel Alexander's floral decorations are designed by a stage set designer. No wonder that it has an artistic reputation: it is a firm favorite with artists and filmmakers, whose visits are not confined to the period of the Berlin Film Festival. Guests are welcomed with a glass of delicious orange punch.

Hotel Askanischer Hof (Charlottenburg)
Kurfürstendamm 53
Tel.: 881 80 33
This is one of the best addresses on the immortal Ku'damm (Kurfürstendamm), Berlin's principal shopping avenue. It still retains some of the glamor of its 1920s heyday. The comfortable rooms are generously proportioned and the furniture is of the kind highly sought after by collectors.

Hotel Hackescher Markt (Mitte)
Große Präsidentenstr. 8
Tel.: 28 00 30
This charming little hotel benefits from a great location in the new theater quarter, where cafés, bars, and restaurants abound.

Hotel Kronprinz (Charlottenburg)
Kronprinzendamm 1
Tel.: 89 60 30
This small hotel caters for the mid-to-high price range. It is tastefully decorated, with a beautiful garden out front. It is not far from the small Halensee.

Hotel-Pension Elba (Charlottenburg)
Bleibtreustraße 26
Tel.: 881 75 04
This old town house just off the Ku'damm is now a guesthouse with a lovely family atmosphere. Their slogan is "comfort needn't be expensive." The sixteen rooms are cosily furnished in a modern style.

Hotel Pension Imperator (Charlottenburg)
Meinekestraße 5
Tel.: 881 41 81
This guesthouse near the Ku'damm is in a beautiful building typical of old Berlin, reminiscent of the city's imperial past.

Hotel Pension Kastanienhof (Prenzlauer Berg)
Kastanienallee 65
Tel.: 44 30 50
A charming small guesthouse in an old Berlin townhouse in the Prenzlauer Berg quarter, in Berlin's historic heart, near Alexanderplatz. The rooms are perfectly up-to-date and decorated in a modern style. The service is warm, and the owners even propose a handy bicycle-hire service. In the summer months, cycling is probably the best and quickest way of getting around the city.

Hotel-Pension Wittelsbach (Wilmersdorf)
Wittelsbacher Straße 22
Tel.: 861 43 71
Unlike certain hotels, families are positively encouraged in this guesthouse. It also calls itself the "fairy-tale hotel" and is decorated in accordance. There is a "Sleeping Beauty" bedroom, a "feudal manor," and every room contains a selection of toys. Quiet, child-free rooms and a refreshing courtyard terrace are also on offer. The guesthouse is accessible to wheelchair users.

Hotel Riehmers Hofgarten (Kreuzberg)
Yorkstraße 83
Tel.: 78 09 88 00
Peace and quiet are guaranteed at this small hotel, dating from the 1870s, with its lovely garden in the inner courtyard. For those who don't want to venture out into the hustle and bustle, meals are available in the hotel's own restaurant, named after the famous Romantic author E.T.A. Hoffmann (of Tales of Hoffmann fame).

Kempinski Hotel Bristol (Charlottenburg)
Kurfürstendamm 27
Tel.: 88 43 40
This top-class hotel has long enjoyed legendary status—since the end of the nineteenth century, in fact. It was supposed to prove the supremacy of the West over the East in the bad old days before reunification, and indeed faces from the media and politics were often seen in its chic English-style lounges. It has recently undergone a total renovation, and is destined to reclaim its rightful place among the crème de la crème of Berlin hotels.

Paulsborn (Zehlendorf)
Am Grunewaldsee/Hüttenweg
Tel.: 818 19 10
This mid-range hotel has something rather unusual to offer the traveler used to city-hopping: a breath of fresh air. It is located in Berlin's Grunewald forest, and is a favorite destination for days out in the summer. Its rustic yet perfectly comfortable rooms (ten in all) are a haven of peace, and the large garden terrace is the perfect place to unwind after a hard day's visiting, shopping, or whatever.

Residenz (Charlottenburg)
Meinekestraße 9
Tel.: 88 44 30
Based in an 1870s town house, this hotel located near the Ku'damm has all the charm of the Belle Epoque. The rooms and service are both worthy of the highest praise, and if that is not enough to convince you, try the hotel's own restaurant, the Grand Cru.

Savoy Hotel (Charlottenburg)
Fasanenstraße 9-10
Tel.: 31 10 30
This top-class hotel, right by the Zoologischer Garten station, sums up the noble charm of the old West Berlin. It is near the famed KaDeWe department store and the Paris Bar.

Sorat Spreebogen (Tiergarten)
Alt-Moabit 99
Tel.: 39 92 00
In the Spreebogen urban development zone, this hotel is in the mid-to-upper price range. Its view over the River Spree guarantees peace and tranquility in the hustle and bustle of the city. The German Interior Ministry recently moved in opposite, and the hotel's terrace is a good place to spot famous political faces at midday. After a workout in the fitness studio, assuage your well-earned hunger in the hotel's own restaurant "Alte Meierei."

Even though the Berlin Wall has been torn down, traces of it remain.

Steigenberger Berlin (Charlottenburg)
Los-Angeles-Platz 1
Tel.: 212 71 17
A large, modern, conventionally furnished hotel, roomy, and with good food: ideal for congresses and conferences. It is near the zoo, in the center of the western part of town, yet manages to give the illusion of secluded isolation. Its romantic evenings in the piano bar are legendary.

Stuttgarter Hof (Kreuzberg)
Anhalter Straße 9
Tel.: 26 48 30
This traditional hotel was a favorite place for guests arriving at the nearby Anhalter Station, even back in the nineteenth century.

The Westin Grand (Mitte)
Friedrichstraße 158-164
Tel.: 202 70
Formerly known as the Grand Hotel, the Westin Grand was the flagship hotel of the GDR, where the VIPs were given a taste of luxury East German style. The octagonal, pink marble lobby, with its imposing staircase, is still impressive. It is but a short walk from here to the Comic Opera. The interiors of the generously spaced rooms are decorated in the style of the eighteenth century.

Wenzel (Schöneberg)
Fuggerstraße 13
Tel.: 218 70 93
This hotel may be relatively small compared to others in this guide (only forty-seven rooms), but it is nevertheless perfectly comfortable, and is handily located near the KaDeWe department store.

GUESTHOUSES

Belvedere (Wilmersdorf)
Seebergsteig 4
Tel.: 826 00 10
A welcoming, well-run small guesthouse,

charmingly decorated with old-fashioned furniture and brocade wall hangings, surrounded by greenery, yet right near the Ku'damm. Breakfast on the terrace is especially tempting.

Pension Dittberner (Charlottenburg)
Wielandstraße 26
Tel.: 884 69 50
A traditional Berlin guesthouse with a cozy atmosphere. The lovely old building offers spacious bedrooms with typical high ceilings.

Pension Funk (Charlottenburg)
Fasanenstraße 69
Tel.: 882 71 93/883 33 29
This sweet, comfortable guesthouse is typical of Berlin. It is in the old center of the western part of town, and is well able to hold its head up in this rather desirable neighborhood.

Pension Merkur (Mitte)
Torstraße 156
Tel.: 282 82 97
This plain but friendly guesthouse is a good place to get a taste of the center of the old Berlin before the Wall came down. Nowadays, the new center round about the Hackeschen Höfe is just round the corner.

GOURMET RESTAURANTS

Alt-Luxemburg (Charlottenburg)
Windscheidstraße 31
Tel.: 323 87 30
The solid, comfortable interior dating from the end of the nineteenth century breathes self-assurance. The top-notch cooking is based on the French and German culinary traditions. The fish and seafood are especially good. Try a wine from Baden or the Rheingau.

Au Lac (Charlottenburg)
Lietzenseeufer 11
Tel.: 32 00 21 77
Here, you're right in the center of the city, but you could be a million miles away. This restaurant is part of the Hotel Seehof, right on the lake front. The cuisine, mainly traditional German dishes, is excellent, and people come from far and wide to try the *Zanderfilet mit Kurkuma-Fenchel* (fillet of pike perch with kurkuma and fennel).

Bamberger Reiter (Schöneberg)
Regensburger Straße 7
Tel.: 218 42 82
The rustic interior is in dark wood, the terrace is magnificent, and the whole is a most inviting

prospect. Try *Leipziger Allerlei* (a mixed vegetable dish containing carrots, peas, cauliflower, asparagus, and mushrooms), oxtail, or pike perch with sumptuous sauces—just some of the specialties of Tyrolean chef Mr. Raneburger. The wines are selected among the finest Europe has to offer. It is wise to reserve, even for the adjoining bistrot, decorated with large mirrors and with a lovely gallery running round the walls.

Borchardt (Mitte)
Französiche Straße 47
Tel.: 20 38 71 10
This is a good place for people-spotting. The Borchardt brings a touch of Mediterranean flair to Berlin, and is always buzzing. The main room, with its tall marble columns and the beautiful mosaic behind the bar, was originally a meeting place for the Huguenot community. In summer, come and pass the time in the intimate garden courtyard.

Du Pont (Charlottenburg)
Budapester Straße 1
Tel.: 261 88 11
Near the zoo, in the heart of the old west part of town, this restaurant is renowned for its fortunate marriage of French and German cooking. The Duck à la Nantaise (or *Nanteser Ente*, if you're looking at the menu) is highly recommended. The décor aims at uncompromising modernity: glass, chrome and mirrored surfaces rule.

E.T.A. Hoffmann (Kreuzberg)
Yorckstraße 183
Tel.: 78 09 88 09
Those in the know say this restaurant, a temple to the gourmet tradition, has the most creative chef in town, even if it's a little far from the center.

Guy (Mitte)
Jägerstraße 59/60
Tel.: 20 94 26 00
This is the place to come to eat fine fish, especially in the summer. Fish and shellfish are presented on a display rack for clients to choose from. The charming inner courtyard is reached through a light, airy gallery behind a curving glass wall.

Grand Cru (Charlottenburg)
Meinekestraße 9
Tel.: 88 44 39 00
This is the restaurant of the Hotel Residenz. First-class food is served in exquisite surroundings: Art Nouveau paintings, mirrored

walls, and flower arrangements. The seafood and game (specially brought in from the Brandenburg region) are particularly recommended.

Grand Slam (Zehlendorf)
Gottfried-von-Cramm-Weg 47-55
Tel.: 825 38 10
Despite the name, this restaurant is not just for tennis fans: it takes its name from the tennis club it is attached to. It's one of the best and classiest restaurants in town. The cooking is original and extremely good: critics rave over the duck tartlets with glazed carrots. The relaxed, unpretentious décor is in the style of an English country house, and the view over the Hundekehlesee in summer is superb.

Harlekin (Tiergarten)
Lützowufer 15
Tel.: 25 47 88 58
The Harlekin is every bit as classy as the Grand Hotel Esplanade, which it is attached to. The Mediterranean-style cuisine is creative and innovative. The chef's use of fresh herbs is especially good. The wine waiter will propose great wines, some from relatively unknown vineyards.

Heising (Schöneberg)
Rankestraße 32
Tel.: 213 39 52
Mr. and Mrs. Heising have been running this small restaurant near the Wilhelm Memorial Church for years. Just like in the days when visitors rolled up in a coach and four, you enter a lounge decorated in the Wilhelmine style, where your hosts seat you at a round mahogany table with a wonderful bouquet of fresh roses. You feel as if you have stepped back a hundred years. The impeccable service is equally old-fashioned and charming. The menu is imaginative, and the food beautifully cooked. Ladies are presented with a rose as a farewell gift. Advance booking essential.

Margaux (Mitte)
Unter den Linden 78
Tel.: 22 65 26 11
Exquisite food in a central location from an inventive young chef who has won several awards. What more could you ask for?

Maxwell (Mitte)
Bergstraße 22
Tel.: 280 71 21
Modernity is the key word here: you can check out the menu online, at maxwell.berlin.@t-online.de. It is best to come at night, as the old brewery building with its skillfully restored inner courtyard is then spectacularly lit up.

Paris-Moskau (Tiergarten)
Alt-Moabit 141
Tel.: 394 20 81
The surroundings may not be great, but the food in this excellent restaurant is worth the effort. The dilapidated half-timbered building along an old railway line is rather plain inside, apart from the huge flower-bedecked bar. The heavy damask tablecloths and expert waiters perfectly complement the delicious poultry and game dishes. The desserts are worth reserving some of your appetite for.

Ponte Vecchio (Charlottenburg)
Spielhagenstraße 45
Tel.: 342 19 99
Good food and good service in simple surroundings. The kitchen team is small but well knit, and excels in fish and game.

Quadriga (Wilmersdorf)
Eislebener Straße 14
Tel.: 21 40 56 50
This small, elegant restaurant in the late-nineteenth-century Brandenburger Hof mansion serves meals of the highest caliber on equally noble porcelain with the royal coat of arms. Advance booking essential.

Remise (Zehlendorf)
Königstraße 36
Tel.: 805 40 00
After a visit to Schloß Glienicke, eat in this restaurant, offering uninterrupted views over the castle's grounds, fine food, and carefully selected wines, and dream the rest of the afternoon away.

Seasons (Mitte)
Charlottenstraße 49
Tel.: 20 33 63 63
This is the restaurant attached to the Hotel Four Seasons. The dining room, with its Canadian oak fittings and marble flooring, is as elegant as the hotel's Langhans and Gontard lounges, and the cooking easily matches the highest expectations. The ambience of nineteenth-century splendor is completed by wood-burning stoves, chandeliers, Biedermeier furniture, and mirrors in huge frames. The terrace looks out over the Gendarmenmarkt.

Vivaldi (Wilmersdorf)
Brahmsstraße 10
Tel.: 89 58 44 00
Designed by Karl Lagerfeld, this first-class gourmet restaurant within the Ritz Carlton has one of the most beautiful restaurant interiors in town. The food is a match for the highly elegant surroundings. Probably Berlin's most luxurious restaurant.

RESTAURANTS

Abendmahl (Kreuzberg)
Muskauer Straße 9
Tel.: 612 51 70
Nouvelle cuisine is on offer here, but with a twist: they specialize in vegetarian or fish dishes. The food is a treat, as are the surroundings. A special mention for the desserts, particularly the unusual ice cream creations.

Adermann (Mitte)
Oranienburger Straße 27
Tel.: 28 38 73 71
A good place to come for decent French cooking. Go up the short flight of steps into the upper rooms with the chandeliers, or eat in the "Glass Room." Admire the Biedermeier inlaid wood paneling dating from 1839 (behind glass, as it's protected under heritage laws).

Aigner (Mitte)
Französische Straße 25
Tel.: 203 75 18 50/51
A lovely place to come and sit in summer, under the arcades, overlooking the Gendarmenmarkt. Try their specialty, *Tafelspitz* (boiled topside of beef). If you do sit outside, be sure not to miss the original Art Nouveau interior, just like an authentic Viennese coffeehouse.

Alter Dorfkrug Lübars (Reinickendorf)
Alt-Lübars 8
Tel.: 40 20 84 00
In the bad old days when the Wall was still standing, people would come to the village of Lübars (just on the west side of the Wall) for a taste of the country life, without having to cross the border. The Alte Dorfkrug, with its solid, dependable German fare, was always full to bursting of city dwellers looking for a bit of the good life. Things have calmed down today, but it's still well worth a visit.

Altes Zollhaus (Kreuzberg)
Carl-Herz-Ufer 30
Tel.: 692 33 00
The Altes Zollhaus, a culinary pioneer in the Kreuzberg quarter, is picturesquely located along an old canal in a half-timbered house. The chef is a representative of the "New German" school of cooking—and since he has his very own jetty, you can go for a boat trip after your meal.

Bieberbau (Wilmersdorf)
Durlacher Straße 15
Tel.: 853 23 90
This restaurant occupies the former exhibition

space of a certain Herr Bieber, who made a killing in late-nineteenth-century Berlin by creating a craze for stucco in interior decoration. He always gave his clients a drink: this restaurant is just the logical extension of that.

Bovril (Charlottenburg)
Kurfürstendamm 184
Tel.: 881 84 61
One of the finest bistros on the Ku'damm. It offers good, modern, Mediterranean cooking, with only the freshest of ingredients.

Brunello (Charlottenburg)
Knesebeckstraße 18
Tel.: 312 93 81
A fine Italian restaurant, where all the produce is of the freshest, and the pasta is homemade, *naturalmente*. The pasta Brunello with langoustines is a sheer poem.

Café de France – Peugeot (Mitte)
Unter den Linden 67–68
Tel.: 206 41 391
The *brasserie* of the Café de France is part of the Peugeot showroom on Unter den Linden. It is a fine ambassador for French gastronomy, serving excellent cuisine at reasonable the prices.

Castros (Wilmersdorf)
Pfalzburger Straße 72a
Tel.: 882 18 08
A rare taste of Creole cooking in Berlin. This Cuban-style restaurant proposes dishes such as red snapper in fermented banana leaves or yam soufflé. After your meal, move into the lounge for a fine Cuban cigar or a Mojito at the bar.

Chez Martial (Charlottenburg)
Otto-Suhr-Allee 114
Tel.: 341 10 33
The choice is deliberately limited at this small French restaurant near Schloß Charlottenburg, so the chef can concentrate on what he does best. The Day's Specials are listed on a blackboard, and the charming owner is always on hand to give explanations, which he does with evident pleasure. The *Assiette de la Mer* (seafood platter) is particularly to be recommended, as are the wines.

Chez Maurice (Prenzlauer Berg)
Bötzowstraße 39
Tel.: 42 80 47 23
The crates of wine here are piled up to the ceiling, and it is usually almost as full of people too. The crockery may be plain, the tablecloths may be paper, but you can't fault the French cuisine.

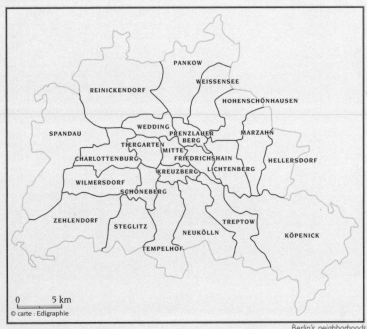

Berlin's neighborhoods

Cri-Cri am Engelbecken (Kreuzberg)
Erkelenzdamm 17
Tel.: 61 65 86 89
If you're hankering after Austrian or Alsatian cuisine, this is the place to come. You can also eat outside under the birch trees, where, even at the height of summer, it is always cool and refreshing.

Diekmann (Charlottenburg)
Meinekestraße 7
Tel.: 883 33 21
Classy French and German cuisine are on offer here, in this converted grocery store. The place is decorated with old-fashioned grocery wares, some of them for sale.

Dieckmann im Weinhaus Huth (Tiergarten)
Alte Potsdamer Straße 5
Tel.: 35 29 75 24
Apart from the Grand Hotel Esplanade, the Huth wine bar is the only old building surviving from the Potsdamer Platz. There are two terraces where you can enjoy a choice of French and German dishes, the specialty being black pudding in pastry with potatoes and mustard vinaigrette.

Dressler (Mitte)
Unter den Linden 39
Tel.: 204 44 22
Carefully decorated in the Art Deco style, this restaurant serves reliable French and German specialties. In summer, you can eat outside on the sidewalk.

Edd's (Tiergarten)
Lützowstraße 81
Tel.: 215 52 94
This is the best Thai restaurant in town—it enjoys cult status among Berlin's foodies. Airy rooms with high ceilings, lots of gold, and dark wood provide the setting for food that is the genuine article: hot and spicy. The service is somewhat brusque, but then that's the way the regulars like it—and they keep on coming back.

Edogawa (Steglitz)
Lepsiusstraße 36
Tel.: 79 70 62 40
Edogawa is an import from Düsseldorf, which has strong links with Japan. The food is exceptional, as testified by the large numbers of Japanese who come here to eat (always a good sign). The Udon noodles are made fresh on the premises.

Feinbeckerei (Schöneberg)
Vorbergstraße 2
Tel.: 784 51 58
This restaurant is always full of homesick southerners eager for a taste of Swabian cooking to remind them of back home. The *Maultaschen* (a variant of ravioli) and *Spätzle* (fried egg noodles) are worth tasting. Harking back to when the building was a bakery, there is still a bread oven set into the brick walls.

Florian (Charlottenburg)
Grolmanstraße 52
Tel.: 313 91 84
This place acts like a magnet for people from the film industry, maybe because of the solid, hearty German fare that keeps their feet on the ground. The *Nürnberger Würstchen* (Nuremberg sausages) and perch in tarragon sauce are especially nourishing.

Französischer Hof (Mitte)
Jägerstraße 56
Tel.: 204 35 70
Located on one of the loveliest squares in Berlin, this restaurant is decorated in Art Deco style over two floors. The food is German, but shows a definite French influence.

Gugelhof (Prenzlauer Berg)
Knaackstraße 37
10435 Berlin
Tel.: 442 92 29
This is one of Berlin's hottest restaurants since Bill Clinton dined here with Chancellor Schröder in 2000. It serves Alsatian and south German cuisine.

Hackescher Hof (Mitte)
Rosenthaler Straße 40/41
Tel.: 283 52 93
If you want a taste of the vibrant new Berlin, you will be right in the heart of the action here in the large dining room and bar.

Hakuin (Schöneberg)
Martin-Luther-Straße 1
Tel.: 218 20 27
An interesting concept: the restaurant is run by a Buddhist community, who wait on the clients. In the center of the non-smoking dining room is a Zen stone garden and a pond, which you can contemplate while you eat the fabulous Japanese food.

Haus Sanssouci (Zehlendorf)
Am Großen Wannsee 60
Tel.: 805 22 90
This is said to be the world's first prefab house, dating from 1889. Times have changed, and now it serves high-flying German cuisine. The view over the lake is as lovely as ever, however.

Kabale (Charlottenburg)
Schillerstraße 34
Tel.: 312 81 33
Uncluttered surroundings, decent typical Swabian dishes, and seven different beers on tap. Simple but effective.

Kellerrestaurant Brecht-Haus (Mitte)
Chausseestraße 121
Tel.: 282 38 43
The place for fans of Bertolt Brecht: the cooking is based on his wife Helene Weigel's recipe book, and shows Austrian influence. It'll cost you more than a threepenny opera, though.

Langhans (Mitte)
Charlottenstraße 59
Tel: 20 94 50 70
A new frontier in fusion food: Japano-Italian. The result can be astonishing, like their young chicken with ginger risotto. Frosted glass tiles in the ceiling cast a flattering light over the proceedings.

Lutter & Wegner (Mitte)
Charlottenstraße 56
Tel.: 202 95 40
Hard by the Gendarmenmarkt, this is an ancient house, founded in 1811, somewhere between a wine shop, an inn, and a restaurant. E.T.A. Hoffmann trod the boards here as Falstaff in Shakespeare's *Henry IV*. It was destroyed during the war, and only opened again recently. Apparently, Pierce "007" Brosnan has been known to put in an appearance.

Ottenthal (Charlottenburg)
Kantstraße 153
Tel.: 313 31 62
Austria in Berlin. Near the famous Paris-Bar and just opposite the overblown Delphi arthouse cinema is this small, highly praised restaurant with irreproachable cooking. The wines are produced by the owner's family, who reserve the best bottles for him.

Pasternak
Knaackstraße 24
Tel.: 441 33 99
The Russians in Berlin serve specialties such as *pel'meni* and *borshch*, accompanied by Russian music. In summer, the restaurant spills out onto the sidewalk. The restaurant is situated not far from Kollwitzplatz.

Portalis (Mitte)
Kronenstraße 55-58
Tel.: 20 45 54 96
You enter this restaurant on a side street off Unter den Linden through a kind of brightly colored portal. The chef is every bit as colorful. The food is flavorsome, well-spiced, and first class.

Raabe-Diele
Wallstraße 70
Tel.: 24 06 20

The art'otel Ermelerhaus has a fine restaurant on the first floor. The atmosphere is rococo, especially in the Rose Room, while the cooking is deliberately rustic--but still excellent. In the summer, guests can eat on the hotel's own boat anchored in front of the hotel.

Restaurant Enterrasse du Bundestag (Tiergarten)
Platz der Republik
Tel.: 22 62 99 33
It is recommended to try this restaurant, which is open to the public, after a visit to the Reichstag. Diners can sample the excellent cuisine, prepared according to recipes by the Munich chef Käfer, while enjoying the superb panoramic views offered by the rooftop terrace.

Restaurant im Logenhaus (Wilmersdorf)
Emser Straße 12-13
Tel.: 873 25 60
Good German food served with good German wines. Perfect.

Sale e Tabacchi (Kreuzberg)
Kochstraße 18
Tel.: 25 29 50 03
This is a real hotspot for journalists, intellectuals and all sorts of media types, drawn by the great Italian cooking. Apparently, rucola with parmesan and *penne con funghi* are great brain food. In the summertime, the courtyard is open and guests can eat under a vine-covered bower.

Schwarzenraben (Mitte)
Neue Schönhauser Straße 13
Tel.: 28 39 16 90
Cool, modern, efficient. The illustrious clientele seems to like it that way. The breast of duck Lombardy-style (*Entenbrust nach lombardischer Art*) is excellent. Down a flight of steps you will find the Engelspalast bar, where you can sample one (or more) of over 140 cocktails.

Siekes Weinhaus (Mitte)
Chausseestraße 15
Tel.: 30 87 29 80
This traditional inn and adjoining wine shop serves up solid, dependable, typical German fare, and wines to match.

Soup Kultur
Kurfürstendamm 224 (Charlottenburg)
Tel.: 88 62 92 82
Katharina Körner's "soup kitchen," opened in 1999, is already a popular feature of the Berlin landscape: as proof of the formula's success, Katharina has opened two further branches, in Rosa-Luxemburg-Straße and Kantstraße. These

tiny, colorful eateries with their wooden counters propose ten freshly prepared soups, and the menu changes daily: hot or cold, vegetarian, exotic. Also to take out.

Storch (Schöneberg)
Wartburgstraße 54
Tel.: 784 20 59
Come to the Storch to sample traditional Alsatian cooking, such as *Flammkuchen* (a Nordic cousin of the pizza), served at great wooden tables. It is well frequented, and you are advised to book ahead.

Trenta Sei (Mitte)
Markgrafenstraße 36
Tel.: 20 45 26 30
This light, bright, modern Italian restaurant lies on the southern side of the Gendarmenmarkt. The large windows give an excellent view of Berlin's loveliest square. The food is worthy of the view, especially the quail in port *jus*. It also proposes some typically German dishes, such as fillet of catfish on a bed of root vegetables.

Vau (Mitte)
Jägerstraße 54/55
Tel.: 202 97 30
High ceilings, minimalist design, and excellent, light Mediterranean and Asian cooking, combined with a list of over 400 wines, make this a popular spot for Berliners.

Viehhauser im Presseclub (Mitte)
Schiffbauerdamm 40
Tel.: 206 16 70
A certain Prussian sense of reserve means that there are no extraneous decorations here, either on the walls or the plates—but the cooking is refined in the extreme. The large windows give onto the new government buildings (or rather, what is currently a large building site).

Wannsee Terrassen
Wannseebadweg 35
Tel.: 803 40 24
Although this restaurant is in the forest, it offers a superb panoramic view of the Havel and the Wannsee. Apart from French dishes featuring wild duck, fish, and game, the tenderloin of beef is particularly delicious.

Werkstatt der Kulturen (Neukölln)
Wissmannstraße 32
Tel.: 622 90 88
This rather unusual eatery is a training school for chefs, set up in a former brewery with an adjoining intimate little garden. The menus that

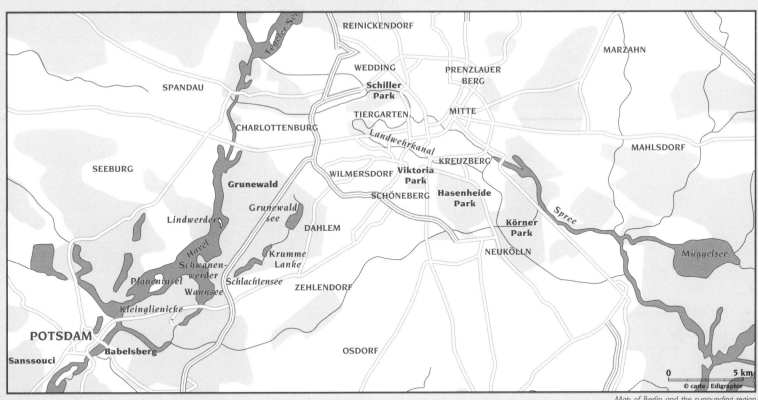

Map of Berlin and the surrounding region

change daily are meant to showcase the talents of the up-and-coming generation of master chefs. The service is equally as good.

Weyers (Wilmersdorf)
Pariser Straße 16
Tel.: 881 93 78
The area around Ludwigskirchplatz is highly sought after, as it is friendly, vibrant and full of surprises. Weyers has a terrace that gives directly onto the square. The typical German food and the wine list are just as friendly as the neighborhood.

Zillemarkt (Charlottenburg)
Bleibtreustraße 48a
Tel.: 881 70 40
Good, reliable, German dishes, in the best sense. Simplicity is the Zillemarkt's watchword. This restaurant near Savignyplatz has a garden for *al fresco* summer dining, and if the heavens open, there is a fabulously decorated conservatory to retreat into, so your lunch is safe.

Zur Letzten Instanz (Mitte)
Waisenstraße 14
Tel.: 242 55 28
Founded in 1621, this is Berlin's oldest restaurant (rebuilt after the war). It lies near the Berlin law

courts. It serves traditional Berlin dishes such as *Rinderschmorbraten mit Rotkohl* (beef pot roast with red cabbage). The old stoves with their wonderful glazed tiles fill the air with delicious warming aromas that certainly whet the appetite.

Zwölf Apostel (Charlottenburg)
Bleibtreustraße 49
Tel.: 312 14 33
This is a large, long-established pizzeria opposite the viaduct of the Savignyplatz S-Bahn station. It is always crammed with locals, as the pizzas are very popular, and if they stay there long enough, they are bound to bump into someone they know. In the summertime, long tables are set up in front of the restaurant and in the garden: breakfast in the garden is especially good.

TAVERNS AND BARS

At the end of the nineteenth century, Berlin could boast over 13,000 taverns and bars: one for every 150 inhabitants! They served up typical Berlin fare such as *eingelegte Eier* (pickled eggs), *Schrippen mit Hackepeter und Zwiebeln* (Berlin bread rolls with steak tartare and onions), *Buletten* (meatballs) and *Schusterjungs mit Schmalz und Röstzwiebeln* (a "cobblers' apprentice," or

bread roll dusted with flour, with goose dripping and roast onions). Today, many bars still provide good, hearty fare at competitive prices: look out for *Spreewälder Gurken* (cucumbers from Spreewald) *Teltower Rübchen* (turnip from Teltow), *Quark mit Leinöl und Schnittlauch* (soft cheese with flax oil and chives) and, in early summer, Beelitz asparagus.

Café Rix (Neukölln)
Karl-Marx-Straße 141
Tel.: 686 90 20
This is the place to come for great salads, homemade cakes and marinated roast beef from the Rhine after a visit to the Neuköllner Opera or the Böhmischen Dorf. The bar hosts temporary exhibitions, which are also worth a look.

Diener (Charlottenburg)
Grolmannstraße 47
Tel.: 881 53 29
Unchanged for decades, this bar belonging to former heavyweight boxer Franz Diener is short on space but big on camaraderie. Many Berlin writers, actors, and other professions where "resting" is the norm treat it as an extension of their living room.

E. & M. Leydicke (Schöneberg)
Mansteinstraße 4
Tel.: 216 29 73
A typical Berlin bar in the western part of town, worth a visit for its vintage interior if nothing else. On offer are homemade eggnog, gooseberry and blackberry wine, and *Persiko* (blackcurrant wine with cherry brandy).

Gasthaus Ranke (Charlottenburg)
Rankestraße 2-3
Tel.: 883 88 82
This inn has made a specialty of a dish many associate with Germany: *Eisbein* (pig's knuckles) with purée of peas and horseradish.

Henne (Kreuzberg)
Leuschnerdamm 25
Tel.: 614 77 30
You may bump into the Mayor of Berlin in this bar that stood in No Man's Land right by the Wall. John F. Kennedy, who famously declared "Ich bin ein Berliner," informing the delighted German crowds he was a type of doughnut, also stopped by here. Over the bar, you can see a letter he wrote, regretting missing dinner. The roast chicken is a delight—only organically raised birds are used.

Herta (Charlottenburg)
Schlüterstraße 78
Tel.: 312 37 76
The Herta is a favorite meeting place for local beer swillers and nostalgic old revolutionaries. The bar is rather dingy and smoky, but the *Rostbratwürstchen* (sausages) are tasty nonetheless.

Kaffee Burger (Mitte)
Torstraße 60
Tel.: 28 04 64 95
After seventy years in the driving seat, the Burger family sold on to a poet from the Prenzlauer Berg quarter, Bert Papenfuß, who made Kaffee Burger the place to be seen. It combines gastronomy and culture, hosting poetry readings, dances and concerts. Bert says you can tell who's from which part of town by what they drink: *Wessis* drink cocktails, and *Ossis* prefer beer.

Leuchtturm (Schöneberg)
Crellestraße 41
Tel.: 781 85 19
This inviting establishment in the calm Kiez part of town has been serving beer to its regulars for over a hundred years. New faces are perfectly welcome, though!

Radkes Gasthaus (Schöneberg)
Marburger Straße 16
Tel.: 213 46 52
The place to come for ballast to accompany your beer intake: warming stews, hearty *Schmalzstullen* (goose dripping tarts!) and *rote Grütze* (redcurrant and raspberry creams).

Schöneberger Weltlaterne (Schöneberg)
Motzstraße 61
Tel.: 21 96 98 61
The charm of this Berlin institution attracts regulars and tourists alike. The décor is a guide to furniture design over the last century. It specializes in good Berlin cooking. Wednesday is cabbage roulade day: cabbage leaves stuffed with minced beef and pork.

Ständige Vertretung (Mitte)
Schiffbauerdamm 8
Tel.: 282 39 65
This spacious, welcoming bar is a corner of the Rhine transplanted to the Spree—literally: it is right on a bend in the river opposite the Friedrichstraße station. Ambience guaranteed.

Torpedokäfer (Prenzlauer Berg)
Dunckerstraße 69
Tel.: 444 57 63
This is a bar with attitude. In its lounge-cum-bar,

authors read from their latest polemical works, and the debates often run high.

Van Loon (Kreuzberg)
Carl-Herz-Ufer 5
Tel.: 692 62 93
From April through October, when the weather is clement enough, this bar on a boat takes visitors on a culinary tour round Berlin's rivers and canals. An original way to see the city from an unusual angle.

Volksgaststätte Zimmermanns (Mitte)
Rosa-Luxemburg-Straße 41
Tel.: 24 72 20 37
The name comes from the theater, which is right opposite. This place offers good food at decent prices, and the interior decoration is rustic in style, yet pleasingly simple and modern. There is a copious breakfast buffet on Sundays.

Yorckschlößchen (Kreuzberg)
Yorckstraße 15
Tel.: 215 80 70
A rather smoky but very old bar that hosts jazz concerts, even at breakfast time, with live music every Sunday afternoon. A very musical clientele.

Zum Nußbaum (Mitte)
Am Nußbaum 3
Tel.: 2 42 30 95
This typical Berlin *Kneipe*, said to be the oldest hostelry in Berlin, serves good-quality German cuisine, notably marinated herring and aspic. In keeping with tradition, marinated eggs and meatballs are kept on the counter for customers who are fond of such things or who simply want to uphold tradition.

BARS AND CLUBS

Bar am Lützowplatz (Tiergarten)
Lützowplatz 7
Tel.: 262 68 07
An authentic bar which consists of little more than the bar itself and which was awarded the title of best bar in Germany.

Bar jeder Vernunft (Wilmersdorf)
Schaperstraße 24
Tel.: 883 15 82
Bar jeder Vernunft is a cabaret/vaudeville-type theater, whose luxurious interior resembles a mirrored tent from the 1920s. It hosts exhibitions and concerts. Many artist and actor types come here to see and be seen.

b-flat (Mitte)
Rosenthaler Straße 13
Tel.: 283 31 23
A jazz bar that is justly proud of its cocktails, where you can dance not only jazz, but also to the strains of salsa and tango tunes.

Blue Note (Schöneberg)
Courbiérestraße 13
Tel.: 218 72 48
A fine cocktail bar with highly skilled bartenders and an agreeably mixed crowd.

Galerie Bremer (Wilmersdorf)
Fasanenstraße 37
Tel.: 881 49 08
A bar in an art gallery? Why not. This one was designed in an asymmetric 1950s style by Hans Scharoun.

Hausbar (Prenzlauer Berg)
Rykestraße 54
Tel.: 44 04 76 06
The Hausbar is decorated in red and gold and has plenty of comfy armchairs for late-night or early-morning lounging.

Junction Bar (Kreuzberg)
Gneisenaustraße 18
Tel.: 694 66 02
The Junction Bar hosts live jazz and other concerts till the wee small hours, almost on a daily basis.

La Casa del Habano im Savoy Hotel (Charlottenburg)
Fasanenstraße 9/10
Tel.: 31 10 36 46
This is one place that really merits the name "lounge," as that is exactly what the clients do here. It celebrates a serious Cuban cigar and whisky cult.

lore.berlin (Mitte)
Neue Schönhauser Straße 20
Tel.: 28 04 51 34
This bar is dominated by black, chrome, and white neon. The bar itself is very, very long. The chic crowd is usually dressed in black to match. The entrance is well hidden, perhaps to discourage the riffraff.

Newton (Mitte)
Charlottenstraße 57
Tel.: 20 61 29 90
This bar belongs to world-famous photographer Helmut Newton, who spent his youth in Berlin and has now returned to settle here. The walls

are covered with his famous photographs. Enjoy one of the very popular cocktails at the long bar or in one of the comfortable club chairs.

Oxymoron (Mitte)
Rosenthaler Straße 40/41
Tel.: 28 39 18 86
Another restaurant in royal red and gold hues, this time specializing in French and Italian cookery. Come and dance in the club, every evening from Wednesday to Saturday.

Paris Bar (Charlottenburg)
Kantstraße 152
Tel.: 313 80 52
The Paris Bar is a major meeting place for actors and artists: some of them have been coming here for over fifty years. The place is always full, and you're bound to make some interesting new friends.

Paris 15 (Wilmersdorf)
Pariser Straße 15
(no telephone)
Paris 15 is an understated, elegant piano bar with exquisite cocktails mixed to decades-old recipes. The well-heeled public enjoys the classics tinkled out by the resident pianist in a highly refined ambience.

Pinguin Club (Schöneberg)
Wartburgstraße 54
Tel.: 781 30 05
This club is a real institution in the Kiez quarter. A bijou in the 1950s style, like they don't make any more.

Quasimodo (Charlottenburg)
Kantstraße 12a
Tel.: 312 80 86
International stars often drop into this legendary jazz club in the basement of the trendy Delphi movie theater.

Reingold (Mitte)
Novalisstraße 11
Tel.: 28 38 76 76
Another place that prides itself on its discreetly understated 1930s atmosphere. You have to ring at the heavy iron doors for admittance, but it's perfectly friendly inside. Portraits of Klaus and Erika Mann (son and daughter of Thomas) gaze down at you from the walls.

Riva (Mitte)
Dircksenstraße, S-Bahnbogen 142
Tel.: 24 72 26 88
This well-hidden drinking spot boasts a huge oval

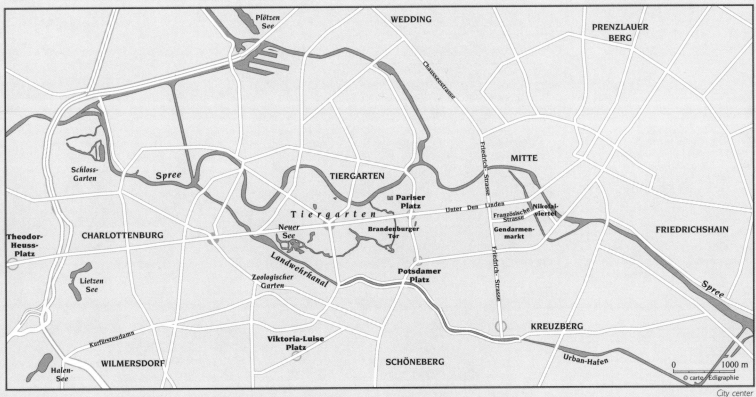

City center

bar in the center of the room. The curved ceiling is covered in great splashes of color, giving the impression of some sci-fi stage set. Turn up when the bar opens at 6 PM and enjoy the last rays of the sun from the terrace.

Roter Salon (Mitte)
Rosa-Luxemburg-Platz
Tel.: 24 06 58 06
A bar within the Volksbühne national theater, with its many sofas and dimly lit ambience, reminiscent of Berlin in the 1920s. Laid-back people stop by here for a casual beer or a glass of wine. From poetry readings, cabaret performances and punk concerts to techno and house discos, Roter Salon offers a little something to suit everyone's taste. Very interesting.

Trompete (Tiergarten)
Lützowplatz 9
Tel.: 23 00 47 94
This elegant bar belongs to popular German actor Ben Becker, and is a great hanging-out spot for thespians of all sorts. Live music at weekends.

Umspannwerk.Ost (Friedrichshain)
Palisadenstraße 48
Tel.: 42 08 93 23

Unusually, this bar is located in a nineteenth-century transformer station, and the building is today protected by law as a site of national interest.

Wasserwelt (Tiergarten)
Altonaer Straße 20
Tel.: 39 90 69 33
This cool, elegant lounge and bar has its own in-house DJ, who beavers away in a kind of submarine engine room. The food is pretty good.

Zucca (Mitte)
Am Zwirngraben 11/12
Tel.: 24 72 12 12
Decent Italian food is on offer in this tastefully decorated bar with north- and south-facing terraces.

808 Bar and Lounge (Mitte)
Oranienburger Straße 42
Tel.: 28 04 67 28
A real home-from-home lounge, where you can sit and sip a cocktail in the comfortable armchairs. If you require extra soothing, the giant aquarium in the back room will do the trick, otherwise you can do your own impression of a goldfish in the front room, with windows all the

way round. The friendly service makes guests really feel at home.

925 Loungebar (Mitte)
Taubenstraße 19
Tel.: 20 18 71 77
The bright red décor of this bar is a mixture of Constructivism and Bauhaus. From the comfort of the leather benches, you can sample one of their forty-year-old whiskies and admire the beautiful view of Gendarmenmarkt through the large bay windows.

BEER GARDENS

Beer has been brewed in Berlin since the thirteenth century. At first, the wheat beer was over-fermented and very bitter—which is why innkeepers came to mix it with different syrups, mostly raspberry and woodruff, to take the edge off the bitterness and improve the color. The famous Berlin *Bockbier* was invented in the mid-nineteenth century. This is a dark, spicy beer with a very high alcohol content, ready to drink in spring, when it is downed by the gallon at the *Maibockfest* beer festivals, both in Germany and abroad, wherever there are nostalgic Berliners thirsty for a pint or two. Today, beers from all

over the world find their way to Berlin's bars: wheat beer, black beer, lager, even exotic beers with a slice of lime. However, these foreign pretenders have a way to go before they dethrone the King of the Beers: Radeberger Pilsener—not native to Berlin, coming from Saxony, but a firm favorite nonetheless.

Alter Krug (Zehlendorf)
Königin-Luise-Straße 52
Tel.: 84 31 95 40
This is a traditional German beer garden—it was built in 1848, the year of the revolution. Customers come here to enjoy the excellent German bourgeois cuisine. In the summer, the tables in the garden accommodate up to 700 diners.

Alte Welt (Neukölln)
Wißmannstraße 44
Tel.: 622 63 96
Near the "Neue Welt" concert venue, this charming little beer garden has found a niche in a gap between two buildings, and welcomes guests with enchanting strings of fairy lights.

Blockhaus Nikolskoe (Wannsee)
Nikolskoer Weg
Tel.: 805 29 14

Frederick William III had the Blockhaus (a large wooden chalet) built for his daughter Charlotte and her husband, Czar Nicholas I, in 1819. The view over the Grunewald and the Havel is spectacular.

Café am Neuen See (Tiergarten)
Lichtensteinallee 2
Tel.: 254 49 30
One of Berlin's most popular bars, the Café am Neuen See is in a lovely leafy spot, right near the zoo, by an artificial lake. It is a great place to hang out on warm summer evenings.

Gasthausbrauerei Luisenbräu (Charlottenburg)
Luisenplatz 1
Tel.: 341 93 88
Near Schloß Charlottenburg, this small, intimate hostelry with rustic wooden benches is a delight. It offers a Berlin buffet with a wide selection of salads for those who need some ballast for their beer.

Gasthaus Ranke (Charlottenburg)
Rankestraße 2-3
Tel.: 883 88 82
This typical Old Berlin inn's specialty dish is that German classic, pig's knuckles with purée of peas and horseradish.

Golgatha (Kreuzberg)
Dudenstraße 48-64
Tel.: 785 24 53
Fancy a beer fresh from the barrel at six in the morning? This is the address for you, but only during the summer months (from April onwards). The bar is well hidden in the Viktoriapark, but you just need to follow the aroma of the barbecue wafting over the grass, and your nose will lead you there.

Loretta am Wannsee (Wannsee)
Kronprinzessinenweg 26
Tel.: 803 51 56
Big place, big atmosphere, all in the shade of some wonderful old trees. Delicious grilled meats get the juices flowing.

Luise (Zehlendorf)
Königin-Luise-Straße 40
Tel.: 841 88 80
If it's fine, sit out in the garden: if the weather lets you down, move inside to enjoy a crisp *Flammkuchen* (a kind of pizza). The charming Old Berlin interior will make up for the rain.

Prater (Prenzlauer Berg)
Kastanienallee 7-9
Tel.: 448 56 88

At a venerable 160 years of age, the Prater is Berlin's oldest beer garden. Under the shade of mighty oaks, come and dance, snack on grilled meats, and above all, get on with the serious business of beer drinking.

Reinhards Biergarten (Mitte)
Poststraße 28
Tel.: 242 52 95
This is a favorite dropping-in spot for many of Germany's former chancellors: the present one, Herr Schröder, has been known to look in on occasion, too. The typical Berlin dishes draws the crowds.

Rübezahl (Köpenick)
Am Großen Müggelsee
Tel.: 65 88 24 72
On the shores of the Müggelsee, Berlin's largest, this bar is characterized by a serene, idyllic ambience. The beer garden and restaurant are (literally) big enough to seat whole villages, so there should be enough room for a few select overseas visitors, too.

Schleusenkrug (Charlottenburg)
Müller-Breslau-Straße/Tiergartenschleuse
Tel.: 313 99 09
Lying between the zoo and the Landwehr canal, this is a favorite spot for a day out. Sit out under the trees or on the terrace and watch the boats passing through the lock for a taste of true relaxation.

Toulouse (Tegel)
Schwarzer Weg
Tel.: 433 70 63
This idyllic spot in the Tegeler Wald forest offers French cuisine in the upper price range. Gourmets will appreciate the setting as much as the food.

Wirtshaus Moorlake (Wannsee)
Moorlakeweg 1
Tel.: 805 58 09
This charming beer garden is already 150 years old. It is on the banks of the Klein-Glienicke and even has its own mooring place. During the winter, stars from stage and screen are often invited to read from their favorite books.

CAFÉS

Apotheke (Friedrichshain)
Wühlischstraße 32
Tel.: 29 00 70 62
The décor is dominated by a huge cabinet full of drawers with mysterious labels, just like in an old

apothecary's shop (as the name indicates). The menu lists all the dishes' ingredients, some of which are brought in specially from Spain and Italy.

Café Aedes
Savignyplatz 599
Tel.: 312 55 04
If you have an interest in architecture, be sure to drop in here: the café regularly hosts exhibitions about Berlin's latest building projects. The coffee is said to be especially good.

Café am Schiffbauerdamm
Albrechtstraße 13
Tel.: 28 38 40 49
For the health conscious, freshly pressed fruit juices and organic produce are a great way to start the day in the Café am Schiffbauerdamm.

Café am Ufer (Kreuzberg)
Paul-Lincke-Ufer 42-43
Tel.: 612 28 27
The Café am Ufer, under the trees by the Landwehr canal, is a great spot for breakfast, which it serves even late at night. It also dishes up exotica such as shark steaks. The terrace (open in summer) is fabulous.

Café Bravo (Mitte)
Augustraße 69
Tel.: 28 38 74 40
A pavilion designed by Dan Graham for the 1998 Biennale. Once inside this extraordinary artwork, customers can admire the astonishing light effects. A sign saying "I am a door" indicates the entrance, which is not easy to find.

Café Einstein (Mitte)
Unter den Linden 42
Tel.: 204 36 32
A fine, traditional café in the Viennese tradition, that breathes an aroma of coffee and leather. It looks out over the revitalized Unter den Linden. Understated charm and a relaxing ambience make clients feel at home.

Café Einstein (Tiergarten)
Kurfürstenstraße 58
Tel.: 261 50 96
This coffee house, located in an old villa, exudes the charm of times past. The Viennese-style cakes and pastries, made on the premises, are of the finest. Especially delightful for a copious breakfast, combined with a little idle people-watching.

Café Filmbühne am Steinplatz (Charlottenburg)
Tel.: 312 65 89

This café belongs to the experimental theater of the same name. It is particularly popular with students of the Academy of Fine Arts opposite.

Café im Felleshuset der Nordischen Botschaften (Tiergarten)
Rauchstraße 1
Tel.: 50 500
Located within the shared premises of the Scandinavian embassies, this is certainly not the place to come if you're feeling scruffy. A Bösendörfer grand piano stands in one corner of the reception room, there is an elegant roof terrace, and the café is full of blond wood, gently perfuming the air with the scent of the fjords and the pine forests.

Café im Literaturhaus (Wilmersdorf)
Fasanenstraße 23
Tel.: 882 54 14
Like the Einstein, the Café im Literaturhaus is a legend in its own lunchtime—or rather coffee break. It hosts regular poetry readings and other literary events. The garden, one of Berlin's loveliest, is open in summer, when guests sit outside by the fountain.

Café im Zeughaus (Mitte)
Unter den Linden 2
Tel.: 20 30 40
The Zeughaus, one of Berlin's few surviving Baroque buildings, is home to the Museum of German History. On the ground floor is a spacious café with a pleasant atmosphere, where there is a large variety of breakfast foods and cakes on offer.

Café in der Schwartz'schen Villa (Steglitz)
Grunewaldstraße 54-55
Tel.: 793 79 70
A green island in the heart of Steglitz. The café is in a romantic villa set in an enchanting garden. Breakfast is available until the afternoon.

Café L & B (Köpenick)
Am Kleinen Müggelsee 1
Tel.: 659 82 24
The décor of this lakeside café is greatly enhanced by some superb old furniture. The homemade cakes are excellent.

Café Odéon (Mitte)
Bahnhof Friedrichstraße
Georgenstraße, S-Bahnhogen 192
Tel.: 208 26 00
This café is located under the arches of the subway between Friedrichstraße and Museuminsel. Hanging from the ceiling are a wooden bicycle, a

station clock, and musical instruments. Simple dishes such as quiche, potato soup, and the famous Tyrolean quenelles are served.

Café Orange (Mitte)
Oranienburger Straße 32
Tel.: 28 38 52 42
After a visit to the Heckmannhöfe courtyards or the synagogue, come to this lovely old building, with its high ceilings and warm orange-painted walls, for homemade cakes and a delicious milk coffee.

Café Richter (Charlottenburg)
Giesebrechtstraße 22
Tel.: 324 37 22
The Café Richter's famous cakes and pastries are made on the premises and delivered all over Berlin. What more reason do you need to break your diet?

Café Savigny (Charlottenburg)
Grolmanstraße 53
Tel.: 312 81 95
This 1920s-style café is aimed at an international clientèle: it provides newspapers and magazines in several languages for its guests.

Café Silberstein
Oranienburger Straße 27
Customers are spoilt for choice in this bar, which was opened following the fall of the Wall: they can occupy one of the strange objects made out of old iron that serve as seats at the bar; they can relax on the terrace, which has a superb view of Oranienburger Straße; or they can sit in the peaceful courtyard, where nothing remains of the noise and bustle of the old days.

Café Westphal (Prenzlauer Berg)
Kollwitzplatz
Tel.: 442 76 48
The statue of artist and social reformer Käthe Kollwitz points you straight to the Café Westphal, where you can sit at old wooden tables placed on the broad sidewalk. The café itself is nothing fancy: its fame comes from its role as meeting place for the trendy Prenzlauer Berg scene.

Lebensart (Kreuzberg)
Mehringdamm 40
Tel.: 786 84 80
This café in a fine old building is very popular because of its great breakfasts.

Manzini (Mitte)
Reinhardtstraße 14
Tel.: 28 04 55 10

The Manzini is both a restaurant and a café. It is very spacious, and has a fabulous overgrown garden which provides it with fresh flowers. It is a real haven of peace, and the chef pays great attention to detail—try the potatoes fried in a cast iron pan, and you will understand.

Savarin (Schöneberg)
Kulmer Straße 17
Tel.: 216 38 64
A well-known spot for delicious homemade cakes, as well as a multitude of different types of quiche.

Savo (Schöneberg)
Goltzstraße 3
Tel.: 216 62 25
A taste of Spain in Berlin. A touch of warm yellow paint, large windows, and you can almost hear the cicadas. The breakfast, prepared with all-Spanish ingredients, is worthy of the Sierra Madre.

Schall & Rauch (Prenzlauer Berg)
Gleimstraße 23
Tel.: 448 07 70
This unusual breakfast café was recently awarded a prize for its design. The buffet is well-furnished, and you can even bake your own waffles.

Tadschikische Teestube (Mitte)
Palais am Festungsgraben
Tel.: 201 06 95
Now here's something you don't see every day: this tea shop was a gift from the people of Tadjikistan to the GDR. No chairs: clients sprawl on cushions and thick rugs. The tea is served in samovars.

Theodor Tucher (Mitte)
Pariser Platz 6a
Tel.: 2 48 94 64
The reading-lounge with its huge bookshelves leads directly into the restaurant: here, your meal comes with its own bookshop. Eat and read, read and eat—whichever way round, the welcome is a warm one, and the food is great. Idleness is the order of the day. You can stay as long as you like, and maybe even listen to an author reading aloud from his latest work.

Tomasa (Schöneberg)
Motzstraße 60
Tel.: 213 23 45
This cheery, light café is a haunt for Berlin's bright young things after a spot of brunch. It is near Victoria-Luise-Platz, one of Berlin's loveliest. The food is as easy on the eye as it is on the taste buds: people come from far and wide to eat here.

TOURS

Berlin offers all sorts of themed tours, from Literary Berlin to Famous Crimes, Architecture and History, to Jewish Berlin and (of course) the Divided City. You can even go on a geological tour based on the stones in the cobbled streets! Whether you want to discover the city on foot, by bike or on a bus, you are advised to get hold of a copy of the listings magazines *TIP* or *Zitty*.

Ansichtssachen
Tel.: 429 91 33
This tour promises to take you to the heart of everyday Berlin. Among other things, it takes in the 1920s utopian housing schemes of Bruno Taut and life in Prenzlauer Berg.

Arbeitskreis Geschichtsräume
Murtzaner Ring 8
Tel.: 0177-244 94 05
A tour round places where history was made: the Kaiserhof, Hitler's bunker, Potsdamer Platz, and the site of Hitler's huge Chancellory, designed by Albert Speer, torn down by the Russians.

ArchitekTour Berlin
Tel.: 0172-992 68 36
A detailed architectural guide to the construction of the Reichstag and Pariser Platz.

art:berlin
Oranienburger Straße 32
Tel.: 28 09 63 90
art:berlin offers over thirty different tours, with special emphasis on art and architecture.

City Cycle Tour
Hagelberger Straße 15
Tel.: 78 89 90 59
You can choose your own start and finishing points, but it's a good idea to stick to the guided itinerary, which avoids the main arteries and gives you a chance to discover lovely, quiet spots off the beaten tourist track in a three-hour tour. The bicycle and all gear (including helmets) are provided. One-to-one tours also available.

Führungsnetz
Tel.: 28 39 74 44
This tour takes you on a whirlwind trip through one hundred years of cinema history, or shows you what Unter den Linden looked like a century ago, before the invasion of the tourist buses.

Gangart Berlin
Calandrellistraße 19
Tel.: 32 70 37 83

A walking tour round the Reichstag and the Scheunenviertel quarter, exploring Jewish life in Berlin.

gehen & sehen
Brigitte Polhaus, Schmargendorfer Straße 11
Tel.: 859 31 34
Among other things, this company proposes tours of the Reichstag dome and the new Berlin from the air.

Geschichte(n) im Vorübergehen
Paul-Junius-Straße 49
Tel.: 97 60 22 84
A guided tour that takes in the Hotel Adlon, the Reichstag, and the part of town known as "government quarter" since the move from Bonn.

Kulturbüro
Greifenhagener Straße 60
Tel.: 444 09 36
This operator offers a number of themed tours, such as Famous Lovers, the Dorotheenstädtischer Cemetery, or Crimes and Misdemeanours.

pluspunkt e.v.
Steglitzer Damm 105
Tel.: 774 40 81
A tour of Berlin's most infamous crime scenes—by night.

Schöne Künste
Tel.: 782 12 02
A tour from a musical perspective. If you've always wanted to know what Richard Wagner got up to in Berlin.

Thematische Stadtrundgänge
Tel.: 217 63 20
Another company offering a multitude of themes, among them the history of Prussia and the Hohenzollern family.

Zeit-Reisen
Sewanstraße 175
Tel.: 51 06 86 40
Travel into Berlin's past, and meet the city's famous poets and thinkers.

COURTYARDS

Berlin's hidden courtyards are one of the city's greatest charms. They were formed higgeldy-piggeldy as the city grew, and homes and shops jostled for space. Today, the small shops that once abounded have all but disappeared, to be replaced with expensive art galleries and exclusive boutiques. Suddenly, the word "Hof" (courtyard) in an address gives a certain cachet. The very secrecy of these spaces, hidden behind old façades, has become desirable in keeping the riff-raff out of vernissages and gallery openings. Still, it is worth taking a look past the doorway into these havens of peace in the busy city, and many of them preserve their old-world charm intact.

Barcomis Deli
Tel.: 28 59 83 63
This Jewish café is recommended for its bagels, quiches, and brownies. Thirteen different sorts of coffee are roasted on the premises.

Buchladen im Kunsthof
Tel.: 281 33 76
A bookshop dedicated to the literary Berlin. Here you will find everything you want or need to know about the city: its history, architecture, and art, as well as a fine collection of literary works.

Civan
Tel.: 28 38 77 12
Come and choose the perfect hairstyle in this plain and functional yet bright and welcoming space, and enjoy a free hand massage.

Fahrradstation
Tel.: 28 38 48 48
Every cycle accessory you have ever needed under one roof. It also hires out bicycles and provides a rickshaw service.

Hackesche Höfe (Mitte)
Rosenthaler Straße 40/41
This series of eight courtyards, joined together to make one self-contained whole, is accessible from all sides. Built in 1906-7 in an Art Nouveau style, it covers 10,000 square meters, and is the biggest such space in Europe. Here, you will find everything you could ever need: it houses high-class boutiques, offices, a movie theater, galleries, cafés, hairdressers, restaurants—you name it, there's a shop that sells it here.

Hanleys Hair Company
Tel.: 281 31 79
Deborah Hanley calls herself a "hair artiste," and prides herself on her ability to find a cut to suit everyone's features.

Heckmann-Höfe (Mitte)
Oranienburger Straße 32
These small courtyards connecting Oranienburger Straße to Auguststraße are home to a number of small, innovative galleries.

Hut up
Tel.: 28 38 61 05
Christine Birkle does away with scissors, needle and thread, making hats, dresses, and handbags out of felt. Her work has been spotted in Paris, New York and Japan.

Karin Jordan
Rosenthaler Straße 40/41
10178 Berlin
Tel.: 281 50 43
Karin Jordan's designs are back to basics: clear, strong lines, the finest fabrics, and no surplus frills.

Katharina Sigwart
Tel.: 28 38 45 95
Hats to suit anyone, anywhere, in whatever situation. Here, everyone has a good head for hats.

Kunsthof (Mitte)
Oranienburger Straße 27
Kunsthof was built toward the middle of the nineteenth century. In 1989, it was almost a ruin, and needed a big injection of cash to give it a facelift. Luckily, the government agency for historic monuments and some private donors stepped in. The result is breathtaking: the architects (civitas) have done a fantastic job. The delicate late classical perspective down the courtyard is once again visible in all its glory.

Lisa D.
Tel.: 282 90 61
This talented fashion designer started out with a wild, experimental phase but has now turned her hand to a more classical style, producing long, flowing outfits in subdued colors.

McBrides Brasserie
Tel.: 28 38 64 61
A friendly wine merchant that offers the finest vintages from Germany, France, Italy, the United States, and Australia. It also has a decent menu to mop up all that alcohol.

quasi moda
Tel.: 283 34 47
The four quasi moda designers create elegant outfits that subtly outline a woman's curves in all the right places. They also offer a made-to-measure service, including stage costumes and wedding gowns tailored directly on the fortunate wearer.

Restaurant Hackesche Höfe
Tel.: 283 52 93
Take a look at the parquet floor in this beautiful old building, as it will be some time before you see such a wonderful old patina again. The

restaurant gives a true taste of the old Berlin. The patrons come from all over the world.

Ruby
Tel.: 28 38 60 30
If you're looking for something to give the person who has everything, try this boutique's range of lamps, vases and furniture. Unusual materials and striking colors proliferate, suggesting all sorts of tempting combinations.

Sophie-Gips-Höfe (Mitte)
Sophienstraße 21/ Gipsstraße 12
This former sewing machine factory houses an eclectic mix of apartments, assembly rooms such as the "Handworkers' Union House," cafés, and galleries like the "Sammlung Hoffmann."

Tatem
Tel.: 27 59 60 10
Tatem offers beautifully feminine designs, in particular a range of handbags by Strenesse and Gabriele Strehle.

trippen
Tel.: 28 39 13 37
Shoe designers Angela Spieth and Michael Oehler have won prizes for their audacious creations made using only the finest materials. Their shoes combine beauty with a rare degree of foot-friendliness.

ALTERNATIVE SCENES

When the Wall was still standing, Berlin was a mecca for global dropouts of all sorts: anarchists, artists, punks, musicians, and romantics (sometimes all combined in one person) flocked to the city to seek an alternative lifestyle. They wanted to do away with bourgeois individuality and live in one big happy community, living, loving, and changing the world together. Art, music, and politics made a heady brew that needed room to ferment. People found it in Berlin's numerous empty factories and shops, squatting and renovating them and bringing them back to life. Some of these projects are still extant, such as the Ufa-Fabrik, Mehringhof, and Tacheles. Some of the rebels have gone mainstream, but a healthy alternative scene still thrives in Berlin, if you know where to look.

Kulturbrauerei (Prenzlauer Berg)
Knaackstraße 97
Tel.: 441 92 69
These were originally the premises of the Schultheiß brewery, once the biggest in Europe, designed in 1872 by Franz Schwechten in the

red brick typical of Brandenburg architecture. The building is worth the trip in itself: parts of it have a solemn, cathedral-like air, and it is protected under heritage laws. Today, the four inner courtyards, former factory floors, store rooms, stables and workshops shelter a culture center that provides studios and working and performance spaces for artists of all stripes. It hosts all sorts of readings, discussion groups, concerts and workshops. There is a collection of industrial design from the former GDR which is worth a visit, and should you feel the need for a party while on site, there is a disco in the boiler room.

Mehringhof (Kreuzberg)
Gneisenaustraße 2a
Tel.: 691 50 99
This bar is still run as a collective to this day. In the summer, benches are placed outside in the courtyard, and the fresh-drawn *Pils* is even tastier in the open air. The site also hosts a cycle shop that shows you how to carry out your own repairs, as well as a theater. There are also occasional concerts by a choir that only accepts former squatters into its ranks.

Tacheles (Mitte)
Oranienburger Straße 54
Tel.: 282 61 85
This ruin of a department store was bound for the demolition crew when it was taken over by a group of young artists and creative spirits in 1990. The shell has a certain morbid charm; it has been painted in bright colors, and provides space for various workshops, bars, a theater and a very bizarre disco.

Ufa-Fabrik (Tempelhof)
Viktoriastraße 10
Tel.: 75 50 30
This place was a film reel copying center back in the 1920s. All the big stars flew in to the nearby Tempelhof airport for the previews of their latest magnum opus. By 1979, demolition loomed, but the alternative crowd got there first. Now the complex houses a theater that hosts rock concerts and cabarets, the Café Olé, the UFA circus, and a bakery specializing in wholemeal products. Further education classes and various cultural events are also on site.

FASHION

Back in the 1950s, Berlin was a fashion capital to rival Paris and Milan. So the Germans like to claim, anyway. Its reputation for all things fashion has since gone downhill, but in recent years relatively cheap rents have led to a number of young designers setting up shop. Many of them are graduates of Berlin's six fashion and design colleges, with courses taught by such stars as Vivienne Westwood. Treptow has the Kiefholz workshops, which have become quite a fashion center, where new collections are shown. Such big names as Jil Sander, Joop!, Chanel, Versace, and Donna Karan have made the move to the Ku'damm and the elegant Friedrichstraße. Berlin fashion is back in the news.

Andrea Schelling (Charlottenburg)
Tel.: 313 21 39
Andrea Schelling's collections are based around the finest fabrics, such as silk and chiffon, which she combines in elegant costumes that bring out the best in every figure.

Arnulf (Charlottenburg)
Kurfürstendamm 46
Tel.: 883 92 02
Volkmar Arnulf's main claim to fame is that he has been tailoring Helmut Kohl's suits for twenty years. He still has time to make made-to-measure suits for well-heeled clients, though.

Bassenge (Charlottenburg)
Bleibtreustraße 19
Tel.: 881 54 31
Shoes, clothes, and accessories made by established young designers from Berlin and elsewhere.

Breitenbach (Charlottenburg)
Mommsenstraße 4
Tel.: 88 67 94 34
Breitenbach specializes in made-to-measure shoes, using on the best materials. Clients can have a hand in the design of their own footwear. You can also go directly to the workshop, a romantic, crumbling little boutique at Bermannstraße 30 (Kreuzberg).

Donna Karan (Mitte)
Friedrichstraße 71
Tel.: 20 94 60 10
With the best address in Berlin, Friedrichstraße, Donna Karan has opened her flagship Berlin store. The elegant, stripped-down interior is the perfect foil for her trademark businesswear.

Evelin Brandt (Mitte)
Friedrichstraße 154
Tel.: 204 44 44
Evelin Brandt's creations are classical, elegant, simple, without crossing the fine line to businesslike *ennui*. Her signature is one-color outfits in the finest fabrics, that flatter any

woman. The sales assistants are welcoming without being intrusive.

Fiebelkorn & Kuckuck (Charlottenburg)
Bleibtreustraße 4
Tel.: 312 33 73
Friedrike Fiebelkorn's beautifully made bridal wear is by turns imaginative and classical. She will adapt her made-to-measure gowns for other uses after the wedding. Nanna Kuckuck's elegant, colorful evening gowns are equally desirable. Every item in the boutique is a one-off, so you needn't worry about bumping into someone with the same dress.

Florales & Design (Grunewald)
Douglasstraße 9
Tel.: 89 72 78 90
On the second floor of the Villa Hateneck, which incidentally possesses a magnificent garden, Gisela von Schenk has made her dream come true, in collaboration with Frank Stüve: floral art and beautiful decorative objects for the garden or house.

Glencheck (Charlottenburg)
Joachim-Friedrich-Straße 34
Tel.: 891 21 99
This unique store sells original 1920s to 1940s dresses, shirts, and suits. It also stocks accessories, if you're looking for something to complete that "GI bride" look.

H.J.B. (Charlottenburg)
Sybelstraße 7
Tel.: 21 75 45 07
Herr Bremermann's trademark is clothes in soft fabrics all in one color—either very pale or very dark.

Les Dessous (Charlottenburg)
Fasanenstraße 42
Tel.: 883 36 32
Elegant, discreetly erotic underwear from La Perla, André Sardà, and Moschino.

Nicola Bramigk (Charlottenburg)
Savignypassage Bogen 598
Tel.: 313 51 25
After a visit to Scenario (see below), pop next door to Nicola Bramigk's store under the viaduct. The owner is happy to provide tips and information on her avant-garde designer gear. Every piece is unique.

Scenario (Charlottenburg)
Else-Ury-Bogen 602
Tel.: 312 91 99

This small boutique is located in the passage to the Savignyplatz tramway opposite the huge Zwölf Apostel pizzeria. It sells gift items and fabulous jewelry (often teetering on the brink of kitsch) at accessible prices.

Skoda (Mitte)
Linienstraße 156
Tel.: 280 72 11
Claudia Skoda is a great specialist in thread and fine-quality materials. She turns old garments into fashion items and makes made-to-measure clothes.

Stilwerk
Kantstraße 17
Tel.: 31 51 50
Those interested in good-quality furniture for the home or office will find what they are looking for here. All the major manufacturers are represented, from hi-fi equipment to pianos.

Tagebau (Mitte)
Rosenthaler Straße 19
Tel.: 28 39 08 90
Provocative, vibrant fashion from six ambitious young designers. Every piece is unique.

Tools & Gallery (Mitte)
Rosenthaler Straße 34
Tel.: 28 59 93 43
This is Berlin's number one shop for designer wear. It is unmissable with its enormous cast-iron steps leading up to the shop front. Kenzo, Givenchy, Lacroix, Jeremy Scott, and Vivienne Westwood are among the famous names available here.

Veronica Pohle (Charlottenburg)
Schlüterstraße 46
Tel.: 883 37 49
If you need to find a Lacroix, Vivienne Westwood, Moschino, Bluemarine or Paul Smith outfit in Berlin, look no further. It's somewhat chaotic, but you should visit the room at the back, with last season's clothes at definitely bargain prices.

Von T. Herrenschuhe (Charlottenburg)
Bleibtreustraße 27
Tel.: 881 26 02
Dieter Kuckelkorn's handmade shoes and classic English models from Edward Green pamper men's feet with only the very best, so they can put their best foot forward.

Walter Steiger (Charlottenburg)
Schlüterstraße 48
Tel.: 88 68 00 68

The fabulous lighting in this boutique highlights the clothes laid out on the black shelves or spread out to best advantage on the floor.

ANTIQUES

Berlin's recent history means it is hardly an El Dorado for the antiques hunter. Even the kitsch GDR memorabilia that abounded after the Wall came down is growing scarcer. Still, you can find some lovely antiques and twentieth-century design classics if you know where to look.

Adelbert Stahlmach (Schöneberg)
Eisenacher Straße 119
Tel.: 215 2à 91
This gallery specializes in classical furniture and objets d'art.

Alterna-Kontor für Antike Öfen
Am Rosenanger 81
Tel.: 401 40 80
Eighteenth- and nineteenth-century stoves and garden sculptures.

Art 1900 (Wilmersdorf)
Kurfürstendamm 53
Tel.: 881 56 27
Many of the city's most coveted houses and apartments bear the stamp of the Jugendstil (Art Nouveau) period, particularly visible in the doors, ironwork, and decorative ornaments. This style can be widely seen in the streets of old Berlin. Anyone fortunate enough to acquire one of these Jugendstil apartments should, to decorate it in an authentic way, visit this store in the Kurfürstendamm, where they will find everything that they need.

Antiquitäten im Scheunenviertel
Tucholskystraße 37
10117 Berlin
Tel.: 283 53 53
Valuable furniture and clocks in classical and Biedermeyer styles. Also carries out repairs and restorations.

Art+Industrie (Charlottenburg)
Bleibtreustraße 40
Tel.: 883 49 46
This is another store that pays homage to the clean, functional lines of great industrial design. Now is the time to visit, as 1930s steel furniture, clocks, and crockery seem to be back in fashion.

Asta von Bethmann-Holweg Volker Westphal Kunsthandel
Rehlstraße 11a
Tel.: 321 23 32

Furniture, objets d'art and sculpture from the eighteenth to the twentieth centuries.

Brigitte von Kuhlberg (Charlottenburg)
Suarezstraße 58
Tel.: 323 81 11
Specialist in antique glass.

Claus-Peter Jörger (Charlottenburg)
Pestalozzistraße 53
Tel.: 32 70 16 33
Antique toys and dolls, with a special collection of model railways.

Das Alte Bureau (Schöneberg)
Goltzstraße 18
Tel.: 216 59 50
In the lively and colorful Schöneberger Kiez district, there is something new around every corner. Rummage through the junk shops, and you might just come across a real bargain. Das alte Bureau specializes in "vintage" office equipment and furniture, with some classic pieces that are masterpieces of design.

DM Antiquitäten (Charlottenburg)
Kurfürstendamm 105
Tel.: 891 82 33
This is a good place to come for genuine Meissen porcelain, especially the oldest designs with the crossed swords symbol on the back (known as Schwerter-Meissen). The pieces are rare, and priced accordingly, but collectors looking for an item to finish off their antique dinner service might just get lucky.

Ebner von Eschenbach (Schöneberg)
Eisenacher Straße 8
Tel.: 218 11 17
Typical Berlin and Prussian eighteenth- and nineteenth-century objets d'art.

Gabriele Höche (Schöneberg)
Kälckreuthstraße 13
Tel.: 211 60 68
This gallery sells Biedermeier furniture.

Glanzlichter art deco (Charlottenburg)
Suarezstraße 60
Tel.: 31 80 34 18
The place to come if ever you are seized by the desire to possess a 1930s lamp, vase, tray, or writing-desk.

Holger Martin (Schöneberg)
Eisenacher Straße 118
Tel.: 215 92 95

In addition to objets d'art from the eighteenth and nineteenth centuries, this gallery offers rare objects and curios.

J. Klein (Schöneberg)
Hedwigstraße 16
Tel.: 852 22 70
J. Klein has a fine collection of weighty nineteenth-century silverware, which no enthusiast should miss.

Lehmanns Colonial-Waren (Charlottenburg)
Grolmanstraße 46
Tel.: 883 39 42
Old luggage and globes—the address for long voyages.

Neumanns Antiquitäten (Charlottenburg)
Suarezstraße 57
14057 Berlin
In the area around Suarezstraße, by the dreamy Lietzensee in the center of town, there are plenty of antiques dealers. Most, like Neumanns, welcome browsers.

Olaf Lemke (Schöneberg)
Eisenacher Straße 7
Tel.: 211 20 87
Specialist in frames from the seventeenth to nineteenth centuries.

Plötz-Peters (Schöneberg)
Keithstraße 8
Tel.: 211 44 76
Berlin objets d'art, porcelain, and ironwork.

Schiffsantiquitäten
Gatower Straße 124-126
Tel.: 361 90 96
Since Berlin has a certain number of houseboat dwellers, this shop has decided to cater for all those who live on the water. Why not decorate your barge with antiques gleaned from old steamers and cruisers? Why not indeed?

Seidel & Sohn (Schöneberg)
Eisenacher Straße 113
Tel.: 216 18 50
Furniture and objets d'art from the seventeenth to nineteenth centuries.

Sigrid Kleihues (Charloteenburg)
Bleibtreustraße 19
Tel.: 213 68 62
Silverware from the eighteenth to the twentieth centuries.

Staatliche Porzellanmanufaktur Meissen (Mitte)
Unter den Linden 39 b
Tel.: 229 26 91
Another store specializing in the blue-and-white porcelain with the traditional "blue onion" pattern. Again, pricey, but worth a visit.

Stefano Gozzi (Schöneberg)
Eisenacher Straße 114
Tel.: 216 95 96
Italian objets d'art and furniture from the eighteenth to the nineteenth centuries.

Straße des 17. Juni (Tiergarten)
Saturday and Sunday 8 A.M. to 3 P.M.
For many Berliners, this is the finest flea market in the city, but not the cheapest. Tourists will be able to find typical kitchen utensils and decorative objects.

Sur l'Île des Musées (Mitte)
Kupfergraben
Saturday and Sunday, 11 A.M. to 5 P.M.
This market will delight those interested in everyday life in East Germany.

Susanne Gropp KG (Charlottenburg)
Ernst von Loesch
By appointment only
Fasanenstraße 29
Tel.: 883 35 33
Eighteenth- and nineteenth-century drawings and architectural models.

Trödel S-Bahnbogen (Mitte)
Bahnhof Friedrichstraße
Georgenstraße, S-Bahnhogen 192
Flea market with around 70 top-quality stalls.

Uhren-Kunst Bischoff (Charlottenburg)
Pestalozzistraße 54
Tel.: 323 21 63
For the sale and repair of antique watches and clocks.

Ulf Breede (Charlottenburg)
Fasanenstraße 69
Tel.: 88 68 31 23
Jewelry from the eighteenth to twentieth centuries.

Ulrich Gronert (Schöneberg)
Giesebrechtstraße 10
Tel.: 88 23 68 6
This gallery selling furniture and porcelain from the eighteenth to the twentieth centuries specializes in objects from Berlin.

Uwe Kniess (Charlottenburg)
Bleibtreustraße 40
Tel.: 883 49 46
Can twentieth-century items now be classed as antiques? Uwe Kniess sells classics of twentieth-century industrial design, as well as steel furniture with the purest of lines. He is very clued up on design history and is happy to take customers on a stroll down memory lane.

Wilhelm Weick (Schöneberg)
Eisenacher Straße 10
Tel.: 218 75 00
Eighteenth- and nineteenth-century furniture and objets d'art.

Wittenbron-Czubaszek (Charlottenburg)
Kunsthandel
Fasanenstraße 61
Tel.: 883 1 01
Furniture and objets d'art from the eighteenth to twentieth centuries.

BOOKSTORES

Whatever else may have changed over the course of history, Berlin has always been a major center for learning. And where there are universities, can bookstores be far behind? In the modern culture superstores, you are just as likely to be offered a CD-Rom or Internet facilities as a leather-bound edition of Goethe, but there are still plenty of independent booksellers—more so than in most major capitals—which will please those for whom nothing can replace the knowledge and passion of a specialist bookseller.

Altberliner Bücherstube (Mitte)
Neue Schönhauser Straße 8
Tel.: 282 73 75
The books here are as old as the building, and that's saying something. At least there is a certain sense of continuity outside and in…

Autorenbuchhandlung (Charlottenburg)
Carmerstraße 10
Tel.: 313 01 51
Another shop booklovers will want to spend hours in. You are welcome to rummage around and even get stuck into the books that take your fancy. Most of the titles are literary or scholarly, or otherwise aimed at the more demanding reader; but there is also a cookbook corner and a selection of comic books. You can order any title available in another Berlin bookstore: delivery in most cases within twenty-four hours.

Bücherbogen (Charlottenburg)
Stadtbahnbogen 593
Tel.: 312 19 32
This was one of the first stores to move into the renovated and sanitized spaces under the S-Bahn viaduct. Its specialties are art, theater, photography, design, and architecture, and a good dose of genuine Berlin atmosphere.

Buchhandlung Starick (Mitte)
Torstraße 125
10119 Berlin
Tel.: 282 85 66
This bookshop specializes in well-known authors from the former East Germany, but also has a good selection of works by unknown young writers from all over Germany.

Düwal (Charlottenburg)
Schlüterstraße 17
Tel.: 313 30 30
Bookworms beware. If you visit this secondhand books store, you are almost certain to miss your flight home, as you will be rooting through the shelves for days! It has some rare first editions, though you may have to hunt for them—but that's all part of the pleasure.

Kiepert (Charlottenburg)
Hardenbergstraße 4-5
Tel.: 31 10 09 26
Kiepert is a real Berlin tradition. From the most abstruse technical textbook to monographs on artists you've never heard of, via the special section devoted to maps and route planners, if it's not here, it's not worth having. There is a secondhand book store attached. There are smaller branches at the Freie Universität, Garystraße 46, and the Humboldt-Universität, Georgenstraße 2, and finally, at Friedrichstraße 63.

Literaturhaus Berlin (Charlottenburg)
Fasanenstraße 23
Tel.: 882 65 52
This charming, well-stocked bookstore hosts in-store readings and debates, and has its own bistro with a winter garden. The building itself, an atmospheric old villa set in a small park, is well worth the visit.

Wohlthat'sche Buchhandlung (Mitte)
Budapester Straße 44
Tel.: 262 36 36
This store calls itself "Act of Kindness," and its aim is to make books available to even the slenderest of student budgets. It has several branches, including one at Alexanderplatz 2 (Mitte).

SPECIALIST STORES

Blindenanstalt von Berlin
Oranienstraße 26
Tel.: 25 88 66 21
The residents of this home for the blind make wickerwork furniture of a quality that cannot be matched by industrially produced versions. The technique may not have changed for centuries, but the sheer quality of the result makes it perfect for the modern home.

Bunzlauer Landhauskeramik (Wilmersdorf)
Hohenzollerndamm 197
Tel.: 873 29 57
Sells pretty blue-and-white crockery with a peacock-tail pattern at reasonable prices.

Erich Hamann Bittere Schokoladen (Wilmersdorf)
Brandenburgische Straße 17
Tel.: 873 20 85
Founded in 1912, this shop dedicated to the delights of dark chocolate is now run by the third generation of the same family. The Bauhaus-Art Deco interior is original. They make seventeen different types of pralines and chocolates, each more mouthwatering than the last.

Gipsformerei der Staatlichen zu Museen (Charlottenburg)
Sophie-Charlotte-Straße 17-18
Tel.: 321 70 11
Goethe thought this place would "purify tastes and lead people to the truly beautiful": it sells small-scale plaster casts of the sculptures to be found in museums in Berlin and round about.

Königliche Porzellan Manufaktur KPM (Tiergarten)
Wegelystraße 1
Tel.: 39 00 92 15
The traditions of Prussian porcelain manufacturing have recently been updated and modernized by talented designers. The color known as "sterbende Blau," or dying blue, is still very popular, however: it is said to have been mixed to a recipe concocted by Frederick the Great.

Königsberger Marzipan Wald (Charlottenburg)
Pestalozzistraße 54a
Tel.: 323 82 54
Frau Wald and her granddaughter jealously guard their family marzipan recipe, so your only chance to taste it is to buy some here, in their store.

Knopf-Paul (Kreuzberg)
Zossener Straße 10
Tel.: 692 12 12
This store contains more buttons than you even thought existed-literally millions. Many of them are delightful vintage buttons, and some are real works of art.

Suff (Kreuzberg)
Oranienstraße 200
Tel.: 614 21 48
350 different wines and champagnes, plus a wide range of wickedly alcoholic spirits.

OPEN-AIR MARKETS

Berlin would be unthinkable without its open-air markets on the banks of the Spree and the Landwehr canal, around the Tiergarten and on leafy squares throughout the city. Some specialize in fresh fruit and vegetables, some in modern art, secondhand books, junk, clothes, or flowers. Berliners love to shop in markets, and often stay faithful to their favorite stalls for decades. Since the Wall came down, many new stalls have moved in, selling regional produce. Specialties from the Brandenburg region such as Spreewald cucumbers and garlic, Teltow turnips, fish from the numerous lakes and rivers around Berlin, now abound, and that's not to mention the exotica in the many Turkish markets. Whether you're out to buy or not, a visit to a market is an essential part of any visit to Berlin.

An der Museuminsel (Mitte)
Tel.: 033 41 – 30 94 11
Saturday and Sunday, 11 A.M. to 5 P.M..
For those interested in everyday relics from the former East Germany, this is the place to come.

Karl-August Platz (Charlottenburg)
Wednesday and Saturday

Marheinekeplatz (Kreuzberg)
Monday and Friday

Maybachufer (Kreuzberg)
12047 Berlin
Tel.: 781 58 44
Tuesday and Friday, noon to 3 P.M.
The Turkish market, where haggling is positively encouraged.

Rathaus (Schöneberg)
Tuesday and Friday

Trödelmärkte
Straße des 17. Juni (Tiergarten)
Tel.: 26 55 00 96
Saturday and Sunday, 8 A.M. to 3 P.M.
For many Berliners, this is the most best fleamarket in the city, but it is not cheap. Tourists can find typical Berlin furniture and kitchen utensils here.

Vor dem Roten Rathaus (Mitte)
Tuesday and Saturday

Winterfeldtmarkt (Schöneberg)
10781 Berlin
Tel.: 78 76 28 85
Wednesday and Saturday, 8 A.M. to 3 P.M.
An international range of goods draws people of all hues of the rainbow. Crowded but fun.

Wittenbergplatz (Schöneberg)
10789 Berlin
Tel.: 78 76 28 85
Tuesday and Friday, 8 A.M. to 2 P.M., Thursday, 10 A.M. to 7:30 P.M.
Close to the pretty Wittenbergplatz U-Bahn station, this is the place to come if you suddenly find yourself short of such delicacies as horsemeat sausage. It does have some real treats, though, if that doesn't take your fancy.

MUSEUMS

Berlin's museums are renowned throughout the world for their magnificent collections. Museuminsel (Museum Island), in the heart of the city, is home to a series of prestigious museums in recently renovated buildings. There are also smaller, less well-known jewels in the crown. These may lie off the well-beaten tourist trail, but they amply repay a visit.

Open night at the museum
A few years back, the good folk at the museum schools service had a brilliant idea, whose success surprised even them: twice a year, nearly all the museums in Berlin stay open all night. This feast of culture takes place on a Saturday, in January or February and then in August. The visitors number in the hundreds of thousands. The "open nights" are now an institution, with something of the flavor of a festival. Concerts, readings, and "nighttime safaris" round the event off.

Bauhaus-Archiv-Museum (Tiergarten)
Klingelhöferstraße 14
Tel.: 25 40 02 78
This is where the archives of the Bauhaus movement are stored, detailing the history of the

movement from 1919 to 1933. Come and see the original drawings and sketches that laid the groundwork for one of the twentieth century's most influential design movements, as well as many beautiful objects and items of furniture typical of Bauhaus production. The white, modernist building along the Landwehr canal was designed by Walter Gropius.

Belvedere (Schloß Charlottenburg)
The Belvedere was designed to be a tea pavilion with viewing turret, to plans by Carl Gotthard Langhans, who also designed the Brandenburg Gate. It is on the northern edge of the Schloß Charlottenburg park on the Spree. It houses a permanent display of porcelain from the Königlichen Porzellanmanufaktur (see above, under Antiques) dating from the Rococo to the Biedermeier periods.
April to October open from 10 A.M. to 5 P.M., November to March open from 12 A.M. to 4 P.M. Closed on Mondays.

Bethanien Cultural Center (Künstlerhaus)(Kreuzberg)
Mariannenplatz 2
Tel.: 616 90 30
This international cultural center is housed in a former hospital built between 1845 and 1847. The building, with its twin pointed turrets and yellow brickwork, was designed by Persius and Stüler. It welcomes scholarship students from all over the world, who are selected by a special jury, and is used for art exhibitions and theater productions.

Brecht-Weigel-Gedenkstätte (Mitte)
Chausseestraße 125
Tel.: 28 30 57 00
A small museum in Bertolt Brecht's and his wife Hélène Weigel's former rented apartments in a rather unimpressive block, with the original furnishings as they were when the Meister still lived there. He wrote some of his finest work here.

Brecht-Weigel-Haus (Buckow in Brandenburg)
Bertolt-Brecht-Straße 29
Mr. and Mrs. Brecht's roomy weekend home on the shores of the Schermützelsee.

Bröhan-Museum (Charlottenburg)
Schlossstraße 1a
Tel.: 321 40 29
A private collection of around two thousand Art Deco and Jugendstil objects dating from 1889 to 1939, including paintings by Hans Baluschek and Willy Jaeckel, porcelain, glassware, ceramics, and furniture.

Brücke-Museum (Zehlendorf)
Bussardsteig 9
Tel.: 831 20 29
The setting of this small museum, on the edge of the Grunewald, is delightful. The museum is dedicated to the productions of the German Expressionist group known as Die Brücke (The Bridge), founded in 1905 in Dresden, and including such artists as Kirchner, Heckel, Schmidt-Rottluff, and Bleyl.

Deutsche Guggenheim (Mitte)
Unter den Linden 13-15
Tel.: 20 20 93-0
Rather unusually, this gallery is in the basement of the Deutsche Bank. It presents four exhibitions of contemporary art annually. The café is also pretty good, as is the museum shop.

Deutsches Technikmuseum Berlin (Kreuzberg)
Trebbiner Straße 7-9
Tel.: 25 48 40
This is Berlin's most hi-tech museum. It explores the science behind such things as modern communications, air travel, and computer technology through a range of multimedia displays. Visitors can print, weave, make paper, shred grain, work on computers or even play newscaster in a television studio. The museum is currently being expanded to house an exhibit on space travel. Visitors may be surprised to see half an airplane sticking out of the ground here, a relic of the Berlin airlift that now serves as a sort of signpost.

Ephraim-Palais (Mitte)
Poststraße 16
Tel.: 24 00 21 21
The Ephraim-Palais townhouse is Berlin's finest example of Rococo architecture. It was demolished by the Communists, who then rebuilt it a few feet further down the road in time for Berlin's 750th anniversary celebrations in 1987. Its façade and interior are as fine as any you could wish to see, and it also houses temporary exhibitions by local artists.

Filmmuseum Berlin (Tiergarten)
Potsdamer Straße 2
Tel.: 300 90 30
This fascinating and popular museum dedicated to cinematographic history has greatly benefited from its recent move to its new, central location, near Potsdamer Platz.

Georg-Kolbe-Museum (Charlottenburg)
Sensburger Allee 25
Tel.: 304 21 44

Considered Germany's best sculptor in his 1920s heyday, Georg Kolbe decided to turn his studio into a museum while he was still alive. Sculptures stand in the grounds, as well as examples of his artwork. The café is a lovely place for a quiet cup of coffee.

Gründerzeitmuseum (Mahlsdorf)
Hultschiner Damm 33
Tel.: 567 83 29
It is rather a trek out to this museum, but once you get there, it is charming. It tells the story of Germany's *Gründerzeit* or foundation years, the period between 1871 and 1914 when Germany took shape before the calamities of the twentieth century. It is a delightful snapshot of life as it was for our great-grandparents.

Hamburger Bahnhof (Tiergarten)
Invalidenstraße 50/51
Tel.: 39 78 34 11
The Museum for Contemporary Art is housed in a particularly lovely building: a former train station, built in 1846 in an Italianate style. The building was already home to a museum of railway technology in the nineteenth century, which is why it was the only original train station in Berlin to escape destruction during the war. Today, the building offers a wonderfully surreal view thanks to Dan Flavin's light installation. The newly renovated building contains works by Beuys, Rauschenberg, Warhol, Haring, Lichtenstein, Twombly, and Baselitz, among others.

Jüdisches Museum (Kreuzberg)
Lindenstraße 14
Tel.: 25 99 34 10
The most interesting feature of Berlin's Jewish Museum is the building by Daniel Libeskind. It is based on a broken Star of David layout, and windows are replaced by diagonal viewing slits. The exterior is covered with rough metal plates that hint at the potential to wound. Inside is a series of "voids," empty spaces that cut across the floorspace, symbolizing absence. It attracts huge crowds, who come to contemplate the errors of the past.

Käthe-Kollwitz-Museum (Charlottenburg)
Fasanenstraße 24
Tel.: 882 52 10
Käthe Kollwitz's powerful work is perfectly represented by the 180 drawings and prints held by the museum, which also features sketches and sculptures.

Kunstgewerbemuseum (Mitte)
Tiergartenstraße 6
Tel.: 266 29 51
This museum houses collections of European applied art ranging from the Middle ages and the Renaissance to Baroque and Rococo pieces. In the basement the focus is on twentieth-century developments, including a small but good collection of Bauhaus furniture and a display of contemporary jewelry.

Kunst-Werke Berlin (Mitte)
Auguststraße 69
Tel.: 243 45 90
This art center is one of a kind. It is housed in a former margarine factory, and was opened shortly before the 1998 Biennale. Art-lovers are invited to play on the shiny steel helter-skelters that join the center's two floors, and which are visible from the interior courtyard. Dan Graham's glass pavilion with the Café Bravo is another attraction: two four-meter-high cubes of glass and chromed steel placed next to each other. Both sides of the sheets of glass are reflective, creating extraordinary natural light effects caused. The center also has archive and exhibition spaces.

Lapidarium (Kreuzberg)
Hallesches Ufer 78
Tel.: 25 48 63 50
The Lapidarium was built in 1876 as the pumping station for Berlin's sewage system, which was being entirely overhauled. The men responsible for the major drive to improve the city's sanitation were James Hobrecht, an engineer, and the doctor Rudolf Virchow. The original equipment is still in place, and is protected by law as a national monument. The highly ornamental brick building today houses the statues formerly to be seen along the Siegesallee. Jazz concerts take place there during the summer.

Märkisches Museum (Mitte)
Am Köllnischen Park 5
Tel.: 308 66-0
The contents of this museum are rather unusual: it displays circus and theater memorabilia. Clown costumes from the nineteenth century, posters, even the stuffed body of a circus lion are on show in oddly atmospheric surroundings.

Martin Gropius Bau (Kreuzberg)
Stresemannstraße 110
Tel.: 25 48 60
This grand building, built in 1880, used to house the museum of applied art. The façade, with its refined decoration of ceramic tiles, mosaic and stone friezes, is particularly striking. This large

edifice was seriously damaged during World War II and was threatened with demolition. Finally, it was decided to rebuild and refurbish it. Today it is used for important exhibitions, usually devoted to modern history.

Mies van der Rohe-Haus (Hohenschönhausen)
Oberseestraße 60
Tel.: 982 41 92
Ludwig Mies van der Rohe built this house in 1932 in the eastern part of town known as Hohenschönhausen. Today, it is open to the public. An exhibition explores the building's own architectural relevance, and the museum also hosts temporary displays by leading contemporary artists.

Museum am Checkpoint Charlie (Kreuzberg)
Friedrichstraße 43
Tel.: 251 20 75
This museum, located in the famous Checkpoint Charlie, is essential for anyone interested in the Cold War. There are four permanent exhibitions covering the Wall's and Berlin's history, the Wall and artists, and non-violent protest leaders, including Gandhi and Lech Walesa.

Museum im Wasserwerk
(Friedrichshagen)
Müggelseedamm 307
Tel.: 8644 7612
An old waterworks building that has been converted into a museum. Three machines dating from 1893 have been preserved in the machine room. One of them is still operational.

Neue Nationalgalerie (Tiergarten)
Potsdamer Straße 50
Tel.: 266 26 62
The Old National Gallery, housing nineteenth-century art, was on Museum Island. It was heavily damaged during the war, and has not yet been rebuilt. The New National Gallery, on the other hand, is housed in the Kulturforum at Potsdamer Platz, and makes up for the old Gallery's closure. It has a permanent collection of twentieth-century art, as well as holding temporary exhibitions. The clear, powerful, yet graceful lines of the building by Mies van der Rohe are a visual treat in themselves. Don't miss the avant-garde light installation by Jenny Holzer.

Panke Museum
Heystraße 8
Tel.: 481 40 47
This museum in the bourgeois house of manufacturer Fritz Heyn gives an idea of what family life was like et the end of the nineteenth

century. The living room, bathroom, and master bedroom have been preserved in their original state, with all their furnitures and the large earthenware stoves. The room leading to the wing, which houses a piano and a phonograph, testifies to the high living standards enjoyed by the Berlin middle classes. The visitor will also be able to learn about famous inventors who were born in Berlin, including the film pioneer Max Skladanowsky.

Pfaueninsel (Zehlendorf)
Pfaueninselchaussee
The mini-palace was originally built by Frederick William II for his mistress. It was then used as a summer residence by his successor, the unfortunate Friedrich Wilhelm III and his popular wife Luise. The interior, preserved in the romantic style of the original, is well worth seeing. The garden, with its various follies, was landscaped by Peter Lenné and is a sort of poetic reverie.

Sammlung Berggruen (Charlottenburg)
Schlossstraße 1
Tel.: 326 95 80
This private collection, directly opposite the Bröhan, is home to eighty-eight Picassos, as well as a number of works by Cézanne, Klee, and van Gogh. The owner lives upstairs, which accounts for the intimate atmosphere.

Schinkelmuseum (Mitte)
Werderstraße
Tel.: 20 90 55 55
Berlin's greatest architect, Karl Friedrich Schinkel, designed this brick church built in about 1830. Today, it houses his museum. Architecture enthusiasts should take time to discover Schinkel's beautifully precise drawings.

Schloß und Garten Klein-Glienicke (Wannsee)
Tel.: 805 30 41
A classical palace, designed by Schinkel, set in rather lovely grounds. Prince Karl von Preußen used it as a summer residence. The summerhouses, fountains, and follies make for an enchanting walk, and the grounds (designed by Lenné) are rarely crowded.

Schinkel-Museum (Mitte)
Werderscher Markt
Tel.: 208 13 23
This solemn church, with its twin Gothic-style steeples, was built in 1830 and is considered Schinkel's finest. It now houses an exhaustive museum dedicated to the multi-talented architect. It also features sculptures by German artists.

SIG (Prenzlauer Berg)
Knaackstraße 97
Tel.: 443 93 82
Take a journey back through the history of design since 1945. The museum specializes in the design of everyday objects, which have a big impact on our lives.

Das Verborgene Museum (Charlottenburg)
Schlüterstraße 70
Tel.: 313 36 56
As its name suggests, you really have to look for the "Hidden Museum," as it is invisible from the street. This unusual gallery is located in an inner courtyard, and only shows works by women. The museum's role is to rescue these hidden creators from obscurity.

Vitra-Design-Museum (Prenzlauer Berg)
Kopenhagener Straße 58
Tel.: 473 77 70
Based in a 1925 transformer plant designed by Hans Heinrich Müller, this is an example of industrial architecture at its finest. The levers and machinery that sprout everywhere are reminiscent of Fritz Lang's masterpiece *Metropolis*. The museum only opened in July 2000, but it has already hosted some major exhibitions. Names on the list include Frank Lloyd Wright, Eames and Mies van der Rohe.

Werkbundarchiv (Kreuzberg)
Stresemannstraße 110
Tel.: 25 48 60
The archive in the Martin-Gropius-Bau is a must for all fans of industrial design.

Zuckermuseum (Wedding)
Amrumer Straße 32
Tel.: 31 42 75 74
A whole museum devoted to the history of sugar? The museum does have a range of interesting historical paraphernalia, such as the box Frederick the Great kept his sugar in, and it also examines the global role played by sugar as a commodity, particularly its part in the slave trade.

SMALL GALLERIES

This is a selection of a few of Berlin's two hundred or so private galleries. Since the city's arts scene is so lively, galleries come and go, so do phone ahead and check that the place you want to visit is still there. Most of the galleries are in the upmarket area of Charlottenburg, but an increasing number are moving into funkier parts of town like Scheunenviertel, where Auguststraße is the place to be. To check out the

latest happenings, buy the monthly art listings magazine *Berliner Kunstkalender*, published by Verlag Angelika Heidrich, Friedrich-Wilhelm-Straße 80.
Tel.: 495 85 50.

Barbara Weiss (Kreuzberg)
Zimmerstraße 88–91
Tel.: 262 42 84
Dedicated principally to Conceptual art.

Chouakri Brahms Berlin (Mitte)
S-Bahnhogen 15–18
Tel.: 283 911 53
A young, cutting edge, international programme.

Contemporary Fine Arts (Mitte)
Sophienstraße 21
Tel.: 288 78 70
Painting is the strong point of this gallery focusing on young, new, international art.

DAAD-Galerie (Tiergarten)
Kurfürstenstraße 58
Tel.: 261 36 40
After a break in the Café Einstein, step upstairs to this gallery that features artists invited to Berlin by the German Academic Exchange Service (DAAD).

Diehl Vorderwuelbecke (Mitte)
Zimmerstraße 88-91
Tel.: 22 48 79 22
Where to find up-to-the-minute international art.

Fine Art Rafael Vostell (Charlottenburg)
Niebuhrstraße 2
Tel.: 885 22 80
Works by Francis Bacon, Joseph Beuys, Christo, Yoko Ono, Ben Patterson, and Ben Watts are shown here alongside the creations of unknown young Berlin artists.

Galerie Aedes East (Mitte)
Rosenthaler Straße 40
Tel.: 282 70 15
Combine a visit here with a trip round the Hackesche Höfe, where the architecture is the real star. The gallery's twin, Café Aedes, in the Savignyplatz tramway passage, also hosts architectural exhibitions.

Galerie am Chamissoplatz (Kreuzberg)
Chamissoplatz 6
Tel.: 69 40 12 45
This small gallery is making a name for itself with its art from the comic book and cartoon scene, as well as satirical works. Take the time to stroll around Chamissoplatz while you're there.

Galerie Bassenge
Erdener Straße 5a
Tel.: 89 38 02 90
This is one of the oldest auction houses in the
city. It specializes in books, with rare editions that
date back to the fifteenth century. It is also
possible to buy sculptures, paintings and
photographs old and new.

Galerie Bremer (Charlottenburg)
Fasanenstraße 37
Tel.: 881 49 08
The bar in the gallery begs the question, does a
glass or two encourage the creative process or,
on the contrary, do you need a stiff drink after
seeing some of the works on offer? The gallery
was founded by Anja Bremer soon after the war,
and specializes in modern art.

Galerie Brusberg (Charlottenburg)
Kurfürstendamm 213
Tel.: 882 76 83
East German art is often given a raw deal by
critics. Judge for yourself in these six exhibition
spaces.

Galerie Deschler (Mitte)
Auguststraße 61
Tel.: 283 32 88
The Galerie Dreschler shows paintings,
sculptures, and objects by predominantly local
artists, such as Elvira Bach.

Galerie Eigen & Art (Mitte)
Auguststraße 26
Tel.: 280 66 05
This gallery hosts shows by young artists from
the former East Germany.

Galerie Frank & Schulte (Charlottenburg)
Mommsenstraße 56
Tel.: 324 00 44
Frank & Schulte deal mainly in Conceptual art
such as Mapplethorpe's creations, but also
occasionally has works by younger artists.

Galerie Haas & Fuchs (Charlottenburg)
Niebuhrstraße 5
Tel.: 881 88 06
Great modern art from Max Beckmann to Erich
Heckel and Emil Nolde, as well as contemporary
artists, all shown in a studious, contemplative
atmosphere.

Galerie Nierendorf (Charlottenburg)
Hardenbergstraße 19
Tel.: 832 50 13
Berlin's art scene in the 1920s was vibrant and

acidic: come to the Nierendorf to (re)discover
the works of Otto Dix and the Dadaist circle.

Galerie Nordenhake (Mitte)
Zimmerstraße 89
Tel.: 206 14 83
Works by modern German artists.

Galerie Pels-Leusden (Charlottenburg)
Fasanenstraße 25
Tel.: 885 91 50
This gallery, specializing in well-known modern
names, has been hosting art auctions in the Villa
Grisebach for 150 years.

Griedervonputtkamer (Mitte)
Sophienstraße 25
Tel.: 288 79 380
This open, innovative gallery offers a youthful,
international programme of shows.

imago Fotokunst (Mitte)
Sophienstraße 32
Tel.: 281 48 69
Specialists in contemporary photography.

Klosterfelde
Linienstraße 160
Tel.: 283 53 05
Klosterfelde promotes young, international
artists.

K & S (Mitte)
ZKM Karlsruhe & Akad. Schloss Solitude
Linienstraße 69
Tel.: 28 38 50 96/97
This gallery specializes in works that use
new technology, notably computer graphics
and video art.

Leo Coppi
Hackesche Höfe, Hof III
Tel.: 283 53 31
Opened in 1991, this gallery is devoted to artists
from the former East Germany.

Max Hetzler (Kreuzberg)
Zimmerstraße 90–91
Tel.: 229 24 37
This gallery handles established artists from
various countries. It has a particular interest in
architecture.

Neugerriemschneider (Mitte)
Linienstraße 155
Tel.: 308 728 10
International programme of contemporary art
by young artists.

Picture Show (Mitte)
Oranienburgerstraße 27
Tel.: 288 791 72
This gallery presents a very original and personal
programme.

Springer & Winkler (Charlottenburg)
Fasanenstraße 13
Tel.: 315 72 20
Established artists from all over the world are
presented in this gallery, which is one of the
oldest in Berlin and used to belong to Rudolf
Springer.

Schipper & Krome
Linienstraße 85
Tel.: 283 901 39
Experimental art by young artists.

Wall Street Gallery
Zimmerstraße 12
Tel.: 251 23 87
This young, vibrant gallery with the golden sun
painted on the ceiling is full of all sorts of objects
made from natural or manmade materials.

Wohnmaschine
Tucholskystraße 36
Tel.: 30 87 20 15
Named after Le Corbusier's Living Machine, this
gallery opened back in 1988, before the Wall fell.
It shows German and international art.

Zwinger Galerie (Mitte)
Gipsstraße 3
Tel.: 285 98 907
Open to all forms of experimental art, this
gallery shows mainly contemporary Berlin-based
artists.

DEPARTMENT STORES

Department stores such as Wertheim in
Potsdamer Platz or the legendary KaDeWe were
once the pride of Berlin. However, the Wall
inevitably brought a slowdown in commerce, and
many flagship stores had a very hard time just
surviving. Since reunification, Berliners have
rediscovered the delights of consumerism, and
the total surface of shop floor space has nearly
doubled in the last decade. New star on the
block is the French store Galeries Lafayette: with
its huge food hall, it is giving KaDeWe a run for
its money.

Arcades de la Potsdamer Platz (Tiergarten)
Alte Potsdamer Straße 7
Tel.: 25 59 27-0

This complex in the heart of the Potsdamzer
Platz consists of around one hundred stores,
restaurants, and bars on three levels. For
Berliners, this is one of the most popular spots in
the city.

Dussmann (Mitte)
Friedrichstraße 90
Tel.: 20 25-0
A Mecca for culture vultures that sells books,
CDs (the classical section downstairs is
excellent), videos, DVDs, and software in a 5,000
square meter store. You can peruse you
purchases in the instore café. It has late opening
hours, and at the weekend, invites prominent
authors to give readings.

Fasanen-Uhland-Passage
Tel.: 882 51 50
A rather attractive passage, with well-restored
late nineteenth-century buildings, a courtyard
restaurant, and exclusive boutiques selling Yves
Saint Laurent, Cartier, Fendi, and Chanel.

KaDeWe (Schöneberg)
Tauentzienstraße 21-24
Tel.: 21 21-0
The Kaufhaus des Westens (KaDeWe), or
Western Department Store, is the biggest
department store in mainland Europe, and a
tourist attraction in its own right. Six floors carry
everything you ever needed, and the food hall
on the top floor is justly famed for the range
and quality of its produce.

Peek & Cloppenburg (Schöneberg)
Tauentzienstraße 19
Tel.: 21 29 00
This store, designed by architects Gottfried and
Peter Böhm, has a striking glass façade that goes
well with KaDeWe next door. It sells top-quality
clothes for the whole family.

Quartier 205 (Mitte)
Friedrichstraße 67
Tel.: 20 94 54 06
This and the following two stores are named
for the blocks they occupy along Friedrichstraße.
205 is the largest, backing onto the Gendarmenmarkt. It specializes in high-class fashion
and accessories. It also contains a number of
restaurants and bistros.

Quartier 206
Friedrichstraße 71
Tel.: 428 10-1
Berlin's answer to Fifth Avenue. This is where to
come for designer gear. Donna Karan, Strenesse,

Bulgari, Prada, Guess, and Helmut Lang are just some of the top names on sale here.

Quartier 207 (Galeries Lafayette)
Friedrichstraße 76
Tel.: 20 94 73 21
More fashion for men and women, cosmetics, fine tableware, and a superb food hall. Gautier, Joop!, Dior, Kenzo, Armani, Cerrutti, Burlington, and René Lezard are some of the designers shown.

Potsdamer Platz Arkaden (Tiergarten)
Alte Potsdamer Straße 7
Tel.: 25 59 27-0
Right at the heart of the new Potsdamer Platz, this mall contains over one hundred shops on three floors, as well as a number of attractive cafés. Many Berliners, unused to such consumerist opulence, come to gawp rather than to shop.

Wertheim (Charlottenburg)
Kurfürstendamm 231
Tel.: 880 03-0
The first Wertheim store was one of the wonders of Berlin. Today, its glory has faded, and it is often regarded as a poor man's KaDeWe. It does sell rather less glitz and rather more basics, but it is well laid out, and the building itself is worth a look.

PARKS AND GARDENS

One of Berlin's most charming features is the number of parks of all sizes, from pocket-sized gardens to great historic landscaped estates. Delightful lawns, thickets, flower beds and benches invite you to discover the city's green heart.

Botanischer Garten
Königin-Luise-Straße 6–8
Tel.: 838 500 27
The botanic gardens, created over a century ago, cover 42 hectares and are home to over 20,000 plant species. The glasshouses, notably the tropical one, are particularly impressive.

Ceciliengärten (Schöneberg)
Hidden between Rubensstraße and Hauptstraße.
The idea of the garden city was developed around these gardens. They were laid out between 1912 and 1924, and are still admired today for their generous spacing and freshness. The main feature is the central cherry-tree garden, which is a riot of blossom in the springtime.

Karolingerplatz (Charlottenburg)
Between Frankenallee and Pommernallee near Theodor-Heuss-Platz.
This square was designated to be a park back in 1905, when the city was expanding westward. It was designed in 1912 by the Charlottenburg quarter's head of gardens as a public garden for the local residents. It has quiet nooks, surrounded by rhododendrons and shaded by enchanting birch trees.

Körnerpark (Neukölln)
Between Jonasstraße, Wittmannsdorfer Straße, Schierker Straße and Ilsestraße.
This site used to be a gravel pit run by a certain Franz Theodor Körner. A wealthy man, he eventually donated the site to the city, which turned it into a 3.6 hectare park in a neo-Baroque style. It was renovated in the 1980s, and is now extremely popular with people from all over the city, not just locals. The parkland lies noticeably deeper than the surrounding streets, so visiting is like descending into a pretty little valley. There is a walkway above the park, giving visitors an unusual view of trees, lawns and flowers. The north and south ends of the park are protected by tall, overgrown arcades with benches in recesses. The fountains and flowerbeds are particularly delightful in the summertime, and the park also hosts open-air concerts. There is a pleasant café in the Orangery, which also houses exhibitions. The terrace is used for concerts in the summer.

Lietzenseepark (Charlottenburg)
Right near the Witzleben tram station on Kuno-Fischer-Straße in the refined but very busy quarter of Charlottenburg is this park with its own lake, a real haven of peace. The grounds were laid out in 1912 and are a fine example of garden architecture. It has wonderful old trees, historic park gates (recently restored), and delicious rose borders. Neue Kantstraße leads over the lake on a brick bridge.

Schillerpark (Wedding)
Between Edinburgerstraße, Dublinerstraße and Bristolstraße.
This park was originally created one hundred years ago for the use of the workers who lived nearby and worked in the great manufactories that once dominated in this quarter. It was Berlin's first modern park. The three-pronged terrace is planted with luxuriant flower beds, and there are several delightful walks lined with elms, horse chestnut, and lime trees.

Victoria-Luise-Platz (Schöneberg)
Between Welserstraße, Motzstraße, Winterfeldtstraße and Regensburger Straße.
This lovely garden is a fabulous example of garden planning in the early years of the twentieth century. It was designed to raise the desirability of the Bavarian quarter, a role which it still fulfills today. A double row of lime trees encircles the six-sided square, at the center of which is a fountain with a round basin that sprays water high into the air. Around the edge of the garden are beds containing sweet-scented flowers. This is a very popular meeting-place for Berliners.

Viktoria-Park
Accessible from Katzbachstraße, Kreuzbergstraße and Dudenstraße, this romantic park is the oldest public garden in the city. It is the highest point in central Berlin, and gives great views over the surrounding area. Schinkel built a memorial here to the soldiers who fell in the Napoleonic Wars, in the form of a cross, which gave the hill and the part of town (Kreuzberg, or "cross hill") its name.

POTSDAM

Capital of the state of Brandenburg, the town of Potsdam is one of Berlin's closest neighbors, and one of the city's favorite spots for a day out. It can get very crowded in summer. The fabulous palaces and grounds of Park Sanssouci can take a day to visit in themselves.

PARK SANSSOUCI

Bildergalerie (Picture gallery)
An der Maulbeerallee
Tel.: (0331) 969 41 81
This is the oldest purpose-built museum in Germany. It has a good collection of paintings by Frederick the Great's favorite artists: Rubens, Tintoretto, Caravaggio, van Dyck, and Vasari. The exhibition room itself is breathtaking: it is over eighty meters long, ten meters wide, and sumptuously decorated.

Chinesisches Teehaus (Chinese Tea Pavilion)
Tel.: (0331) 969 42 22
A fine example of the eighteenth-century Rococo fashion for all things Chinese.

Neue Kammern (New Chambers)
Tel.: (0331) 969 42 06
Originally an orangery, later turned into a guesthouse for Frederick the Great's visitors. The Ovid Gallery is worth the visit.

Neues Palais (New Palace)
Tel.: (0331) 969 42 55
This is the largest and most imposing building in Park Sanssouci. Frederick himself was not over-fond of the three-winged design, but today, it really draws the crowds. The little palace theater is a jewel.

Orangerie
Tel.: (0331) 29 61 89
This elegant building, based on the Villa Medici in Rome, was built in 1860 to a design by Stüler. It combines elements of the Italian late Renaissance with Baroque overtones. It houses sculptures and paintings by both German and Italian artists. The Raphael Room in the center of the orangery should definitely not be missed. The gallery in the tower hosts various exhibitions.

Römische Bäder (Roman baths)
Tel.: (0331) 969 42 24
Built in 1830 by Persius, a pupil of Schinkel, this imitation Roman villa and bathhouse has a strangely solemn feel to it.

Schloß Charlottenhof
Tel.: (0331) 969 42 28
This palace, all on one level, is a perfect example of romantic Neoclassicism. Its harmonious design reflects the combined ideas of Crown Prince Frederick William, Schinkel, and the garden designer Lenné. Schinkel decorated the interior as well, and designed the silver-gilt furniture especially for the palace. The highlight of a visit here is the copper engravings room.

Schloß Sanssouci
Tel.: (0331) 969 42 00
This is the reason why people come to Potsdam. Frederick the Great's palaces and grounds draw visitors from all over the world. The gardens are at their best in the fall, when the vines turn gold, bringing a touch of Italy to the banks of the Havel.

NEUER GARTEN

Marmorpalais (Marble Palace)
Tel.: 969 42 46
This is another palace built for Frederick William II, designed by Carl von Gontard in around 1790. It was his summer residence, right on the banks of the Heiligen See. Carl G. Langhans also had a hand in its building. The palace takes its name from the expensive Silesian marble that covers the brick façade.

Schloß Cecilienhof
Tel.: (0331) 96 94 24
This is where the Potsdam Conference was held in 1945. The palace, built in an English country house style, was the last to be built by the Hohenzollern dynasty, in 1914-1917, for Crown Prince Wilhelm and his wife. The interior is in a style known as "Gdansk Baroque," with lots of carved wood. The White Salon is interesting.

PARK BABELSBERG

Schloß Babelsberg
Tel.: (0331) 969 42 50
The view from this Gothic-style fairytale castle is breathtaking. Some of the rooms are set up as a museum of prehistory.

Flatowturm
Tel.: (0331) 969 42 49
This 46-meter tower can be seen from far and wide. It was built in 1856. The views from the top are spectacular, if you can manage the steep spiral staircase.

IN POTSDAM

Dampfmaschinenhaus (Steam engine house)
Breite Straße
Tel.: (0331) 969 42 48
Until the early years of the twentieth century, the steam-powered engines for the Sanssouci fountains were made by the wealthy German industrialist August Borsig. Although they have not been used for decades, they are open to visits. The cast-iron components are decorated with motifs taken from the cathedral at Cordoba, and the building as a whole was built to resemble a mosque. Astonishing.

Einsteinturm
Astro-Physik Institut Potsdam
Albert-Einstein-Straße
Tel.: (0331) 288 23 00
Open to visitors by appointment
This 20-meter observatory tower was designed by Erich Mendelsohn. As the building is still used for scientific work, visits are restricted (it is best to phone ahead). But from the outside it is still possible to admire one of the finest examples of Expressionist architecture in Germany.

Filmmuseum im Marstall
Breite Straße/Schlossstraße 1
Tel.: (0331) 27 18 10
Open Tuesday to Sunday, 10 AM to 5 PM
This museum takes you right into the heart of the German film industry, once one of the most

vibrant in the world. The pride of the collection is the collection of film-making equipment, such as the "Bioskop" double projector by the film pioneers, the Skladanowsky brothers. There is a cinema on-site, which shows silent films with organ accompaniment on Mondays.

Pomonatempel
Pfingstberg
Tel.: (0331) 29 24 68
A must for admirers of Schinkel—his first architectural design (1800).

NEAR POTSDAM

Caputh
Tourist office, Lindenstraße 54
Tel.: (033209) 708 86
The village of Caputh lies between the Templinersee and the Schwielowsee, six kilometers south of Potsdam. The village is graced with a Baroque castle that is now a museum, and which also hosts open-air concerts during the summer months. Its most noteworthy sight is the summer dining room, tiled with over seven thousand blue-and-white tiles. Albert Einstein had a summer home in the village that is now open to visitors, although sadly none of his original furniture remains.

Filmpark Babelsberg
Großbeerenstraße
Tel.: 01805-345672
This is the biggest and oldest film studio in Europe. With the aid of movies such as *Metropolis* and *The Blue Angel*, the development of fil-making techniques is explained. As at Hollywood, you can watch stunts, see what happens behind the scenes during a shoot and attend the production of a talkshow.

HOTELS

Am Jägertor
Hegelallee 11
Tel.: (0331) 201 11 00
This elegant and luxurious hotel, with its extravagant entryway (a listed historic monument), is close to the oldest surviving town gate, the Jägertor (hunter's gate). The hotel's interior is inspired by Italy, whose influence can be seen in the town's architecture as a whole. The lamps are in Murano glass, and the floors are in Shivakashi granite. The ambience is refined but welcoming.

Am Luisenplatz
Luisenplatz 5
Tel.: (0331) 97 19 00

Am Luisenplatz is a comfortable hotel with twenty-two rooms and three suites, near one of the entrances to Park Sanssouci. The imposing, elegantly restored townhouse gives a flavor of Potsdam's status as regional capital.

Art'otel
Zeppelinstraße 136
Tel.: (0331) 981 50
Art'otel stands on the banks of the Havel, near the grain warehouses. The rooms are decorated in a modern, minimalist style, but are nonetheless comfortably, not to say luxuriously equipped.

Ascot Bristol
Asta-Nielsen-Straße 2
Tel.: (0331) 66 91 00
Slightly far from the center, near the Stern hunting lodge, this first-rate hotel has generously proportioned rooms, including one with a fireplace. The building is modern, the rooms are light and airy, and some reduced-mobility accommodation is available.

Hotel am Griebnitzsee (Babelsberg)
Rudolf-Breitscheid-Straße 190
Tel.: (0331) 709 10
As its name, "By Griebnitz Lake," suggests, this hotel is right on the waterfront. It offers boat tours and water sports. The terrace enjoys fabulous views over the lake to the Berlin forest, a choice spot for the private villas of the stars. The hotel restaurant specializes in regional cuisine.

Hotel Voltaire
Friedrich-Ebert-Straße 88
Tel.: (0331) 231 70
Behind the façade of the historic Brühl townhouse is this modern hotel. Meals in the courtyard garden are a real pleasure, and the roof terrace looks out over the picturesque Dutch quarter.

Inselhotel Potsdam
Halbinsel Hermannswerder
Tel.: (0331) 2 32 00
On the southern tip of the Hermannswerder peninsula, surrounded by woodland, lies this luxurious, spacious hotel. The town center is still within easy reach. The view over the Templiner lake is wonderful, and boat trips are available.

Schloßhotel Cecilienhof
Im Neuen Garten
Tel.: (0331) 370 50
This beautiful hotel in one wing of Schloß Cecilienhof within Park Sanssouci is a pure delight. Looking out over the flower beds and

the small lakes in the park, the rooms are all decorated in different styles. The atmosphere is refined, and the food in the hotel restaurant is absolutely first-class.

RESTAURANTS

Alter Stadtwächter
Schopenhauerstraße 33
Tel.: (0331) 280 46 38
This restaurant is in the former gatekeeper's residence, so you just need to walk along the town wall to find it. They serve decent local specialties.

Am Pfingstberg
Große Weinmeisterstraße 43b
Tel.:(0331) 29 12 66
Am Pfingstberg specializes in typical German cuisine, and the poultry and game are particularly to be recommended. They also serve former Chancellor Kohl's favorite: *Pfälzer Saumagen* (a tripe-cum-haggis dish from the Rheinland Pfalz region). The view from the terrace over Potsdam is superb.

Klosterkeller
Friedrich-Ebert-Straße 94
Tel.: (0331) 29 12 18
The Klosterkeller restaurant and beer garden is in a Baroque house with a wonderful vaulted ceiling, that was formerly used as a brewery. Today it serves fine German wines and traditional regional cuisine.

Schloß Cecilienhof
Tel.: (0331) 3 70 50
The Schloß Cecilienhof restaurant serves great international cuisine, and it even has its own in-house patisserie. History enthusiasts might like to try a reproduction of the meal served to those attending the 1945 Potsdam Conference, a meeting of the victorious leaders of the Allies in Europe. The terrace is wonderful in summer.

Speckers Gaststätte
Am Neuen Markt 10
Tel.: 280 43 11
Fine German cuisine, a wide-ranging wine list, and a simple yet refined atmosphere make this place one of Potsdam's nicest places to eat. The fountain in the courtyard adds another touch of charm.

Villa Kellermann
Mangerstraße 34
Tel.: (0331) 29 15 72
The Villa Kellermann proposes good Italian cooking which guests can enjoy in the garden while enjoying the view over the Heiligen See.

BARS AND CAFÉS

Café Heider
Friedrich-Ebert-Straße
Tel.: (0331) 270 55 96
This is Potsdam's oldest café, but the clientele is young and buzzing. The cakes and tortes, doubtless inspired by the Viennese-style décor, are fabulous.

Café Luise
Luisenplatz 6
Tel.: (0331) 227 97
This extremely popular little spot models itself on the ever-delightful Italian café.

Drachenhaus
Maulbeerallee
Tel.: (0331) 2 15 94
This is the ideal place for a break during a visit to Sanssouci. The cakes are especially good, but the café can often get overcrowded, particularly at weekends.

Hohle Birne
Mittelstraße 19
Tel.: (0331) 280 07 15
Housed in a 250-year-old building in the Dutch quarter, the "Hollow Pear" is decorated with nineteenth-century newspapers and posters. The inner courtyard with its winter garden is very popular. It serves all sorts of wines and beers, specializing in local brews and even a notorious cherry-flavored beer.

Matschkes Galerie-Café
Alleestraße 10
Tel.: (0331) 280 03 59
German and Russian cuisine is served here in a beautiful courtyard garden, and the adjoining gallery often hosts interesting exhibitions.

Waage
Am Neuen Markt 12
Tel.: (0331) 270 96 75
A lovely, modestly classical building in the town's most beautiful square. The owner is an artist, and she decorated the fine interior herself. The food is served in small but tasty portions.

FASHION, JEWELRY, AND GIFT BOUTIQUES

Kontrast
Mittelstraße 6
Tel.: (0331) 280 03 65
This boutique sells handmade hats and dresses, as well as interesting jewelry designs.

Kunsttruhe
Mittelstraße 22
Tel.: (0331) 280 32 09
A shop that prides itself on selling elegant items in an country house style. It specializes in antiques and accessories, with a good collection of valuable Biedermeier furniture, and complete tableware services.

Mana Kehr Ô
Gutenbergstraße 26
Tel.: 201 18 99
This designer's jewelry designs are works of art. Clients can watch her at work, creating collections of jewelry in glass and silver. She also has a "button gallery," which attempts to persuade men to do away with their ties in favor of button decorations.

Tafelfreuden & Wohnambiente
Gutenbergstraße 89
Tel.: (0331) 280 20 50
Another boutique dealing in dinner services, silverware, glassware, and antiques, to wow your dinner guests. They also show samples of their wares in the courtyard of the Hotel Voltaire.

Wohnart
Mittelstraße 28
Tel.: (0331) 280 06 07
An interesting store that sells garden furniture, but also specializes in making the most surprising and unusual objects out of paper.

Zeppelin
An der Spandauer Brücke 7
10178 Berlin
Tel.: 422 30 78
Classic fashions in fine, all-natural fabrics.

GALLERIES

Galerie Egon von Kameke
Persiusstraße 7
Tel.: (0331) 270 59 66
Contemporary works from artists of all nationalities.

Galerie Samtleben
Brandenburgische Straße 66
Tel.: (0331) 29 40 75
Ute Samtleben's gallery displays paintings and graphic art by local contemporary artists.

Hiller-Brandtsche Häuser
Breite Straße 8–12
Tel.: (0331) 218 55
Organizes interesting exhibitions on the history of the city.

Waschhaus
Schiffbauergasse 1
Tel.: (0331) 271 56 30
This gallery shows not just pictures, but installation art by artists from all over the world.

ANTIQUES

The center of Potsdam, in particular Friedrich-Ebert-Straße and the Dutch quarter, has become a Mecca for antiques hunters. Lots of fine pieces have been coming onto the market since the Wall came down. Enthusiasts should plan to spend at least half a day rooting round the antiques stores, looking for neglected treasures.

Antikmarkt im Kutschstall
Am Neuen Markt (Saturday and Sunday, 11 A.M. to 6 P.M.)
This market specializes in antique household objects such as toys and furniture. Dealers come from all over the region to offer their wares; haggling welcome.

Antiquitäten
Lindenstraße 11
Tel.: (0331) 280 10 47
This antiques dealer has two departments, one devoted to furniture, and the other a treasure trove of vintage jewelry, watches, old paintings, and a fine collection of busts of the famous deceased.

Antiquitäten-Galerie
Kurfürstenstraße 14
Tel.: (0331) 280 54 69
Antique furniture, lamps, paintings, and tableware.

Antiquitäten im Holländischen Viertel
Benkertstraße 12
Tel.: (0331) 280 03 41
Objets d'art and furniture, some skillfully restored.

Detlef Walinski
Friedrich-Ebert-Straße 24
Tel.: (0331) 29 27 67
Detlef Walinski buys and sells grandfather clocks, pocket watches, and wall clocks, as well as carrying out repairs.

Greulich
Gutenbergstraße 18
Tel.: (0331) 280 99 33
A charming shop selling heavy, solid antique doors, Biedermeier chests, clocks, and other household goods.

Viv'Antique
Hebbelstraße 50
Tel.: (0331) 270 54 57
The very model of a well-stocked antiques dealer: paintings, cutlery, tableware, clocks, jewelry, and furniture. Deliveries within Germany.

Wassermann Geschenke & Wohnen
Jägerstraße 32
Tel.: (0331) 280 43 05
This wonderful shop still has its original decorated ceiling, which complements the grandfather clocks and writing desks. It also sells a range of new items that go surprisingly well with the antiques.

INDEX

The index covers pages 1 to 200 only, not the Visitor's Guide

Aalto, Alvar, 102
Alexejew, Manuela, 105
Altes Museum, 35, 36
Anton, Sabine, 198
Armleder, John, 115
Arsenal, 36, 39
Atrium, 20

Babelsberg, 168-169
Baselitz, Georg, 35, 182
Bassenge, Gerda, 110
Bassenge, Jan, 110
Bassenge, Kiki, 110
Bauhaus, 36
Becq, Henri, 109
Beethoven, Ludwig van, 82
Berggruen, Heinz, 95, 181
Berlin-Est, 41, 52
Bernd, Kurt, 45
Beyer + Schubert, 126
Blanke, Wilhelm, 105
Borchardt, August F.W., 195
Borsig, August, 45, 171
Both, Iris, 116
Brahms, Edzard, 116
Brandenburg, 56
Braque, Georges, 95
Brecht, Bertolt, 177
Buechler, Annette, 118
Buechler, Peter, 118
Büring, 150

Cartier, 198
Cattelan, Maurizio, 115
Cecilie, Princess, 164
Cézanne, Paul, 95, 181
Chancellery, 31
Chanel, 198
Chapu, Henri, 101
Charles of Prussia, Prince, 76
Charlottenburg, 17, 44, 46, 47, 56, 59
Charlottenhof, 141, 150, 153, 154, 155, 160, 168
Checkpoint Charlie, 52, 53
Chinesisches Teehaus, 149
Chipperfield David, 33
Christo, 31
Cobb and Partners, 42
Coenen, Bernhard, 132

Daimler-Chrysler, 20, 21
De Leon, Gonzales, 26
Debis, 20, 21
Dejanov, Plamen, 117
Dessau, Duke of, 168
Deutscher Dom, 14, 36, 41
DG-Bank, 39
Dieterich, Friedrich W., 178
Dietrich, Marlene, 171, 177
Dutch quarter, 162-163
Düttmann, Hans, 132

Eames, Charles and Ray, 117
Ebert, Ulla, 92
Einstein, Carl, 189
Endell, August, 45
Ephraïm, Veitel Heine, 178
Ephraim-Palais, 178
Eyserbeck, Johann A., 164

Fetting, Rainer, 182
Filmhaus, 22
Foster, Norman, 31
Frank, Charlotte, 32
Frederick William I, 160
Frederick William II, 70
Frederick William III, 73, 76, 163
Frederick William IV, 141, 157, 164, 168
Frederick II, 178
Frederick the Great, 81, 141, 142, 146, 154, 160, 199

Galeries Lafayette, 42, 43
Garbo, Greta, 171
Gehry, Frank O., 37, 115, 181
Gendarmenmarkt, 36, 41, 42, 184, 193
Giacometti, Alberto, 95
Glume, Friedrich C., 146
Gontard, 149
Gonzalez-Torres, Felix, 112
Grillitsch, Wolfgang, 129, 130
Gropius, Walter, 178
Gropp, Suzanne, 99
Grottensaal, 150
Grunewald, 63, 65, 81, 188

Haag, Romy, 125
Hackesche Höfe, 44, 47
Hackescher Markt, 45, 46
Havel, 53, 60, 63, 66, 70, 76, 81, 138, 164, 168, 171
Haydn, Joseph, 82
Heger, Swetlana, 117

Hilmer, 45
Hirst, Damien, 192
Hoffmann, E.T.A., 39
Hoffmann, Erika, 110
Hoffmann, Rolf, 112
Hohenzollern, 164
Huth, 20

Imax Kino, 21

Jagdfeld, Anne Maria, 106
Joachim II, 63
Joop, Wolfgang, 92

Klee, Paul, 95, 181
Kleihues, Joseph Paul, 36
Klein-Glienicke, 70, 76
Knöb, Elke, 129, 130
Kokoschka, Oscar, 103
Kolbe, Georg, 177
Kollhoff, 18
Kollwitz, Käthe, 34
Kornerpark, 86, 87
Kreuzberg, 17, 45, 46, 49, 51, 52, 59, 60, 86
Kulturforum, 20, 21, 27

Lagerfeld, Karl, 182
Landwehrkanal, 59, 60, 82
Lang, Fritz, 171, 177
Langhans, Carl G., 37, 39
Legeay, 150
Léger, Fernand, 110
Lenné, Joseph, 70, 76, 86, 153, 168
Locher, Thomas, 112
Loesch, Ernst von, 99
Lubitsch, Ernst, 171
Luise, Queeen, 73, 76, 81

Mäckler, Christoph, 42
Maenz, Paul, 115
Mahlsdorf, Charlotte von, 178
Manger, 150
Mann, Heinrich, 42
Marmorgalerie, 150
Matisse, Henri, 95, 110
Mitte, 17, 32, 45, 48, 49, 52, 196
Moabit, 45
Mosse, Rudolf, 19
Mozart, Wolfgang A., 82
Müggelsee, 60, 66, 67

Nay, Ernst W., 105
Neto, Ernesto, 112
Neue Nationalgalerie, 27

Neue Wache, 36, 37, 38
Neues Palais, 138, 141, 150, 153, 160
Neukölln, 45, 49, 86, 87, 186
Nouvel, Jean, 42

Offenbach, Jacques, 41
Orangery, 141, 157, 164
Ovid, 149

Panton, Verner, 123
Peanutz, 129
Pei, I.M., 40
Persius, Ludwig von, 168
Philharmonie, 27
Piano, Renzo, 20
Picasso, Pablo, 95, 110
Polke, Sigmar, 112
Portzamparc, Christian de, 37
Postdam, 56, 70
Potsdamer Platz, 19, 20, 21, 23, 27, 31, 46
Prenzlauer Berg, 44, 45, 48, 49, 52
Pückler-Muskau de, Prince of, 168

Quartier 206, 42, 43

Rauch, Christian D., 81
Raue, Tim, 195
Récamier, Juliette, 96
Reichstag, 14, 22, 31, 32
Reine, Louise, 73, 76, 81
Reiter, Ludwig, 198
Riedl, Stefan, 100
Riehmer, Wilhelm, 195
Roman baths, 168
Rühmann, Heinz, 177
Russian colony, 163

Sander, Otto, 191
Sanssouci, 138, 141, 143, 147, 153, 157, 160, 164-165, 171
Sattler, 46
Schacht, Martin, 125
Scharoun, Hans, 27
Schenk, Gisela von, 109
Schiller, Friedrich von, 38
Schinkel, Friedrich, 35, 36, 41, 50, 70, 76, 81, 86, 102, 153, 154, 157, 168
Schlüter, Andreas, 38
Schmidt, Erik, 122
Schultes, Axel, 32

Schultze-Naumburg, Paul, 164
Serrano, 27
Sieverding, Katharina, 112
Sombart, Nicolaus, 96
Sony Center, 19, 20
Sophie-Gips-Höffe, 45, 46
Spree, 17, 31, 32, 35, 36, 41, 49, 53, 56, 59, 60, 81, 82
Staël, Germaine de, 96
Stella, Frank, 112, 113
Stendhal, 184
Sterf, Stefan A., 135
Strack, 168
Stüler, Friedrich A., 95
Stüve, Frank, 109

Tiergarten, 17, 19, 21, 22, 28, 31, 39, 56, 81-83, 188
Timmermann, 20
Tinguely, Jean, 20

Unter den Linden, 36, 37, 38, 39, 42

van der Rohe, Mies, 27
van Dyck, 100
van Gogh, Vincent, 95, 181
Varnhagen, Rahel, 96
Viktoriapark, 49, 52
Vitra Design Museum, 181
Vogt, Olivier, 125
Von Arnim, Bettina, 36
Von Knobelsdorff, Georg, 143, 146
Von Mahlsdorf, Charlotte, 178

Wagenbach, Klaus, 191
Wagner, Richard, 82
Wald, Imgard, 198
Wall, 17, 20, 27, 31, 39, 49, 52
Wallot Paul, 31
Walpole, Horace, 70
Walz, Ado, 162
Wannsee, 56, 60, 63, 66-67, 70
Warhol, Andy, 112
Wegely, Caspar, 199
Weigel, Helene, 177
Weizenegger, Hermann, 125
Wenders, Wim, 191
Wiegand-Hoffmann, Nany, 102
William II, 90

Yanagi, Sori, 117

BIBLIOGRAPHY

Neal Ascherson, et al. *Berlin, A Century of Change.* London: Prestel, 2000.

Alan Balfour, ed. *Berlin.* New York: Rizzoli International, 1990.

Stephen Barber, *Fragments of the European City.* London: Reaktion Books, 1998.

Karl Baedeker, *Berlin and its Environs.* Leipzig: Karl Baedeker, 1903.

Berlin Insight Guide. APA Productions, 2001.

DK Eyewitness Travel Guides: Berlin. London: Dorling Kindersley, 2000.

Everyman City Guide: Berlin. Everyman Travel Guides, 1998.

David Fisher and Anthony Read, *The Fall of Berlin.* New York: Da Capo Press, 1995.

Norman Foster and David Jenkins. *Rebuilding the Reichstag.* Woodstock, N.Y.: Overlook Press, 2000.

Derek Fraser. *The Buildings of Europe: Berlin.* London: St. Martin's Press, 1997.

Otto Friedrich, *Before the Deluge: A Potrait of Berlin in the 1920s.* New York: Harper Perennial, 1972.

John Gawthrop and Jack Holland, *The Rough Guide to Berlin.* London: Rough Guides Ltd., 2001

Norman Gelb, *The Berlin Wall.* London: Michael Joseph Press, 1986.

Peter Güttler, et al. *Berlin-Brandenburg: An Architectural Guide.* Berlin: Ernst & Sohn, 1993.

Jurgen Habermas, *A Berlin Republic: Writings on Germany.* Lincoln: University of Nebraska Press, 1997.

Dr. Volker Hassemer. *The New Berlin: Images.* Berlin: Jovis/Deutsches Architektur Zentrum, 2001.

Martin Kieren and Andreas Gottlieb Hempel. *New Architecture: Berlin 1990–2000.* Berlin: Jovis, 1999.

Josef Paul Kleihues. *Berlin/New York, Like & Unlike.* New York: Rizzoli International, 1994.

Brian Ladd, *The Ghosts of Berlin: Confronting German History in the German Landscape.* Chicago: University of Chicago Press, 1997.

Daniel Libeskind, *Jewish Museum Berlin.* London: Prestel, 1999.

Giles MacDonogh, *Berlin.* New York: St. Martin's Press, 1998.

Charlotte von Mahlsdorf, *I am My Own Woman.* Pittsburgh: Cleis Press, 1995.

Anne Massey, *Blue Guide: Berlin and Eastern Germany.* London: A & C Black, 1994.

Michelin Green Guide: Berlin and Potsdam. Michelin Travel Publications Ltd., 2001.

David Murphy et al., *Battleground Berlin: CIA vs KGB in the Cold War.* New Haven: Yale University Press, 1999.

Darwin Porter and Danforth Prince. *Frommer's Portable Berlin.* Hungry Minds, Inc. 1999.

Hermann Pundt, *Schinkel's Berlin.* Cambridge, Mass.: Harvard University Press, 1973.

Alexandra Richie, *Faust's Metropolis.* New York: Carroll & Graf Publishers, 1998.

Andrea Schulte-Peevers, *Lonely Planet: Berlin.* Lonely Planet Publications, 2000.

Uwe Seidel, *Berlin & Potsdam.* Bielefeld: Peter Rump, 1991.

Ronald Taylor, *Berlin and its Culture: A Historical Portrait.* New Haven: Yale University Press, 1998.

Time Out Guide: Berlin. London: Penguin Books, 2000.

Michael Z. Wise, *Capital Dilemma: Germany's Search for a New Architecture.* New York: Princeton Architectural Press, 1998.

ACKNOWLEDGMENTS

We would like to thank all those who generously opened their doors to us, as well as the owners of hotels, restaurants, and cafés and the directors of museums who gave us their support.

Barbara Sichtermann and Ingo Rose thank in particular Janna Dahme for her knowledge and contagious passion for the city of Berlin; she enabled them to see it from a new angle. They would also like to thank another discerning expert, Wolfgang Hebold, for agreeing to read several chapters.

Finally, they would like to express their gratitude to the historian Susanne Pecher, the specialist in religion Ulrike Brunotte, and the publisher Klaus Wagenach, who shared their knowledge about particular aspects of Berlin.

Deidi von Schaewen wishes to thank the following: Manuela Alexejew, Alexandra d'Arnoux, Kiki and Jan Bassenge, Heinz Berggruen, the architects Beyer and Schubert, Marie Claire Blanckaerdt, Iris Both, Edzard Brahms, Peter and Anette Buechler, Genia Chef, Medi Chouakri, Ulla Ebert, Renate Gallois Montbrun, Anette Gerlach, Nina Gerlach, Christiane Germain, Mark Gisborne, Dr. Göres, Wolfgang Grillitsch, Anjana and Michael Hasper, Erika and Rolf Hoffmann, Ben and Nani Wiegand Hoffmann, Anne Maria Jagdfeld, Wolfgang Joop, Mrs. Kamara, Elke Knöss, Mrs. Kompatzki, Matheo Kries, Axel and Sibylle Kufus, Ernst von Loesch, Paul Maenz, Claude Martin, Mr. Pfeil, Andrée Putman, Martin Schacht, Gisela von Schenk, Erik Schmidt, Nicolaus Sombart, Barbara and Rudolf Springer, Bernard and Ranjana Steinrücke, Stefan Arne Sterf, Karoline Stummel, Frank Stüve, Alexander von Vegesack, Irene and Josi Vennekamp, Olivier Vogt, Klara Wallner, Ralph Weiden, Hermann Weizenegger, Jeannette Zwingenberger, and above all her cousin Natasha Struve, whose hospitality made this book possible.

We would also like to thank the following people for their assistance and their competence: Christine Chareyre, Mark Dagobert, Diana Darley, Sylvie Girard-Lagorce, Nicolas Lefort, Carine Panis, Susan Pickford, and Sylvie Ramaut. It would not have been possible to produce this book without them.

The publisher would like to express its warm thanks to Annette Gerlach for her precious advice on living in Berlin, as well as José Alvarez, Françoise Aurivaud, and Dominique Bourgois for their assistance during the creation of this book.

Series editor Ghislaine Bavoillot

Graphic design Karen Bowen

Translated from the French by Deke Dusinberre

Visitor's guide translated by Susan Pickford

Copy-editing Bernard Wooding

Typesetting Studio X-Act, Paris

Cartography Édigraphie

Photoengraving Dupont, Colorway and Compo-Rive Gauche

Originally published as *L'Art de vivre à Berlin*
© Flammarion, Paris, 2001

English-language edition © Flammarion, 2002

ISBN: 2-0801-0676-7   (FA0676-01-X)
Dépôt légal: 03/2002

Printed and bound in Italy